Today's Top Stationery Artists

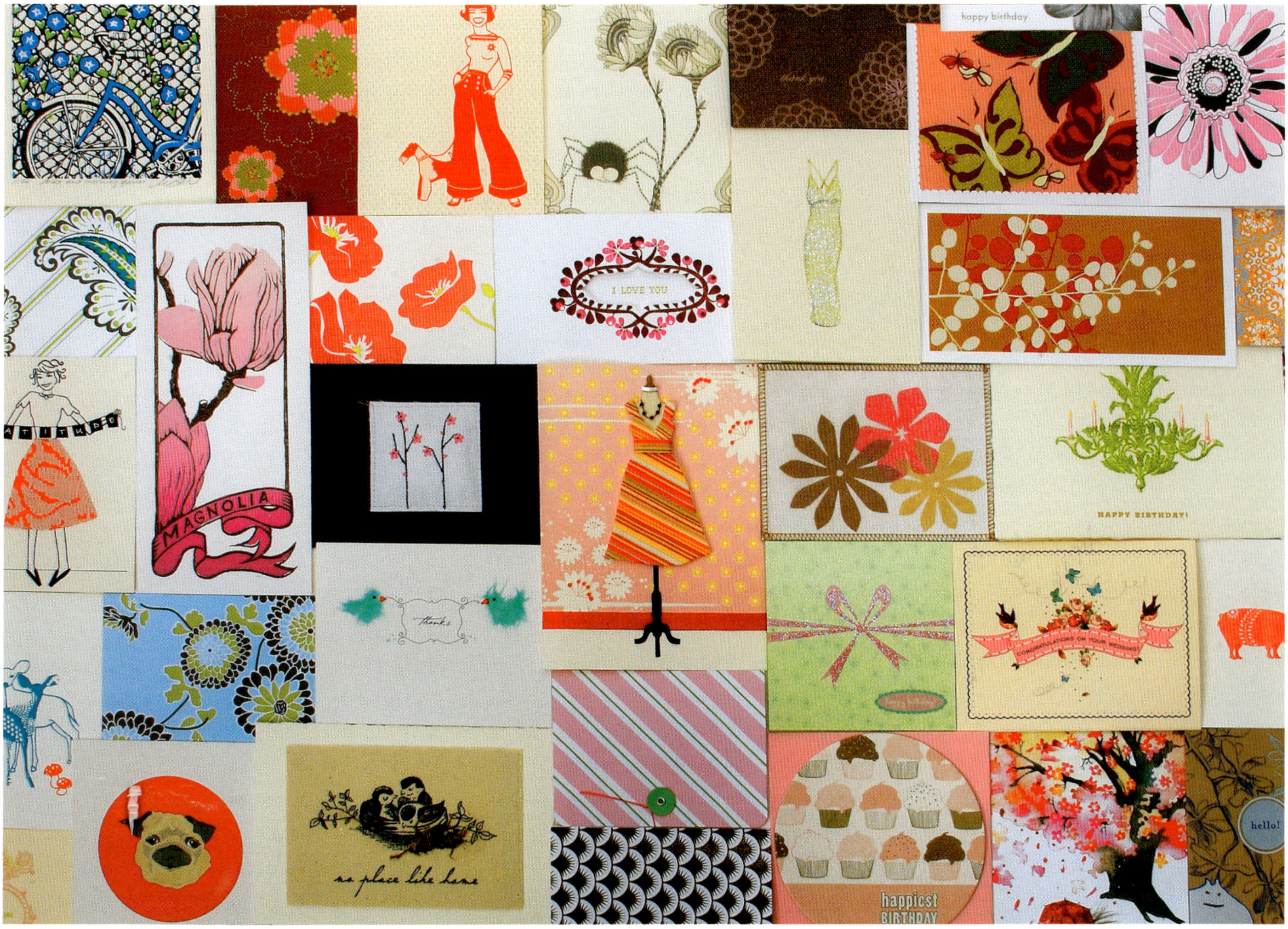

Photograph by Casey Figlewicz.

Tori Higa

Schiffer Publishing Ltd

4880 Lower Valley Road Atglen, Pennsylvania 19310

I0808828

Other Schiffer Books on Related Subjects
Affordable Art Deco Graphics. Susan Warshaw Berman.
Book of American Type Standard Faces. The American Typefounders Company
Christmas Long Ago. Marian I. Doyle
Christmas Household Textiles 1920s-1970s. Jeanette & Donald Michalets
Great Rock and Roll Street Art. Victor Burleigh
Great Street Art: Reggae, Blues, and World Beat Posters, 1977-1989. Victor Burleigh
The Ultimate Fruit Label Book. John A. Baule

Library of Congress Control Number: 2007938038

Covers and book designed by Bruce Waters
Type set in Bodoni Bd BT/New Baskerville BT

ISBN: 978-0-7643-2832-9
Printed in China

Published by Schiffer Publishing Ltd.
4880 Lower Valley Road
Atglen, PA 19310
Phone: (610) 593-1777; Fax: (610) 593-2002
E-mail: Info@schifferbooks.com

For the largest selection of fine reference books on this and related subjects, please visit our web site at **www.schifferbooks.com**
We are always looking for people to write books on new and related subjects. If you have an idea for a book please contact us at the above address.

This book may be purchased from the publisher.
Include $3.95 for shipping.
Please try your bookstore first.
You may write for a free catalog.

In Europe, Schiffer books are distributed by
Bushwood Books
6 Marksbury Ave.
Kew Gardens
Surrey TW9 4JF England
Phone: 44 (0) 20 8392-8585; Fax: 44 (0) 20 8392-9876
E-mail: info@bushwoodbooks.co.uk
Website: www.bushwoodbooks.co.uk
Free postage in the U.K., Europe; air mail at cost.

Dedication

For my best friend and husband, Branden.

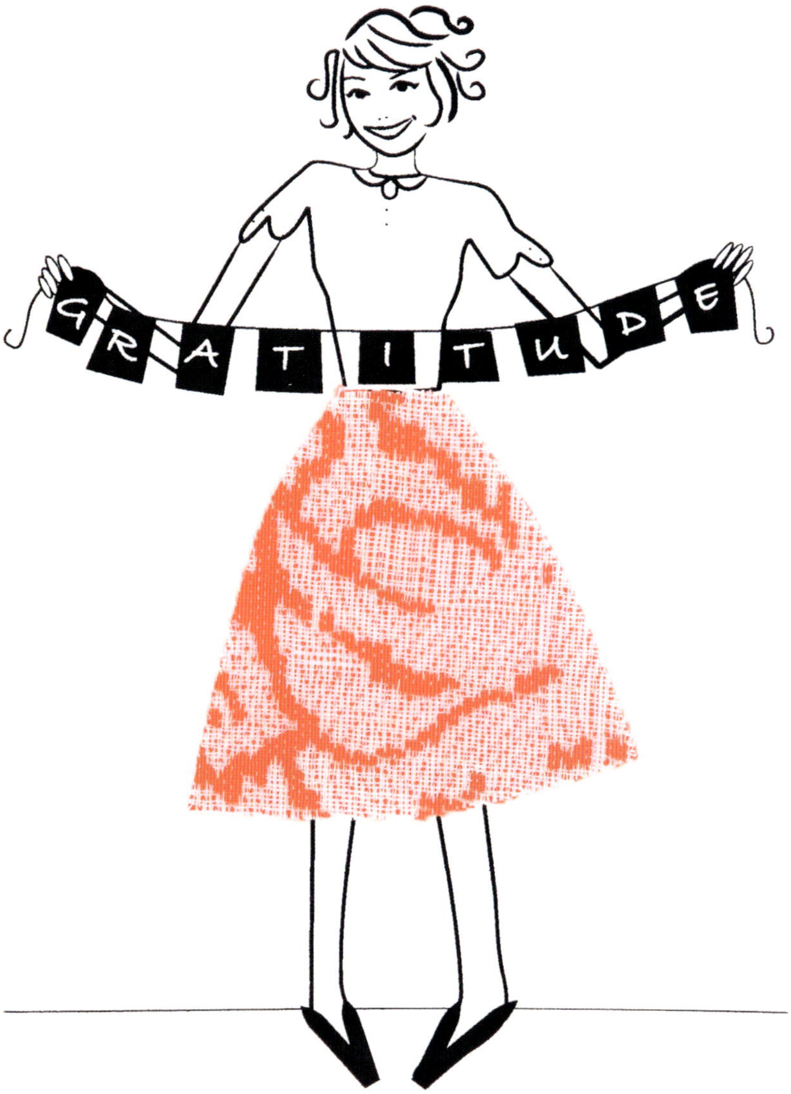

Gratitude. Handmade with vintage fabric. *Courtesy of Tori Higa Stationery.*

Contents

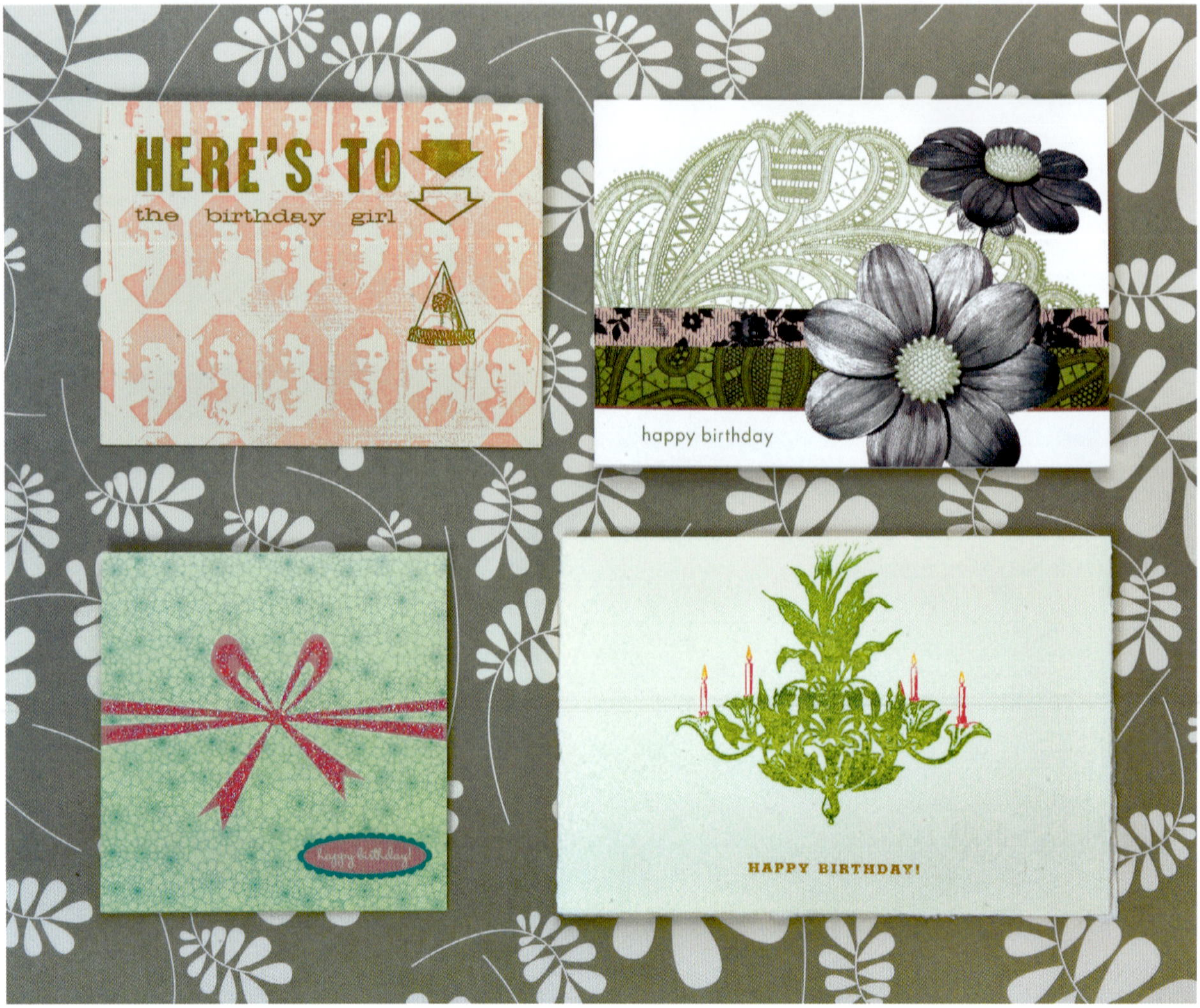

Greeting cards by (clockwise) Hammerpress, Rosebud Design Studio, Saturate, and You Send Me. Wrapping Paper by Snow and Graham. *Photograph by Casey Figlewicz.*

Introduction

Ever since the dawn of recorded time, man has had a desire to communicate through the written word. The use of stationery can be traced back to the civilizations of antiquity. Historians note that early Egyptians sent messages on papyrus scrolls, while the Chinese exchanged written greetings on paper. But it wasn't until the end of the Middle Ages that the predecessor to the modern day greeting card began to take shape. Throughout Europe, handmade notes were given on holidays and special occasions.

With the arrival of the industrial age in the mid-1800s, advances in printing and the advent of the modern postal system allowed for low cost production of greeting cards and the ability to send the card to loved ones far away. Different methods have been used to produce these cards. From being lovingly made by hand, to woodcuts, letterpresses, lithography, and offset printing, the greeting card has endured as a symbol of glad tidings and good will. It is used to celebrate life's milestones, the passing of another year, a new addition to the family, to show appreciation for a kindness received or to just let dear friends know you have been thinking about them. Throughout the ages, the greeting card remains a classic and enduring way to show your regard for one another.

In this modern age of email and text messages, the hand written note takes on added significance. It symbolizes permanence, a part of someone. A person's thoughts flow from pen to paper as a physical, tangible item—something to be treasured, something with flourish, if just for a short time. Maybe it is displayed on a desk so its quality can be appreciated; perhaps it is tucked away in a drawer, hidden until opened again so that a kindness rendered will be remembered once more.

It can't be sent with the push of a button, then quickly forgotten. It must be folded, sealed, addressed, stamped, and delivered to a postal box, so when the message is finally on its way, it truly represents a part of that person. When you receive a card, you receive a part of that person.

Even in today's society of e-mail and e-cards, the greeting card industry remains strong. According to the Greeting Card Association, it is estimated that over 7 billion cards are sent every year, with annual sales topping $7.5 billion.

But beyond this, greeting cards have become an art form all their own. More than their original practical function, greeting cards have evolved into one of the most accessible art forms of our time. These diminutive masterpieces are available for consumption by anyone who wishes to spend a dollar or two to make their loved ones feel special.

Recently, there has been a surge in independent card companies who have taken greeting card design to a new level. By shunning mass production and focusing on unique design and printing elements, the "indies" now offer stationery that have more in common with fine art than with the flat, drug-store counter cards of the past.

It is now time to recognize the efforts of these talented designers and artists.

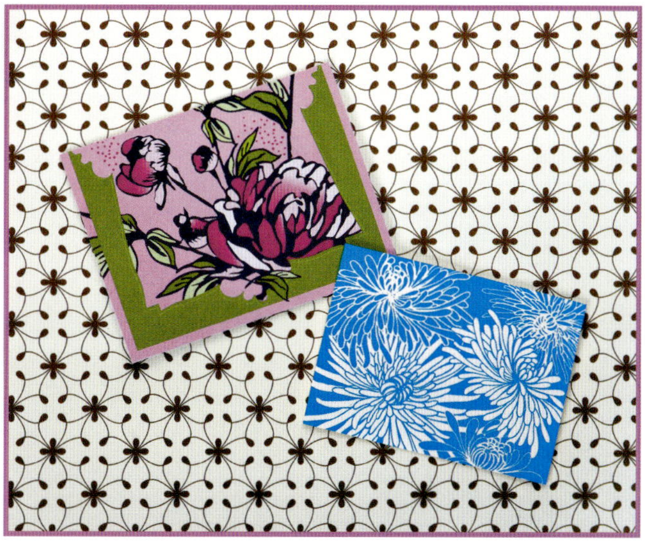

Note cards by Dewey Howard and Elum Designs. Wrapping Paper by Snow and Graham. *Photograph by Casey Figlewicz.*

Chapter One
Graphic Design

This section profiles the many talented graphic designers turned stationery and greeting card artists. Jami Darwin Chiang of *Letterspace* believes, "stationery is such a wonderful mixture of all types of design – it really lets you (as a designer and as the one giving the card) take anything you love in your life and share it with someone else."

Pattern design has become an ever-increasing trend in stationery – especially among graphic designers. Patterns are often inspired by trends in fashion and interior design as well as classic and vintage styles from years past. Because of the familiarity of the patterns portrayed on stationery, this trend will be around for years to come. A classic preppy stripe pattern or a simple floral repeat inspired by vintage wallpaper will always be a timeless way to send a thoughtful note.

Asian Floral, Nico, Petra, and Franz. Offset printed with rounded die cut corners. *Courtesy of Rock Scissor Paper.*

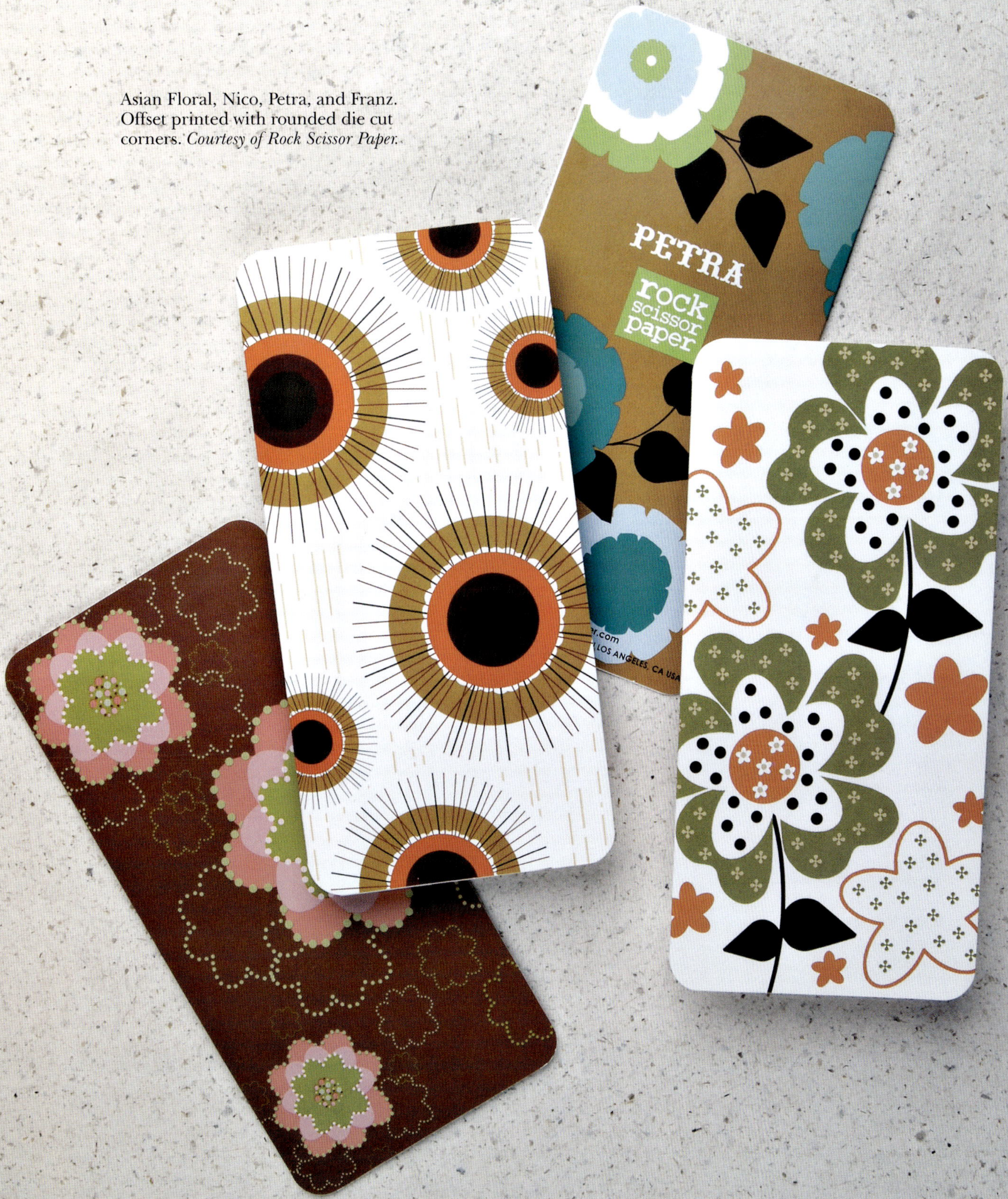

Rock Scissor Paper

www.rockscissorpaper.com

Susie Bauer and Heidi Bauer are the talented, self-taught designers behind Rock Scissor Paper. The two sisters grew up being "crafty" kids. They made many of their own toys as well as gifts and cards for family and friends. Drawing on inspirations such as local architecture, pop culture, and vintage advertisements, they launched their Los Angeles based company in 1993. They now have over 500 designs in their collection.

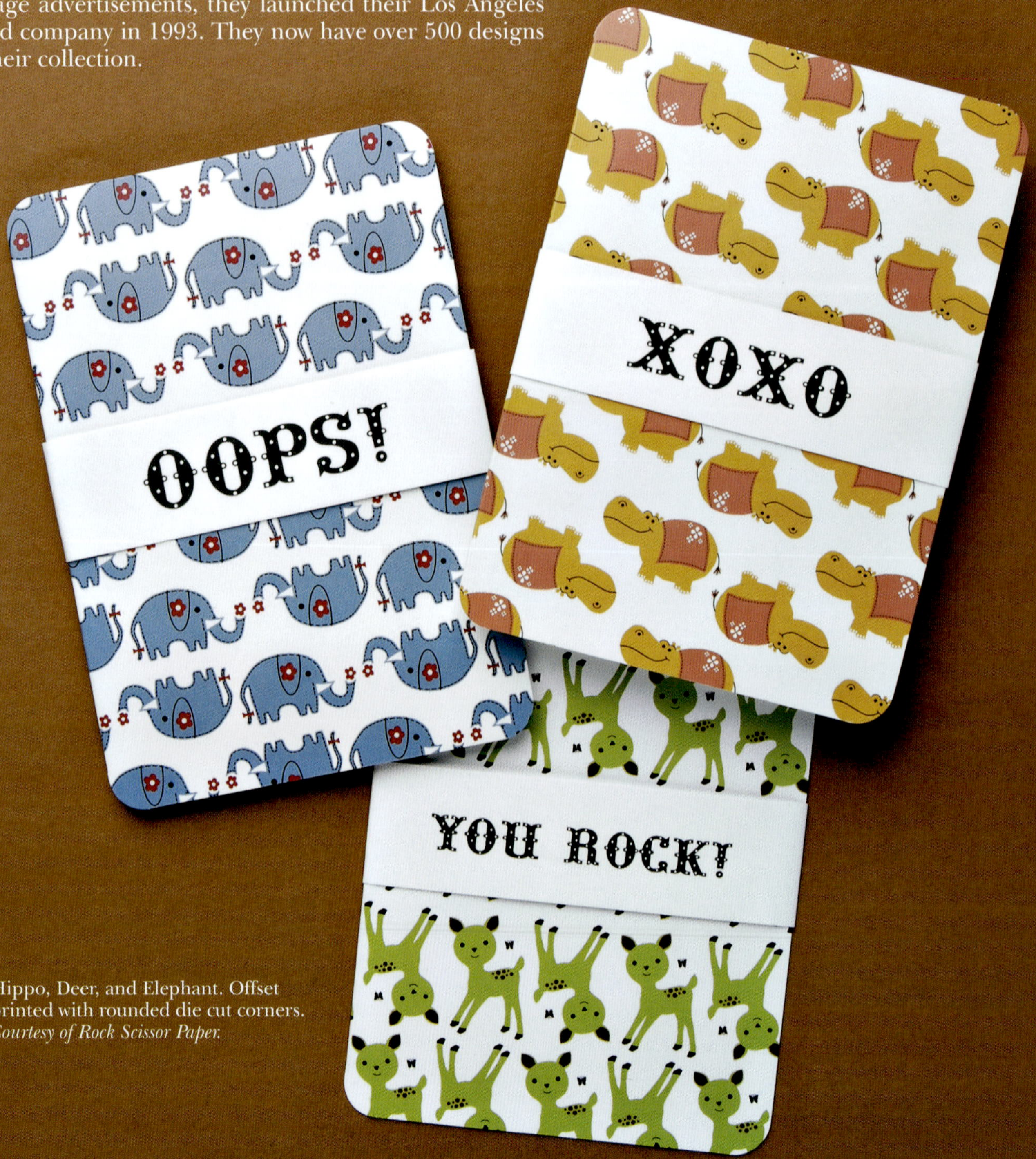

Hippo, Deer, and Elephant. Offset printed with rounded die cut corners. *Courtesy of Rock Scissor Paper.*

Bird Cages, Butterfly Flock, and Spider Mum. Offset printed with rounded die cut corners. *Courtesy of Rock Scissor Paper.*

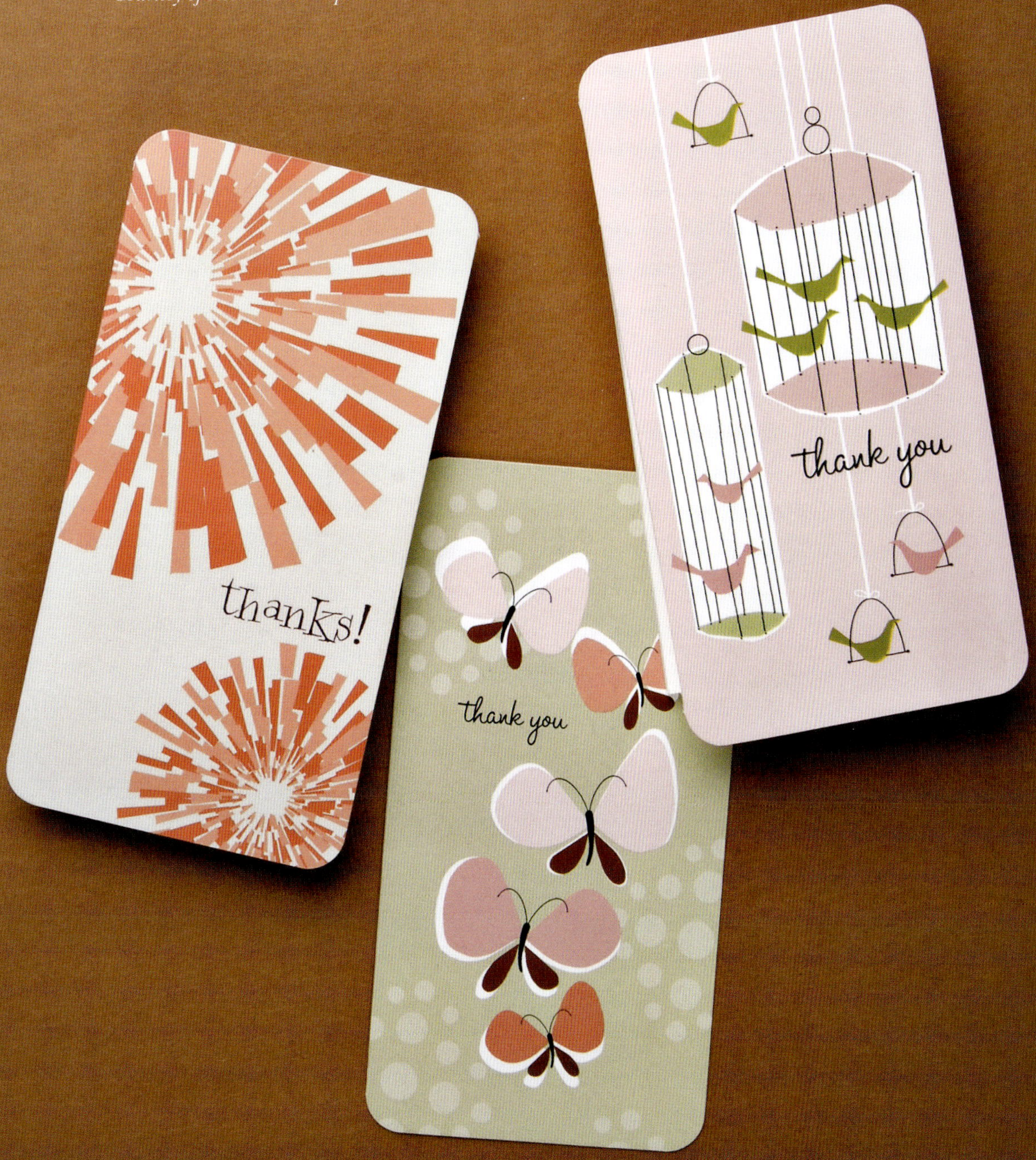

Blanckslate

www.blanckslate.com

Suzanne Blanck of the Gilbert, Arizona, based company, Blanckslate, began her innovative company four years ago. She holds a BFA in Graphic Design, Advertising, and Marketing. She finds inspiration for her designs in patterns of all kinds as well as color, color, and more color.

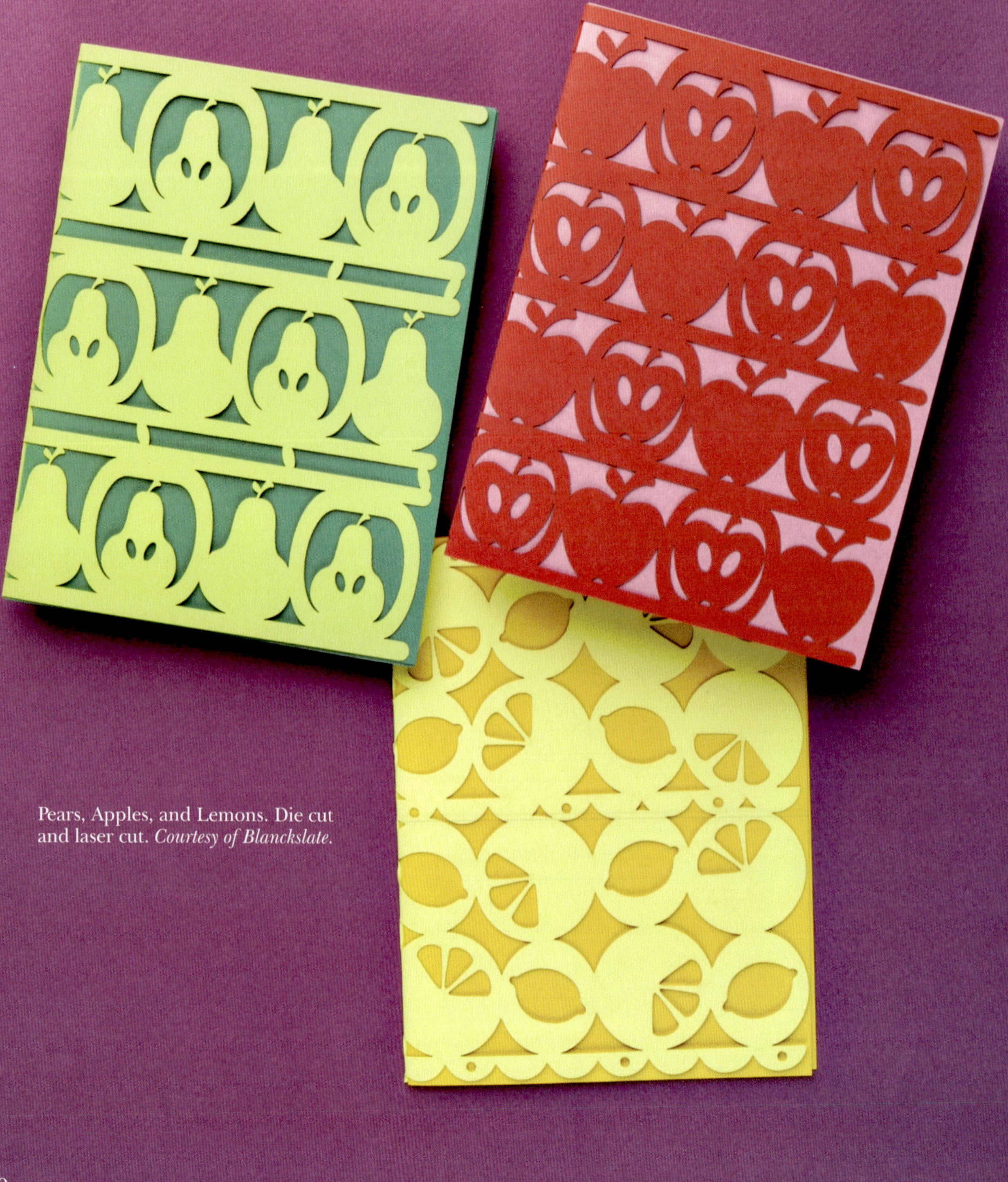

Pears, Apples, and Lemons. Die cut and laser cut. *Courtesy of Blanckslate.*

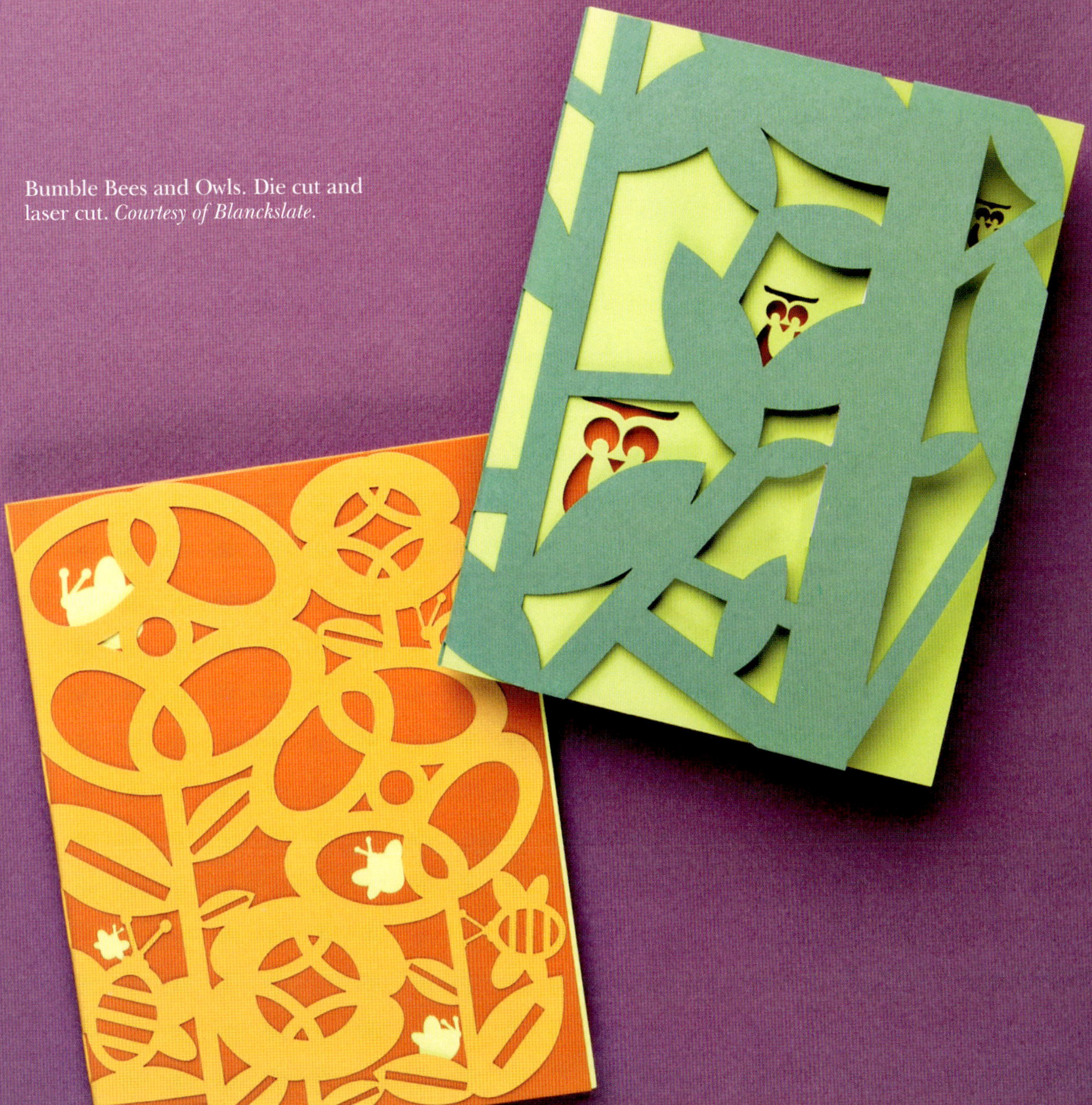

Bumble Bees and Owls. Die cut and laser cut. *Courtesy of Blanckslate.*

Paperdolls Precious Paper Goods

www.paperdollscards.com

Julie Savasky and Meggan Webber are the Dolls behind Paperdolls Precious Paper Goods. Both Julie and Meggan are graphic designers by trade, specializing in book, package, magazine, and catalog design. They have worked together at Pentagram Design in Austin for years and have always appreciated beautiful stationery and paper. Their collection is inspired by vintage textiles and wallpaper.

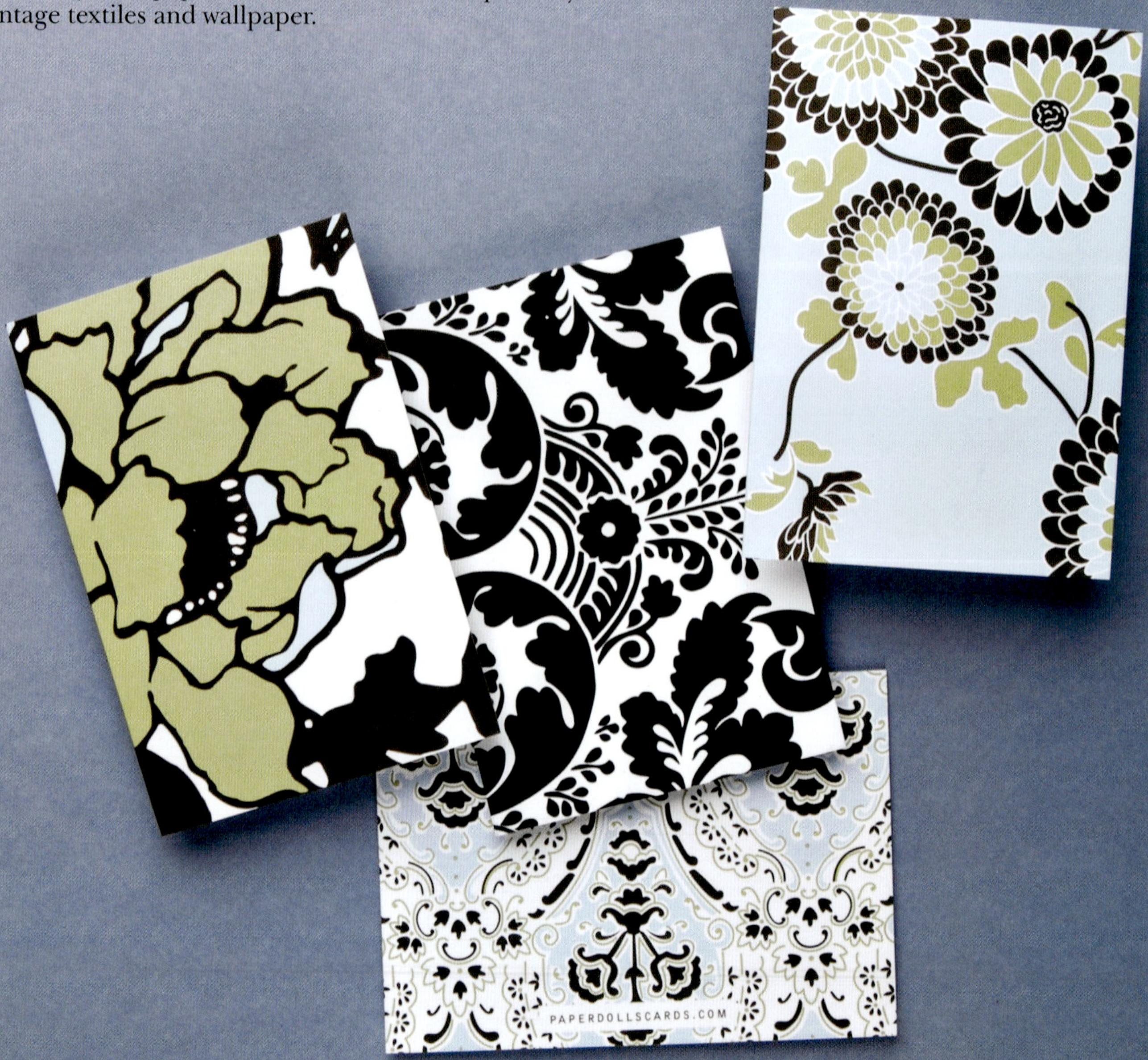

Charlotte, Dotty Black, Camellia, and Frances. Offset printed. *Courtesy of Paperdolls Precious Paper Goods.*

Marjorie Pink, Teal, and Orange. Offset printed. *Courtesy of Paperdolls Precious Paper Goods.*

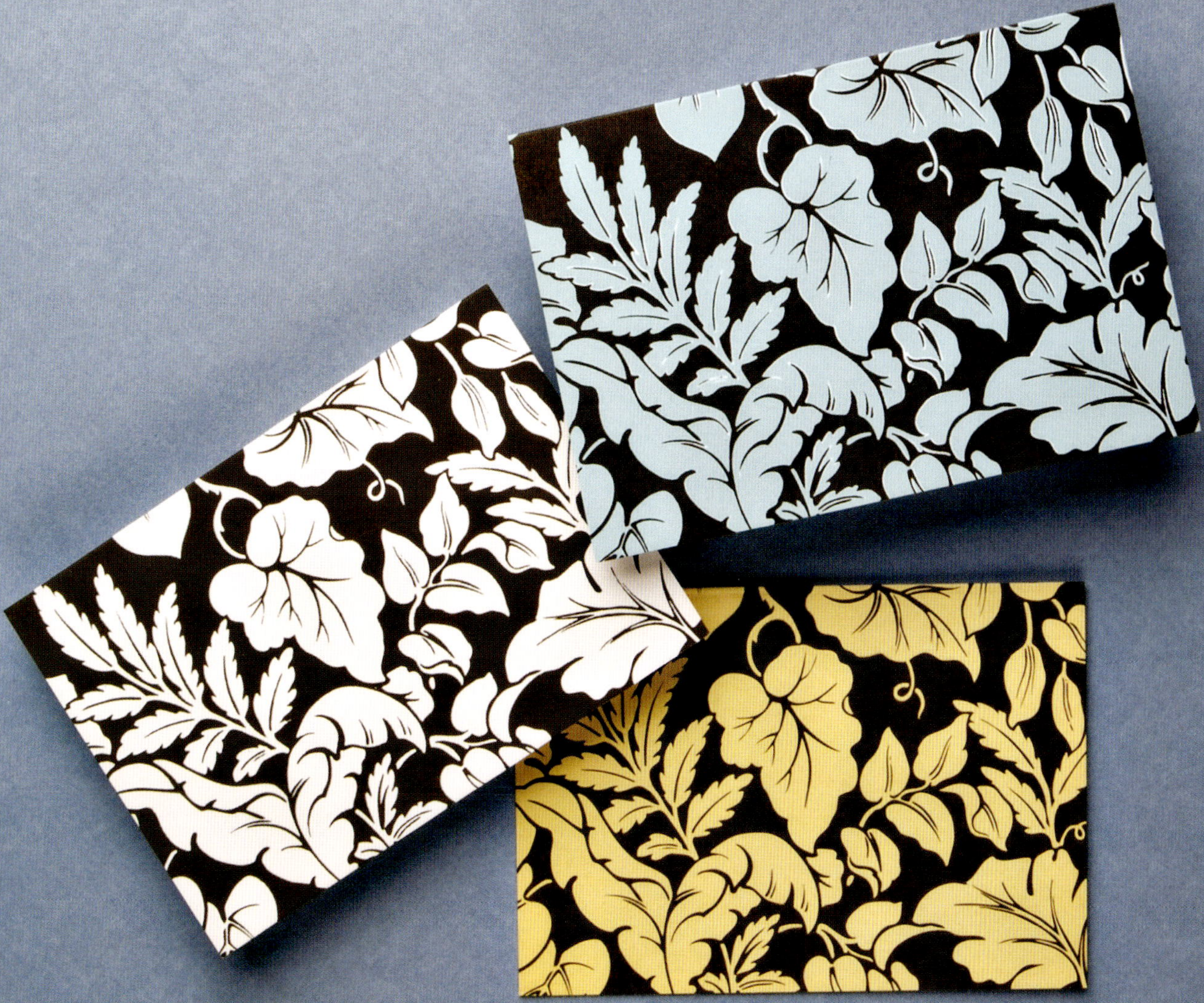

Letterspace

www.letterspacepaper.com

Jami Darwin Chiang studied fashion design in college and soon after graduation went into window display and merchandising. She slowly made her way back into what she has always loved most – paper. She is inspired by vintage textiles, oil paintings, portrait art, architecture, and children's illustration. Jami launched Letterspace seven years ago and currently resides in Chicago, Illinois.

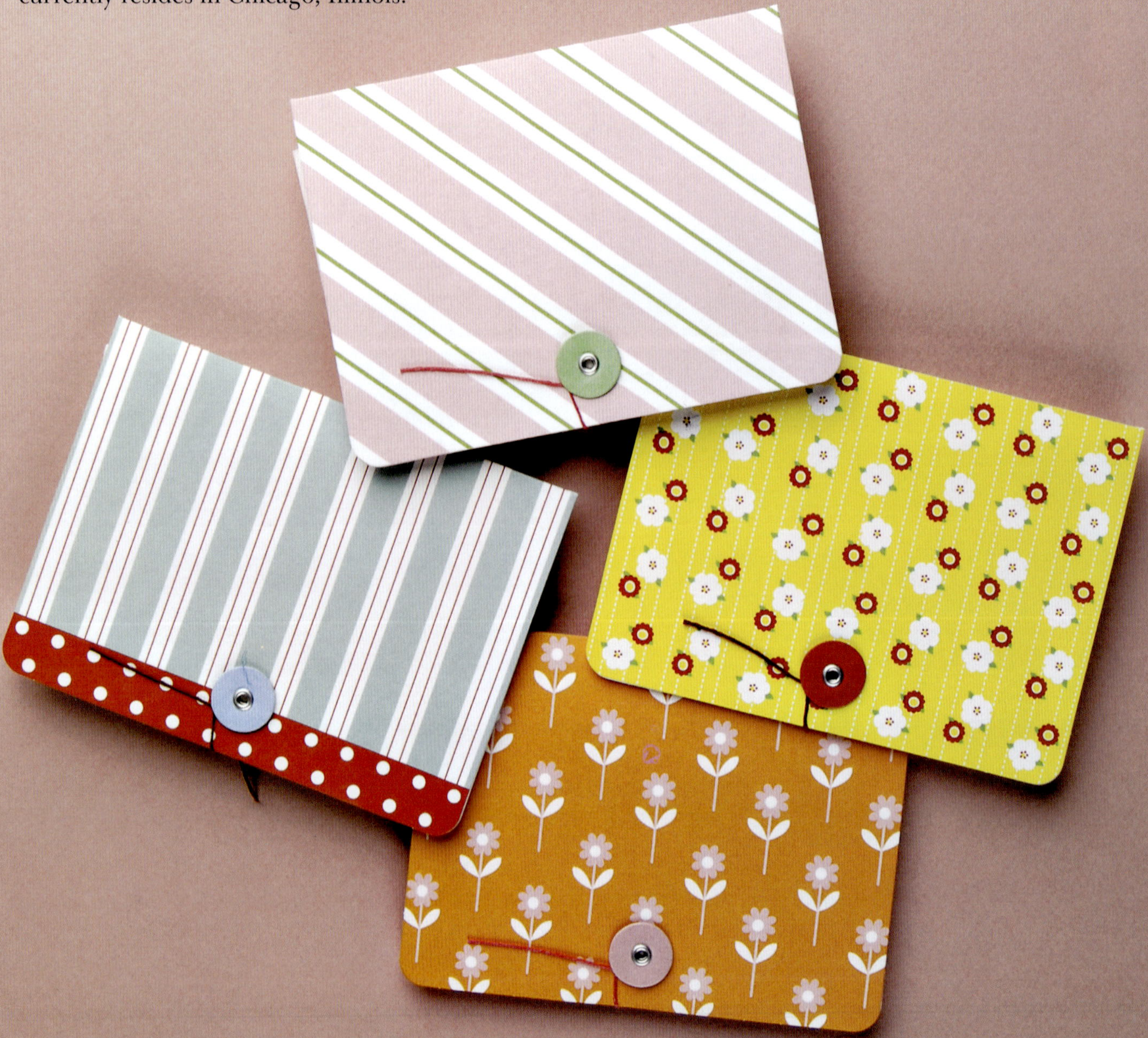

Vintage Kitchen Towel, Pink and Green Stripe, Strawberry Fields, and Tangerine Wallpaper. Offset printed. *Courtesy of Letterspace.*

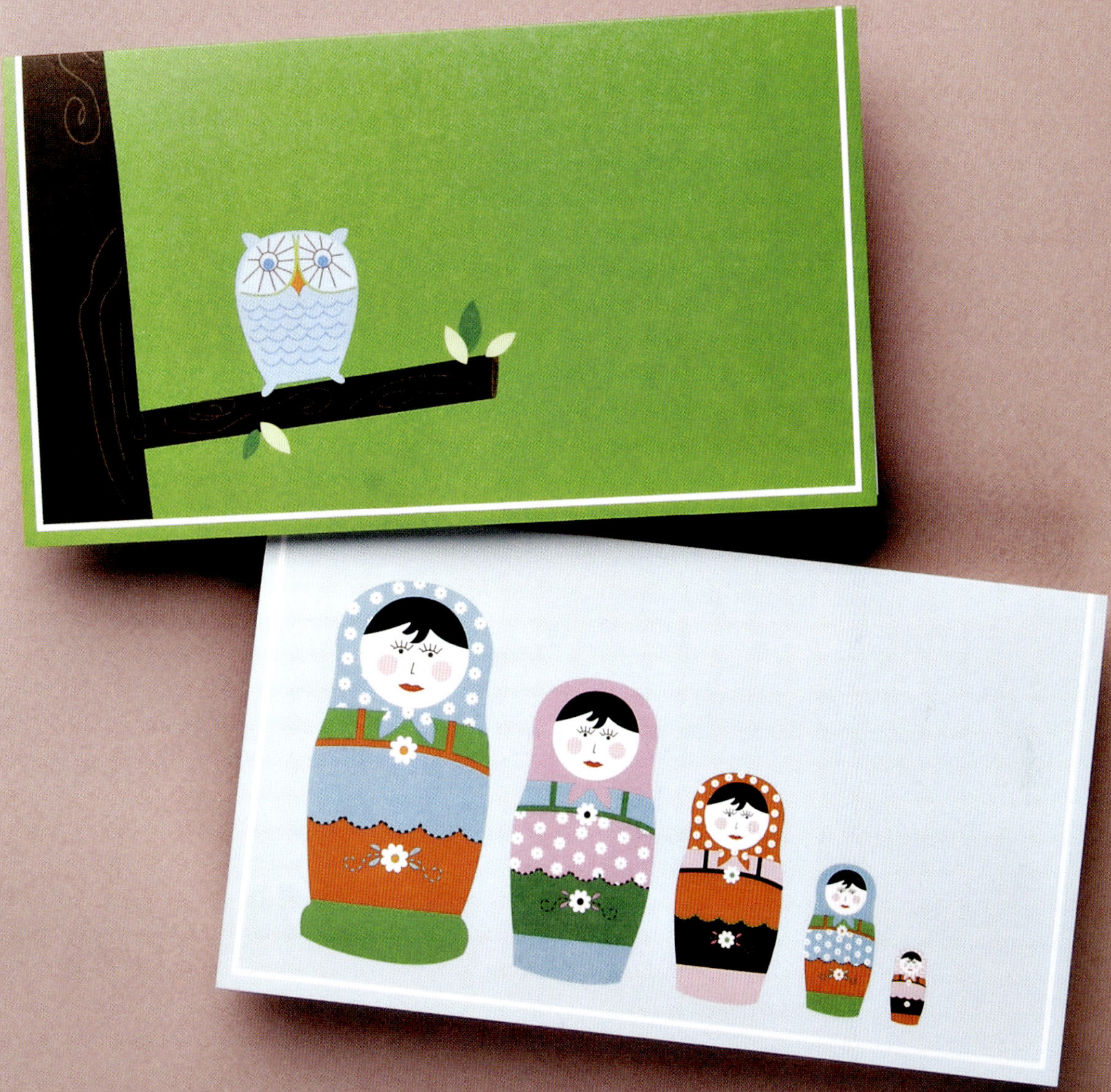

Owl Monarch and Matryoshka Monarch. Offset printed. *Courtesy of Letterspace.*

Herman Yu Design

www.hermanyu.com

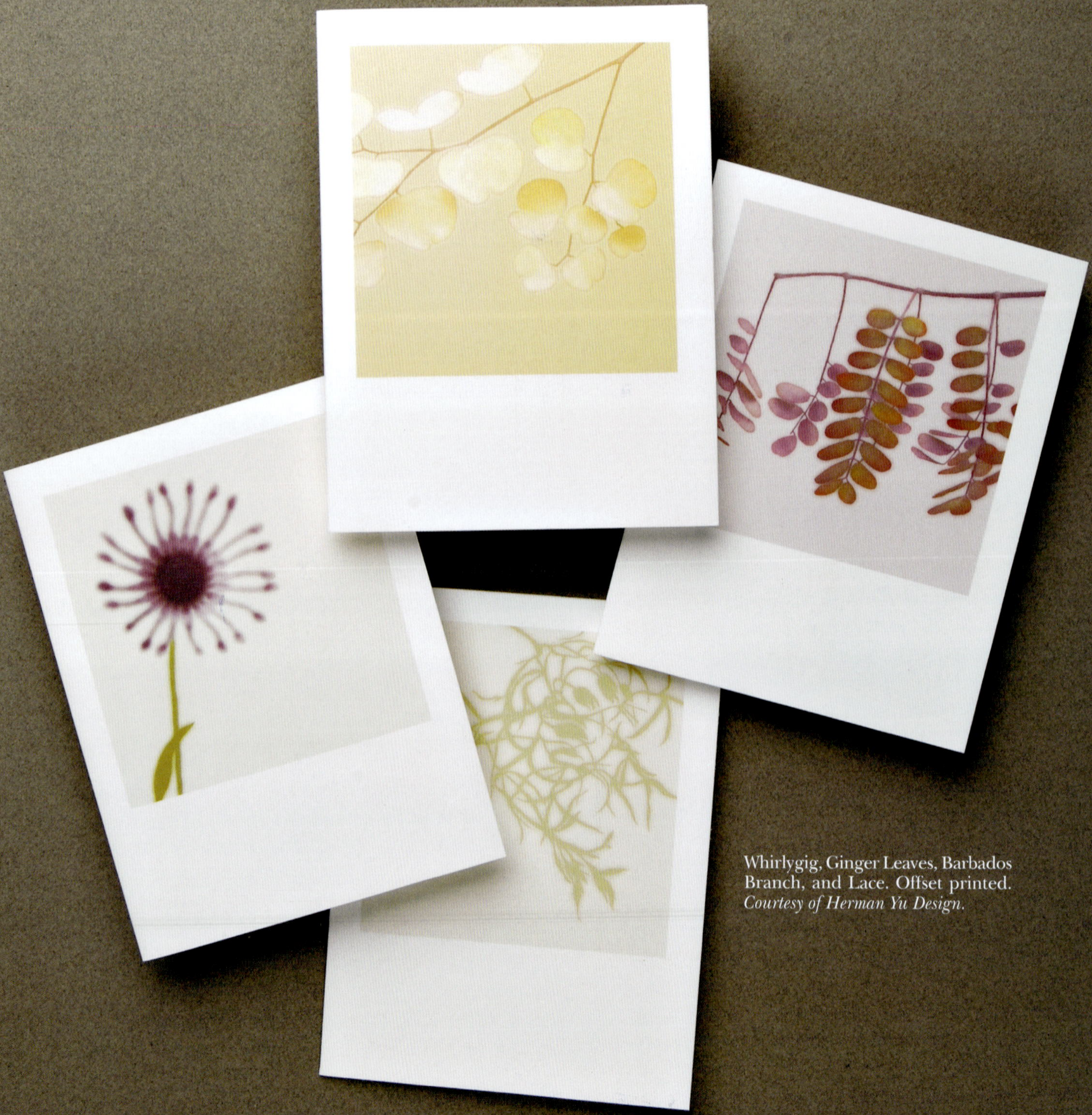

Whirlygig, Ginger Leaves, Barbados Branch, and Lace. Offset printed. *Courtesy of Herman Yu Design.*

Herman Yu is a Seattle based designer who started her company in 2001. After graduating with a degree in Textile Design from the Rhode Island School of Design, she began her career in New York developing decorative interior fabrics. She continued on to work with European and US mills, and designed bedding and decorative accessories for the Calvin Klein Home Collection. She currently designs for Herman Miller and other design savvy companies in addition to designing paper goods.

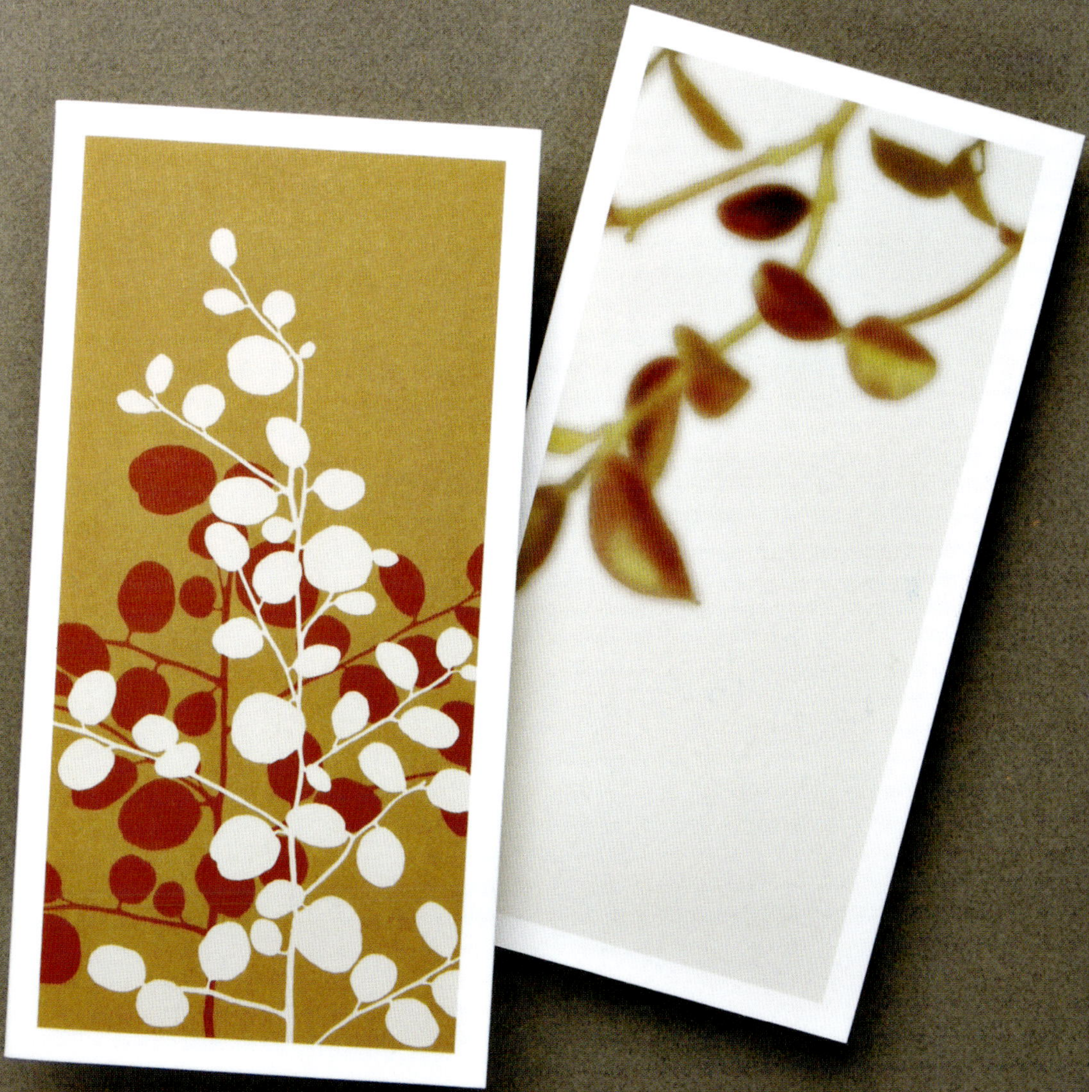

Round Leaves and Red Leaves. Offset printed.
Courtesy of Herman Yu Design.

Joy by Mel Lim

www.joybymellim.com

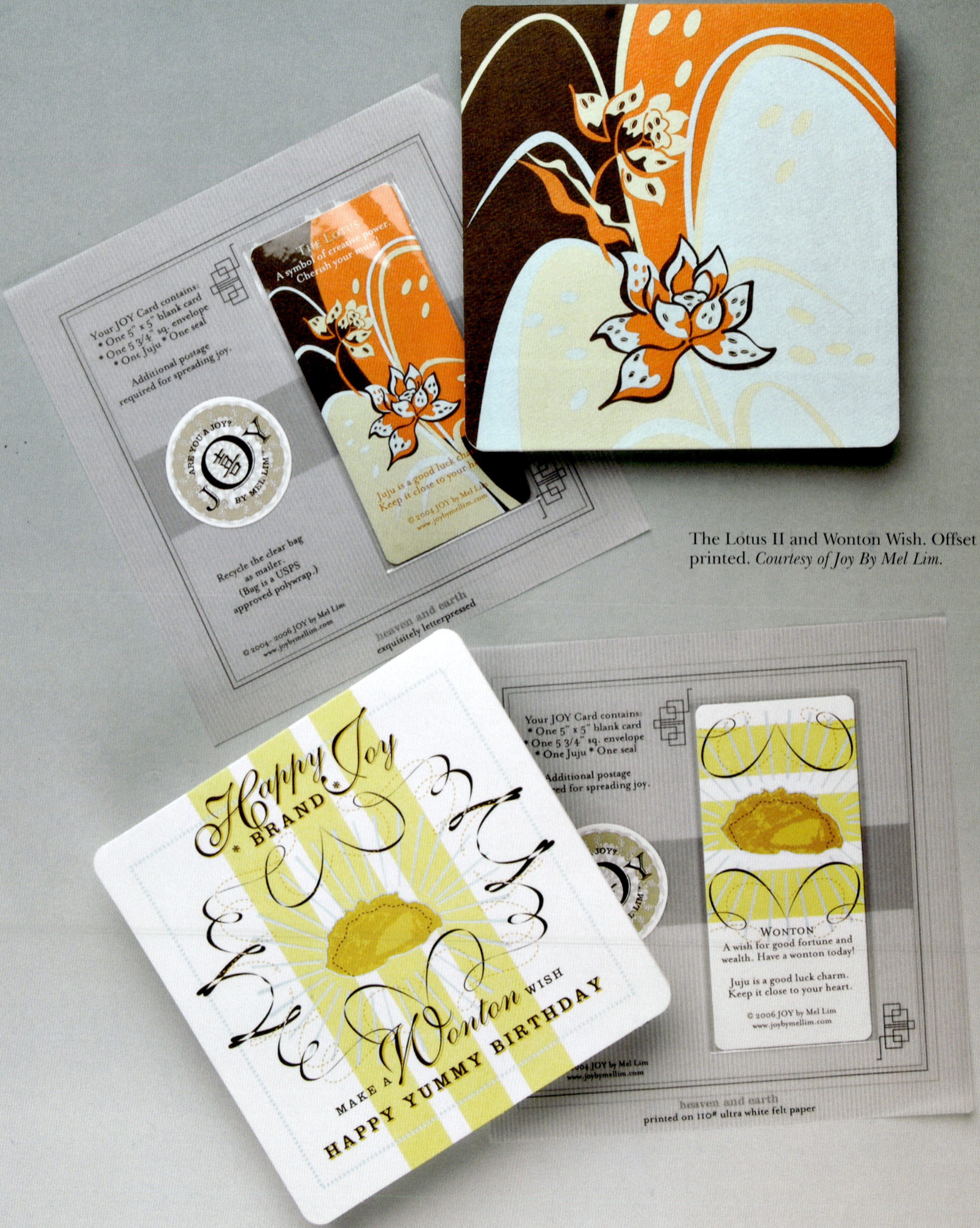

The Lotus II and Wonton Wish. Offset printed. *Courtesy of Joy By Mel Lim.*

Mel Lim began her stationery company in 2005 but has been a designer for the greater part of her life. She started designing interior spaces when she was only thirteen years old, working with her mom at her furniture and interior design studio in Malaysia. She graduated with the highest distinction in Environmental Design from the Art Center College of Design in Pasadena, California. She currently lives in San Diego with her husband Joe and Chihuahua Bambi.

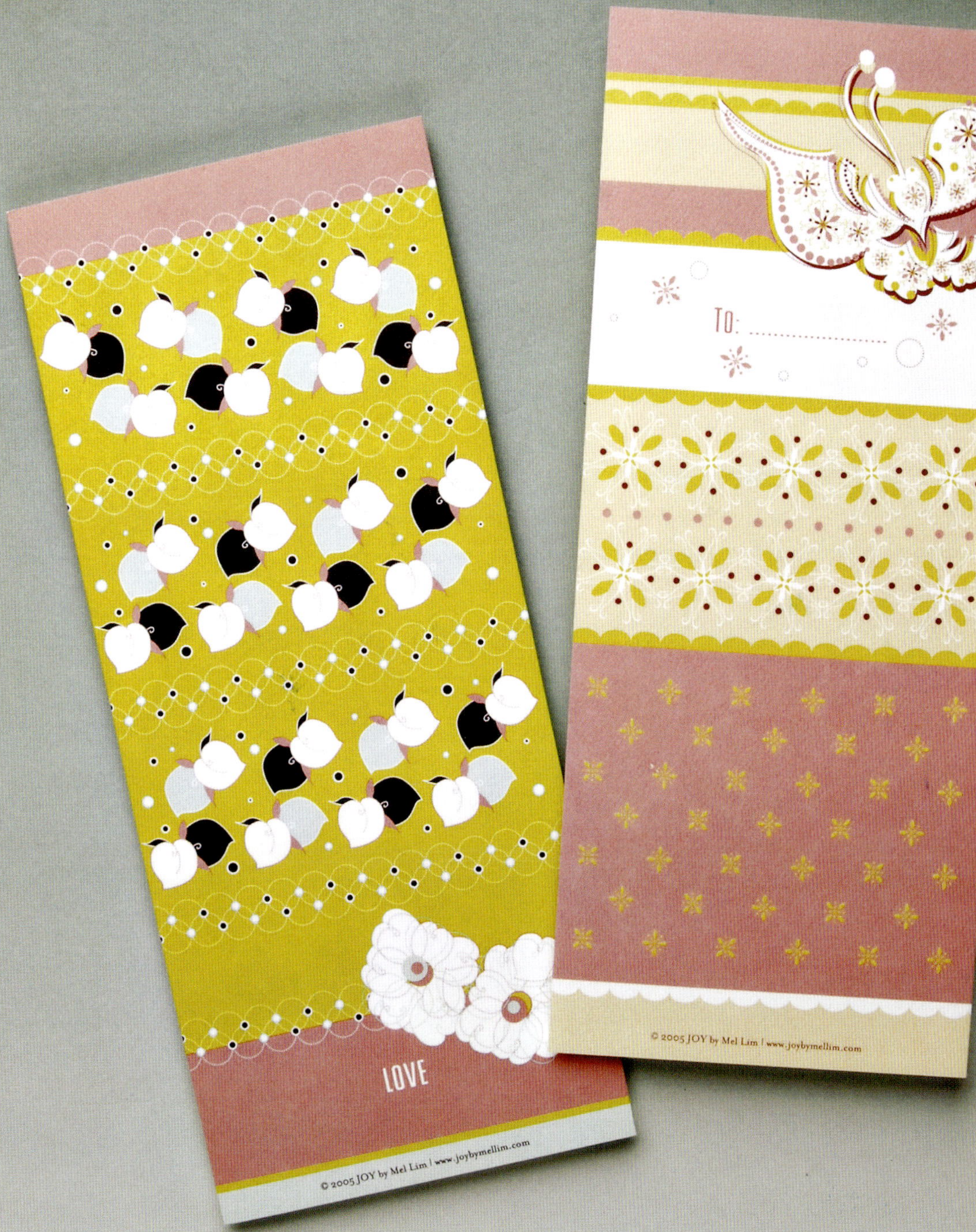

Love and Butterfly. Offset printed. *Courtesy of Joy By Mel Lim.*

Dewey Howard

www.deweyhoward.com

Elizabeth Grubaugh has been designing stationery since 2000 for her New York based company named after her grandfather. She has also designed fabrics for Emilio Pucci in Italy, taught design for two and a half years in Japan, designed snowboards for Burton Snowboards, and designed carpet for a Japanese company. She is now paired with a soap company where she makes scented drawer papers, scented stationery, beeswax candles, and much more. They call their collaboration the "Soap and Paper Factory."

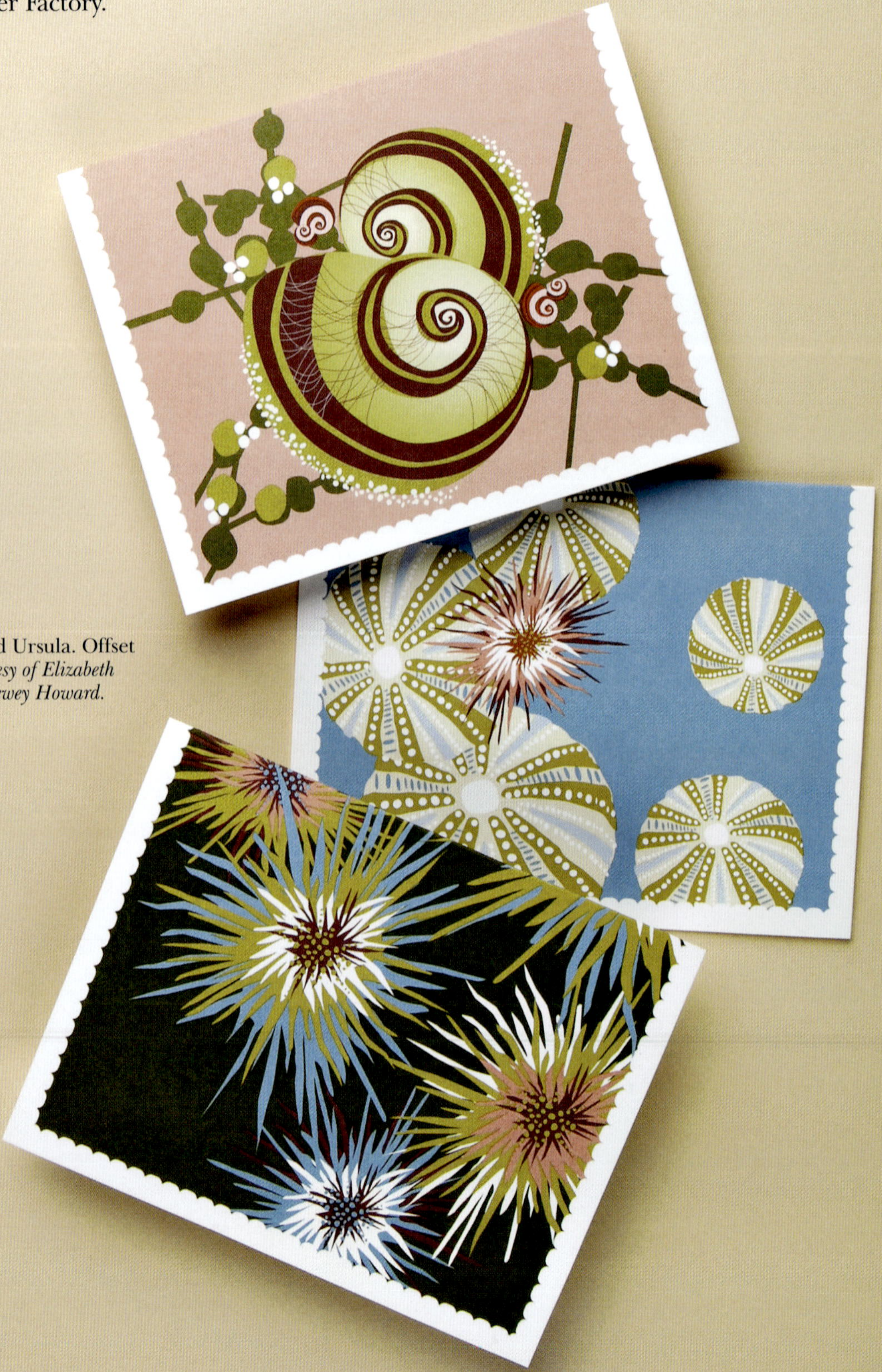

Gail, June, and Ursula. Offset printed. *Courtesy of Elizabeth Grubaugh of Dewey Howard.*

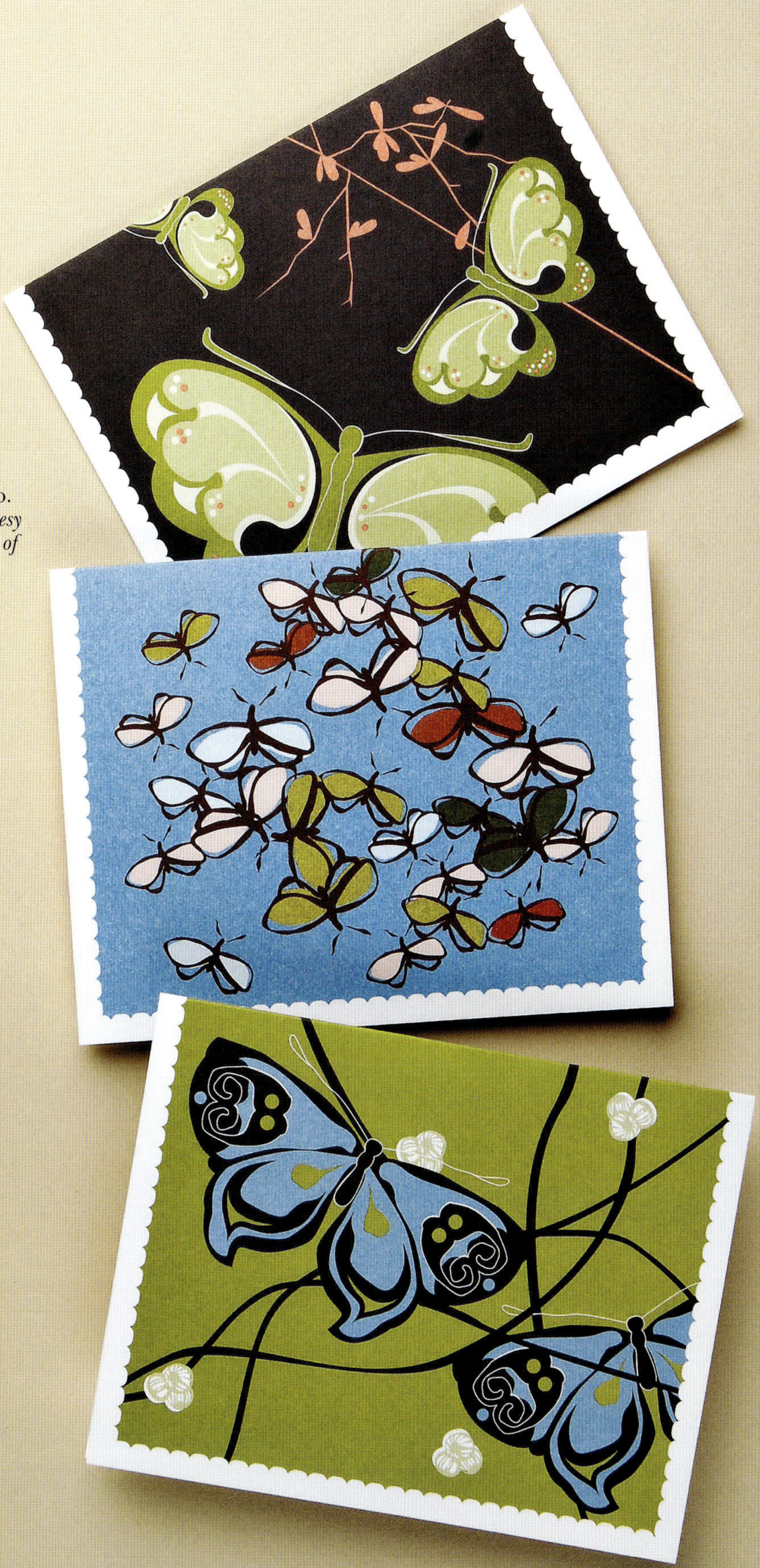

April, Agnes, and Flo. Offset printed. *Courtesy of Elizabeth Grubaugh of Dewey Howard.*

Wooster and Prince

www.woosterandprince.com

Amy Ormond started her company in 2002 and considers herself a self-taught artist who prefers to learn through doing. She has a great love for art and architecture and loves to restore homes. She has completely renovated her loft in SoHo, a beach cottage in Nantucket, and an 1850 farmhouse, where she now lives with her family. When she isn't busy designing in some capacity, she enjoys playing with her two boys, Jack (5) and Bear (4).

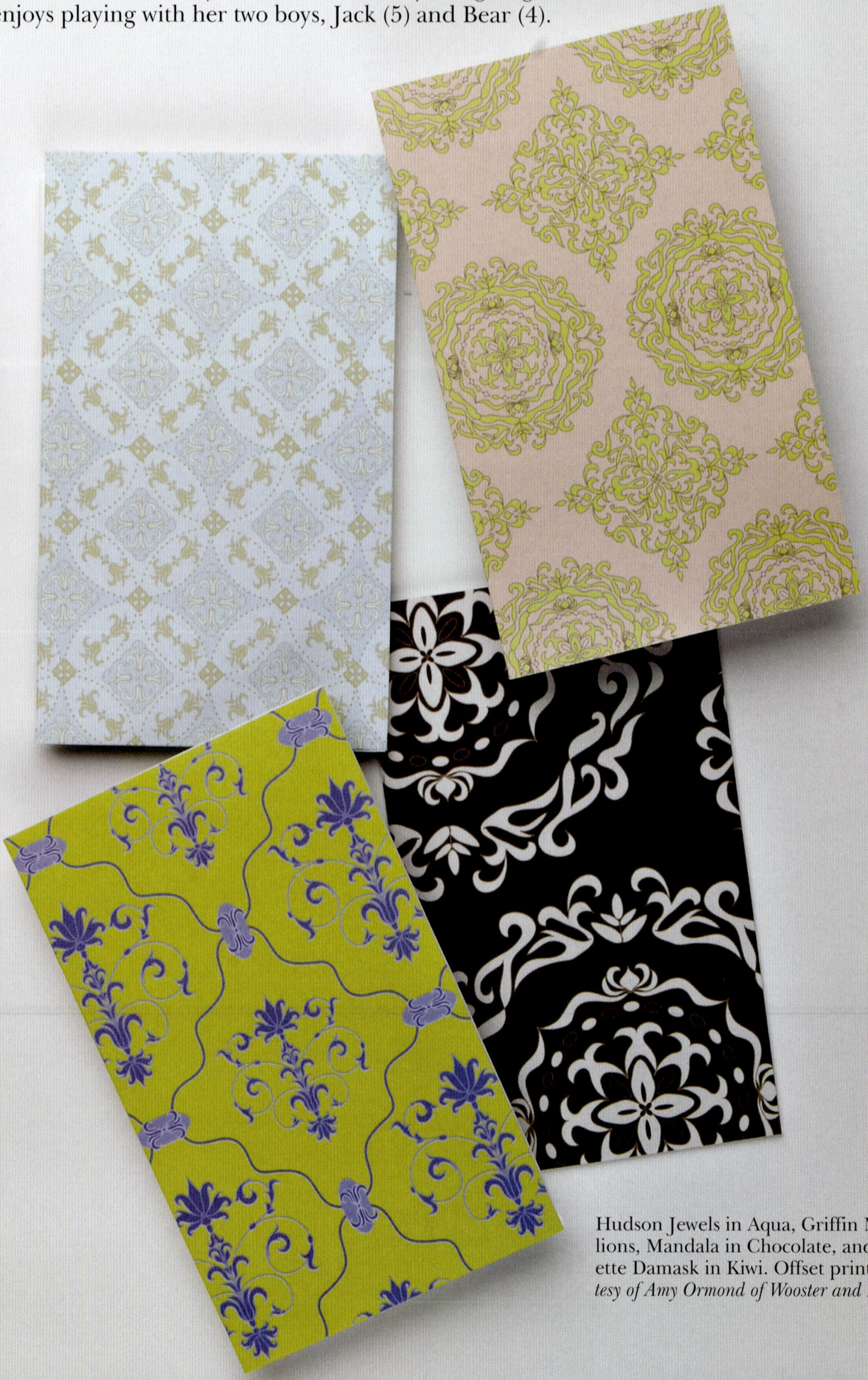

Hudson Jewels in Aqua, Griffin Medallions, Mandala in Chocolate, and Lafayette Damask in Kiwi. Offset printed. *Courtesy of Amy Ormond of Wooster and Prince.*

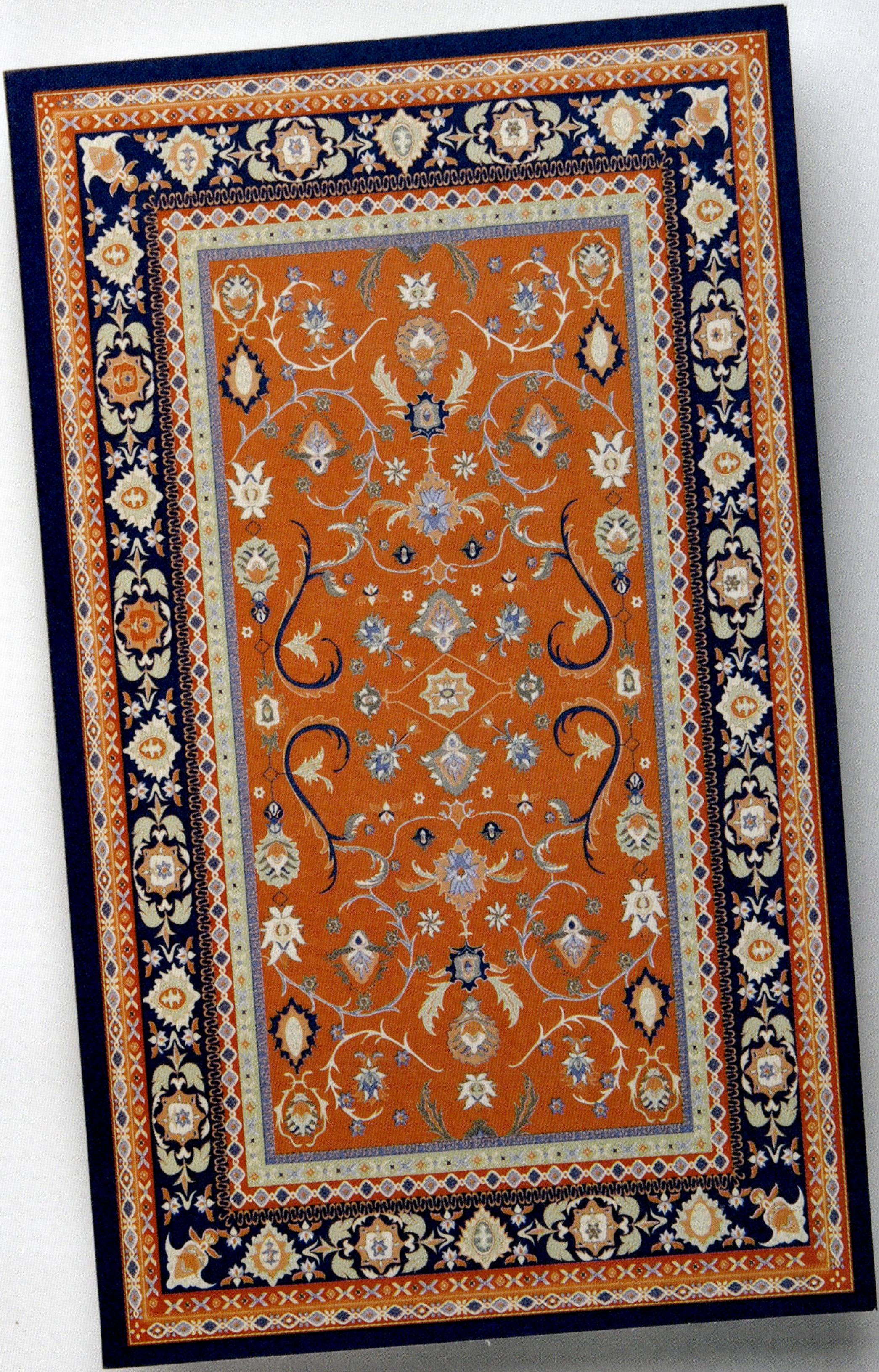

Sultana. Offset printed. *Courtesy of Amy Ormond of Wooster and Prince.*

Rosebud Design Studio

www.rosebud-design.com

Elana Iaciofano has been a stationery designer since 2005 and currently lives and works in Santa Monica, California. She studied Graphic Design and Fine Arts at the University of Pennsylvania and the School of Visual Arts. She went on to work in very creative, small design studios in New York and Los Angeles. Elana draws inspiration for her designs from multi-media collage, textiles and fashion, illuminated manuscripts, vintage graphics, and her small, fluffy, tri-colored dog, Toby.

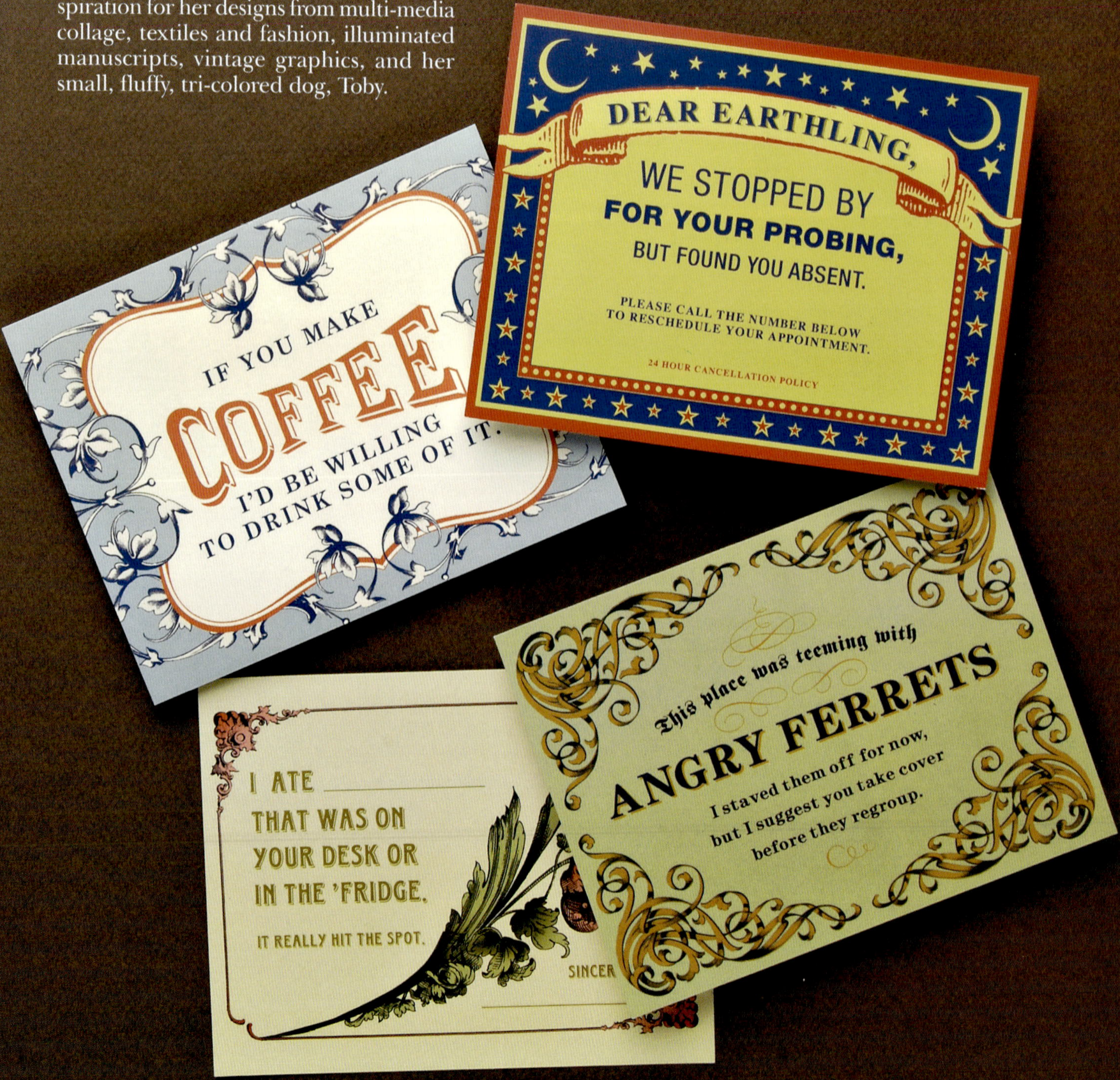

Notes to Self and Others Post Card Collection. Offset printed. *Courtesy of Rosebud Design Studio.*

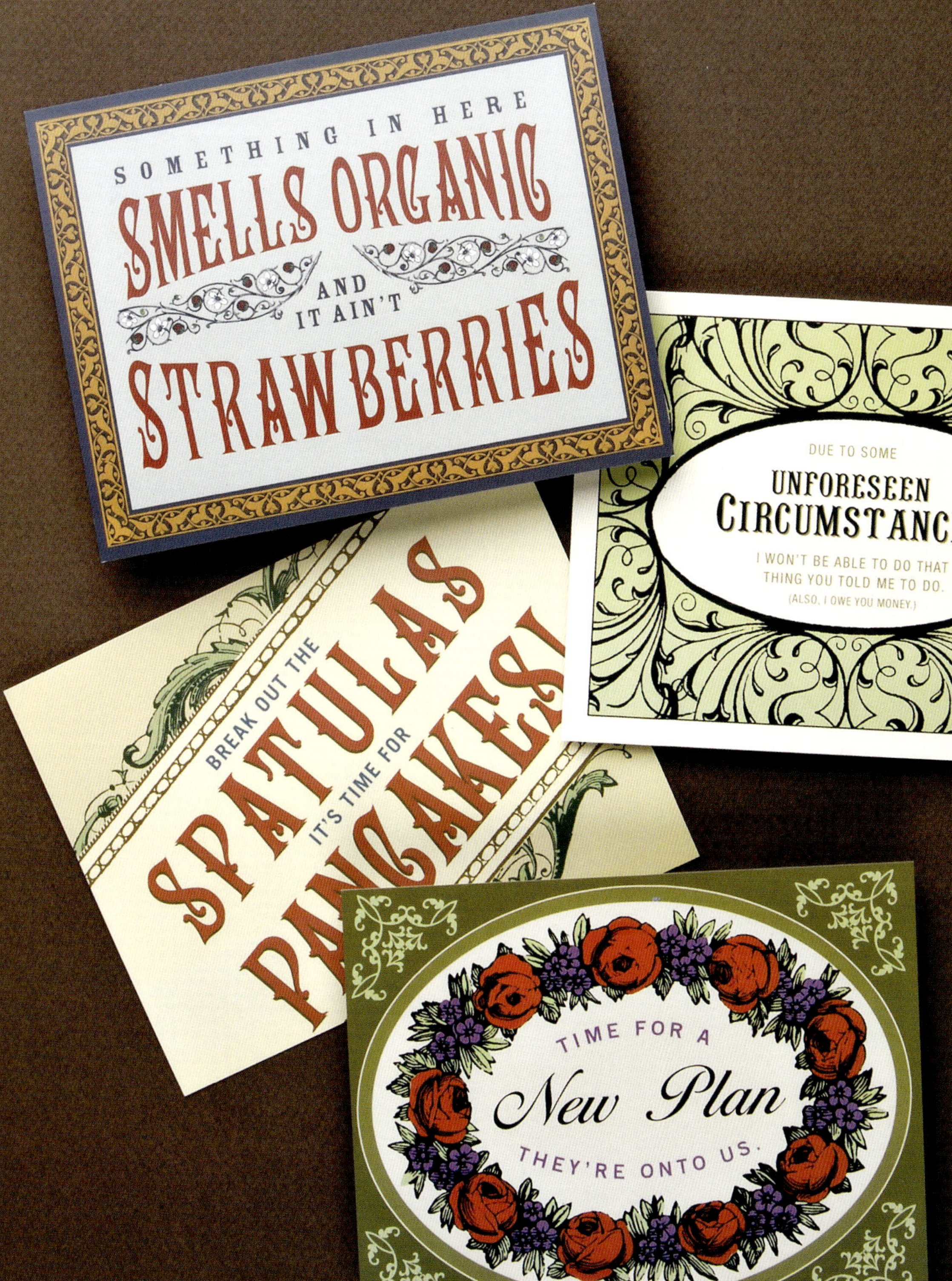

Jezebel

www.ilovejezebel.com

Leigh Batnick resides in Brooklyn and has been designing cards for her line since 2002. She considers herself a bibliophile and is completely obsessed and inspired by books, old films, the French New Wave, seashells, Joseph Cornell, test shots from her grandmother's years as a model, and the space age meeting the decorative age.

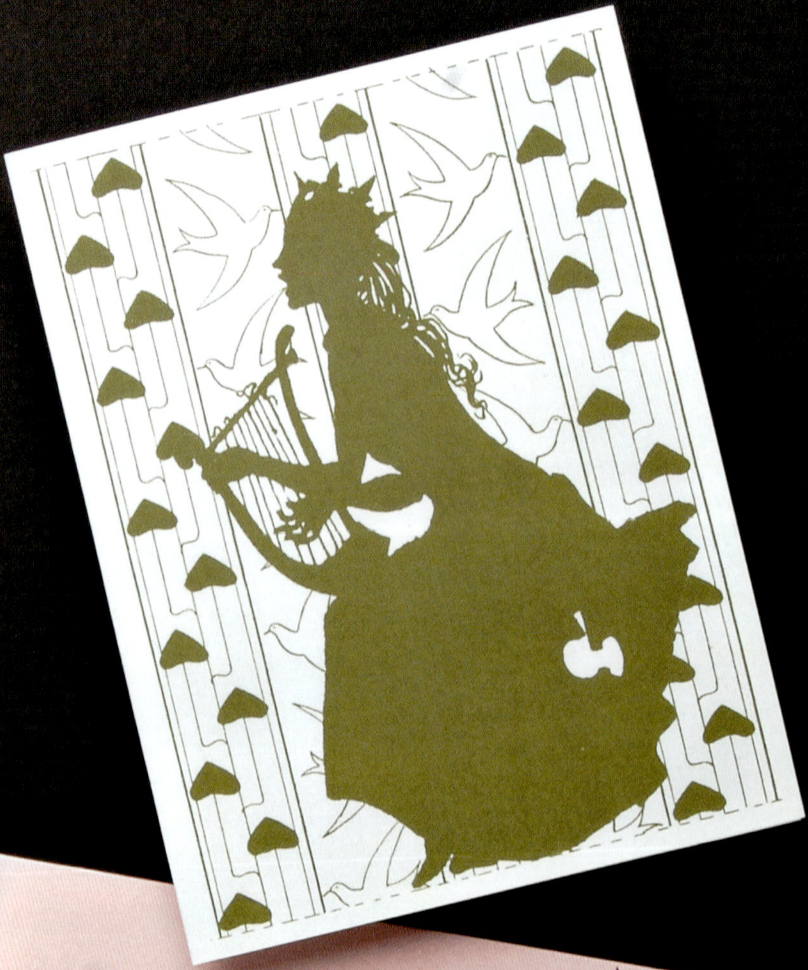

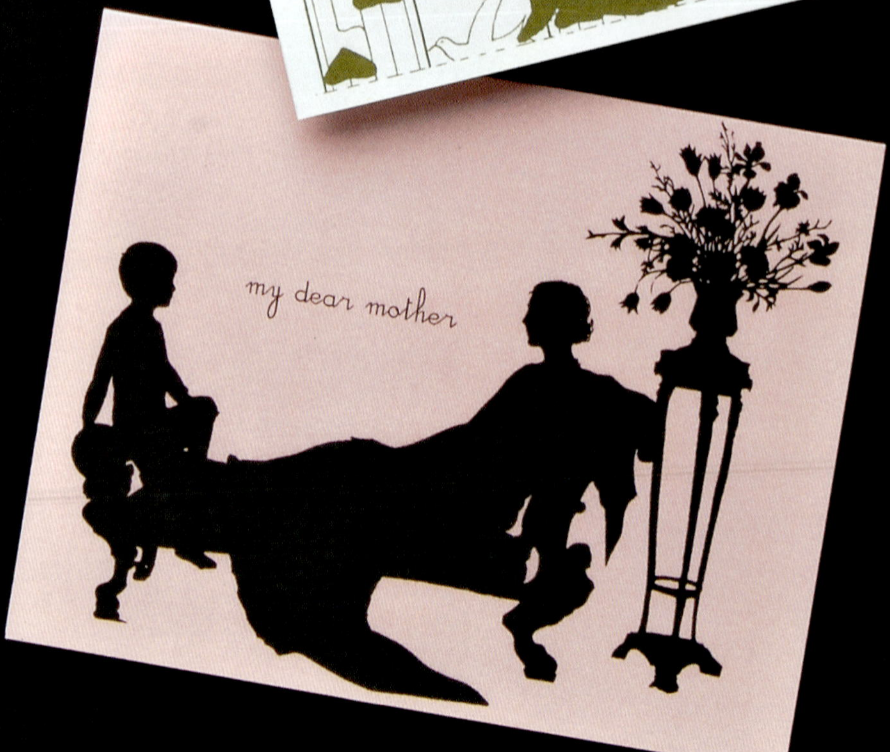

Honey Strums a Creaky Tune for Hannah and Gilda and One Day, Blanche Birthed a Mad, Bad Bibliophile. Iris printed. *Courtesy of Jezebel Stationery.*

Bernice Spoke Latin with Alacrity and Maybelle, Chanteuse. Iris printed. *Courtesy of Jezebel Stationery.*

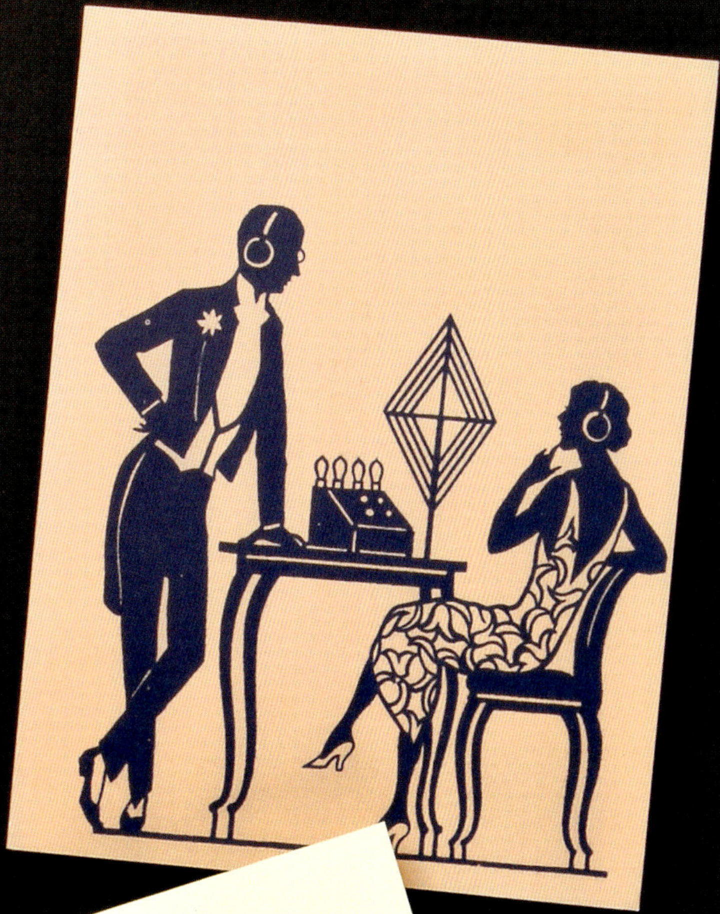

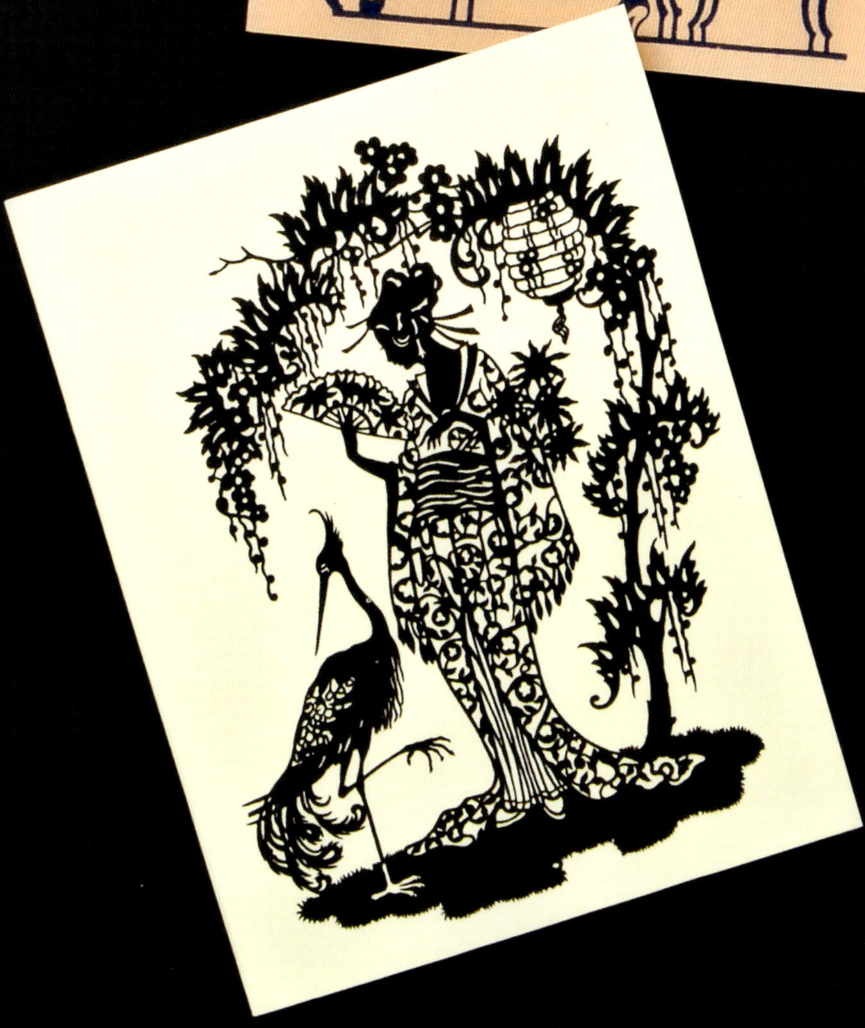

Apiary Design

www.apiarydesign.com

Molly Woodland spent ten years as a graphic designer in the professional services industry before she officially launched her company in 2005. She is a self-proclaimed "old-fashioned girl" with an unabashed love of vintage design and a desire to bring back the lost art of the handwritten note. She currently lives and works in Minneapolis, Minnesota.

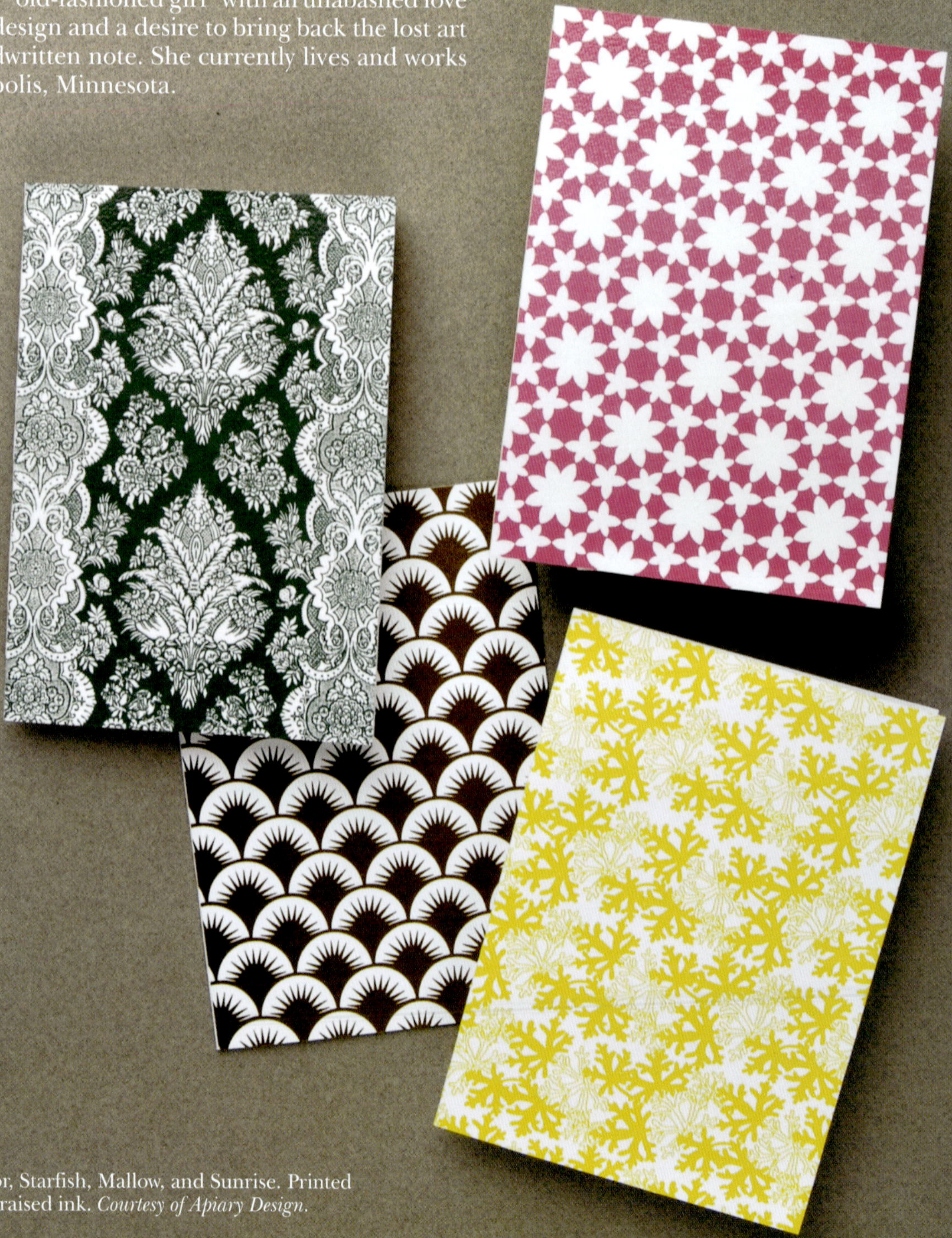

Parlor, Starfish, Mallow, and Sunrise. Printed with raised ink. *Courtesy of Apiary Design.*

Thoughts of You, With Gratitude, Mini Lucky in Love, Mini Birthday Wishes, and Mini Thoughts of You. Printed with raised ink. *Courtesy of Apiary Design.*

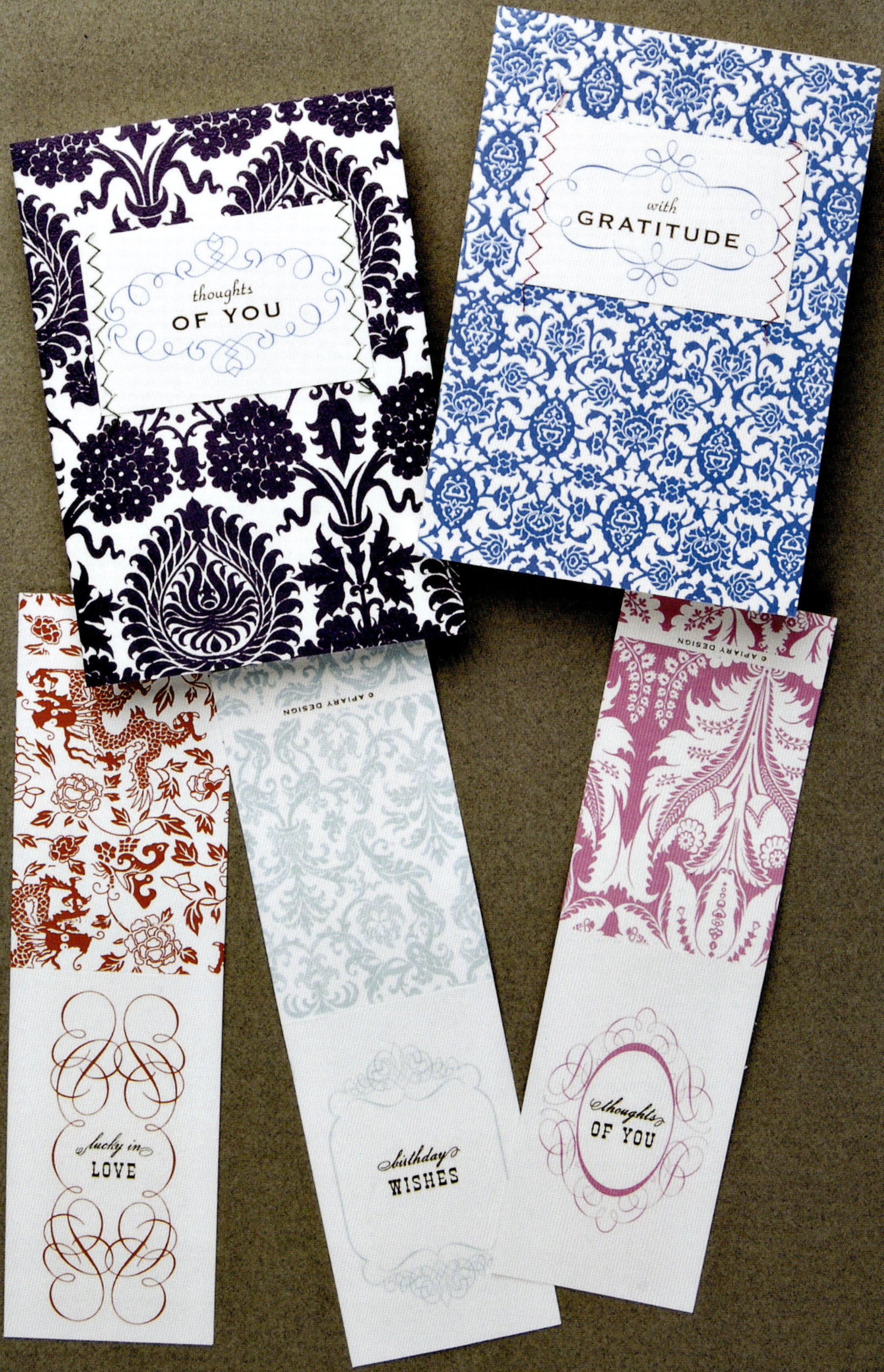

Chapter Two
Handmade

Another popular and ever growing trend in stationery is the handmade greeting card. Most of the designs that are profiled are taken from small stationery studios that manufacture their products by hand in the USA. These cards are hand cut, hand glittered, and even hand sewn. The attention to detail, fine craftsmanship, and innovative use of materials make these cards truly special. Many people feel that purchasing one of these creations is not so much like buying an expensive greeting card, but rather owning an inexpensive piece of art.

Handmade card designers enjoy the art of making each individual card as much as the actual design process. Anne Millett of *Mira Aster* states that "designing was stimulating, but the making was equally rewarding." Many handmade card designers have been "crafty types" since childhood. Jenni Kelly and Karen Leeds of *You Send Me* were friends in junior high and they say that anyone who know them in eighth grade wouldn't be surprised in the least to find out what they are doing for a living as adults.

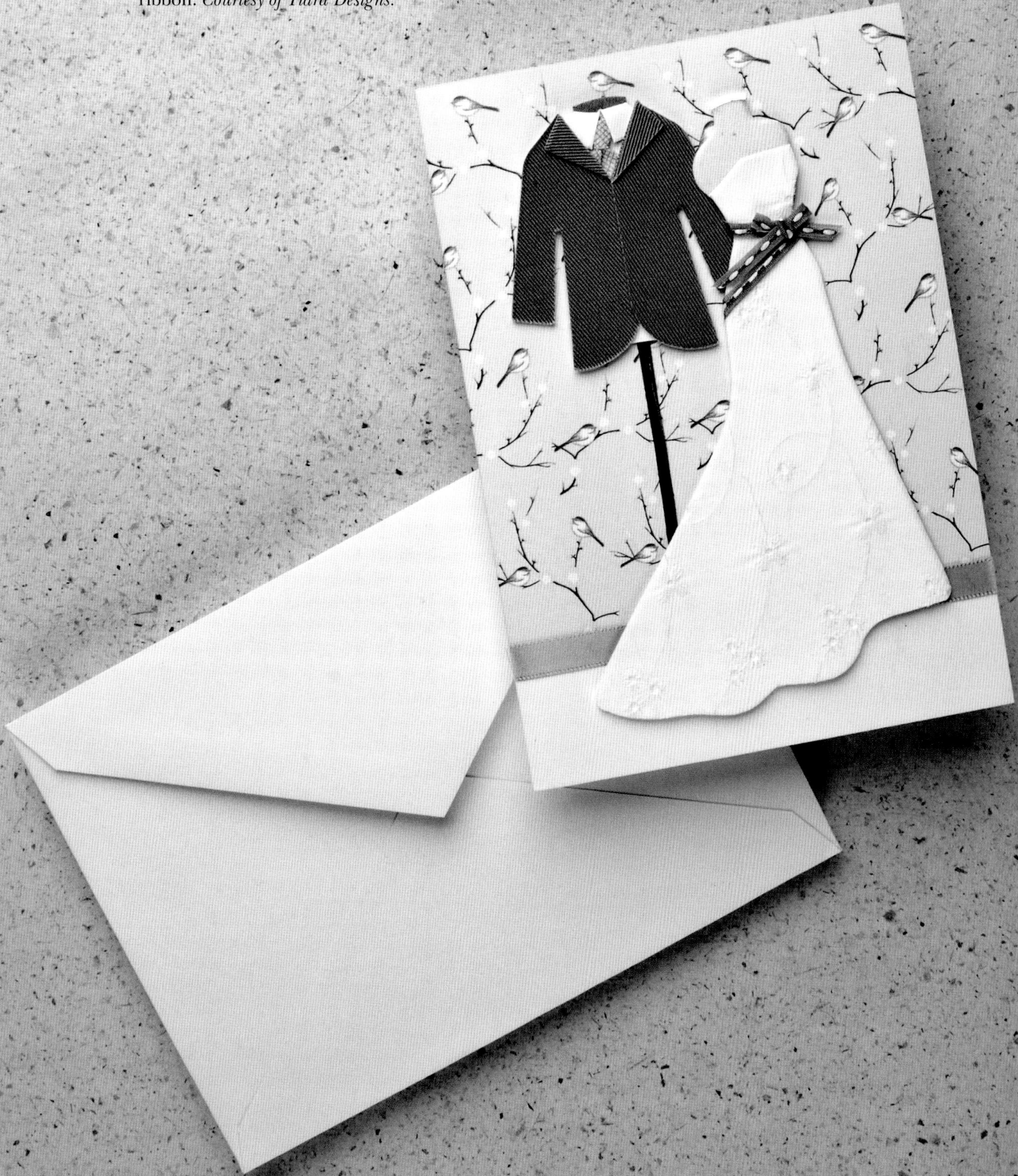

Woodland Bride and Groom. Handmade with fabric, paper, and ribbon. *Courtesy of Tiara Designs.*

Tiara Designs

www.tiara-designs.com

Kira Romashko-Thiel launched her company in 2002 from her dining room table in Milwaukee, Wisconsin. Tiara Designs is a six time Louie Award Winner and nine time finalist. She holds a BFA in painting and has always loved fashion. She is inspired by her vintage kimono fabric collection, the pages in vintage *Vogue* magazines, European interior design, art museums and galleries, the ballet, her cat Yoshi and dog Brandy, and window shopping.

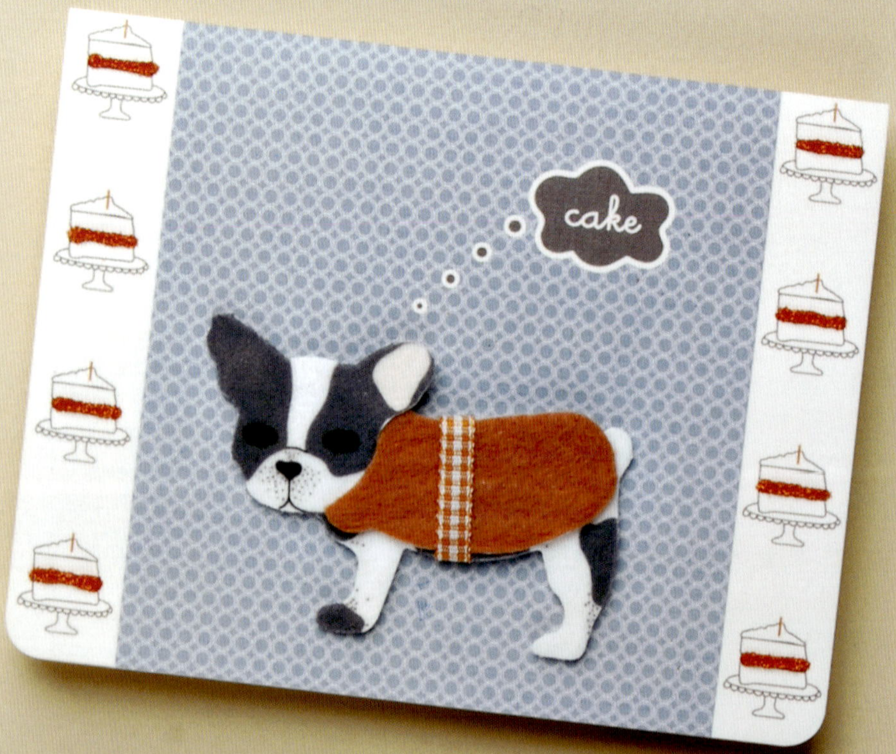

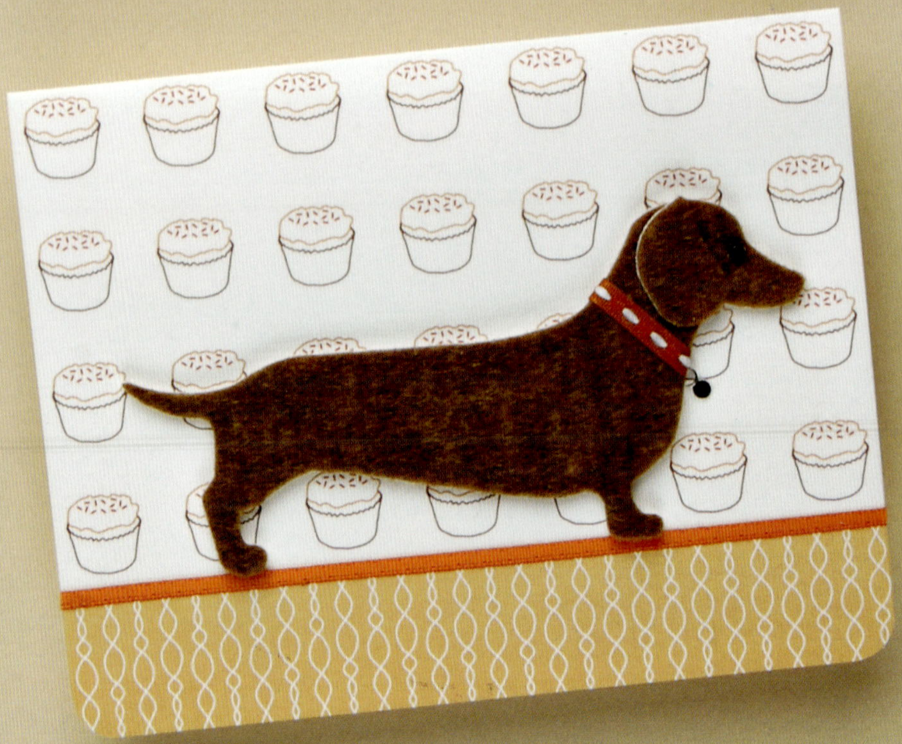

Le Frenchie and Cake, Dachshund and Cupcakes. Handmade with cut fabric and embellishments. *Courtesy of Tiara Designs.*

Striped Sundress, Ditsy Floral Dress and Umbrella, Couture Top and Swirl Skirt with Owls and Trees, Floral Red Skirt and Bag. Handmade with cut fabric and embellishments. *Courtesy of Tiara Designs.*

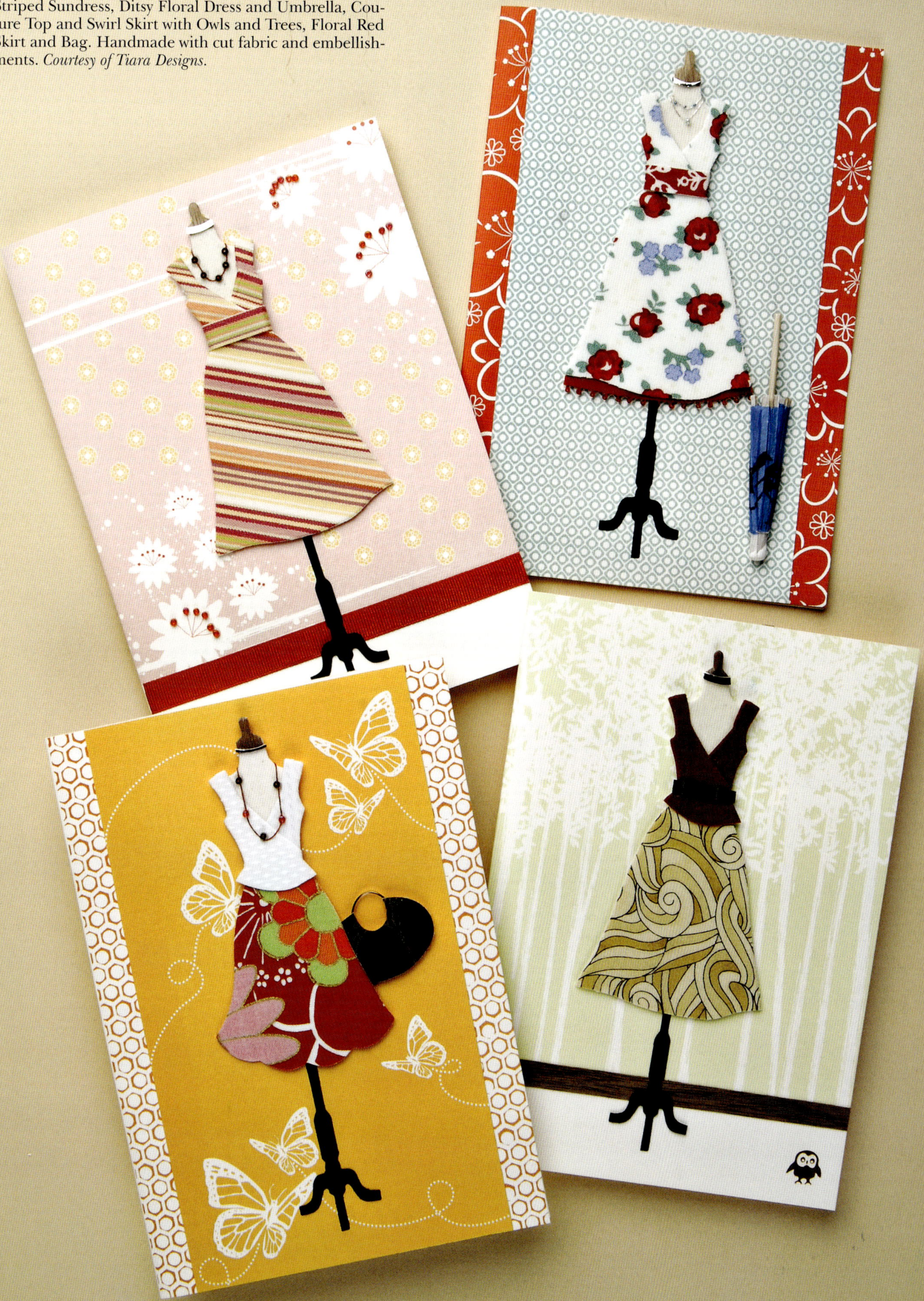

Flaunt

www.flauntcards.com

Shannon Barnes started designing cards for friends and family in 2001. A distributor soon picked her up after getting some initial designs into a local home decor store in Vancouver, British Columbia. She finds inspiration in the small and beautiful things in life, her business minded husband, her Saint Bernard, and her two-year-old (inquisitive) little girl.

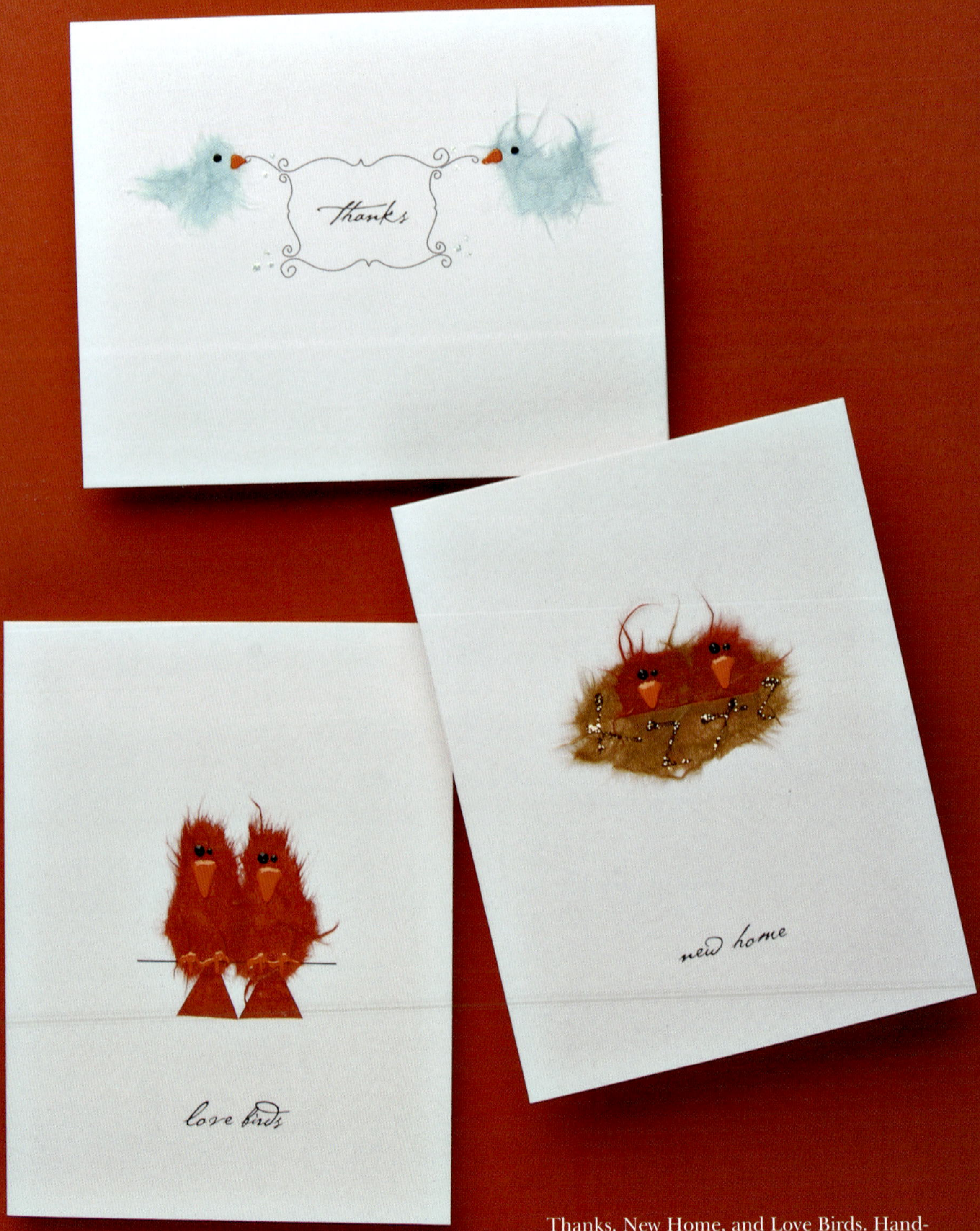

Thanks, New Home, and Love Birds. Hand-torn mulberry paper with fabric paint and glitter. *Courtesy of Shannon Barnes.*

Birthday Wishes, Spring Chicken?, Happy Birthday Two Ewe, and Another Year Wiser. Hand-torn mulberry paper with fabric paint and glitter. *Courtesy of Shannon Barnes.*

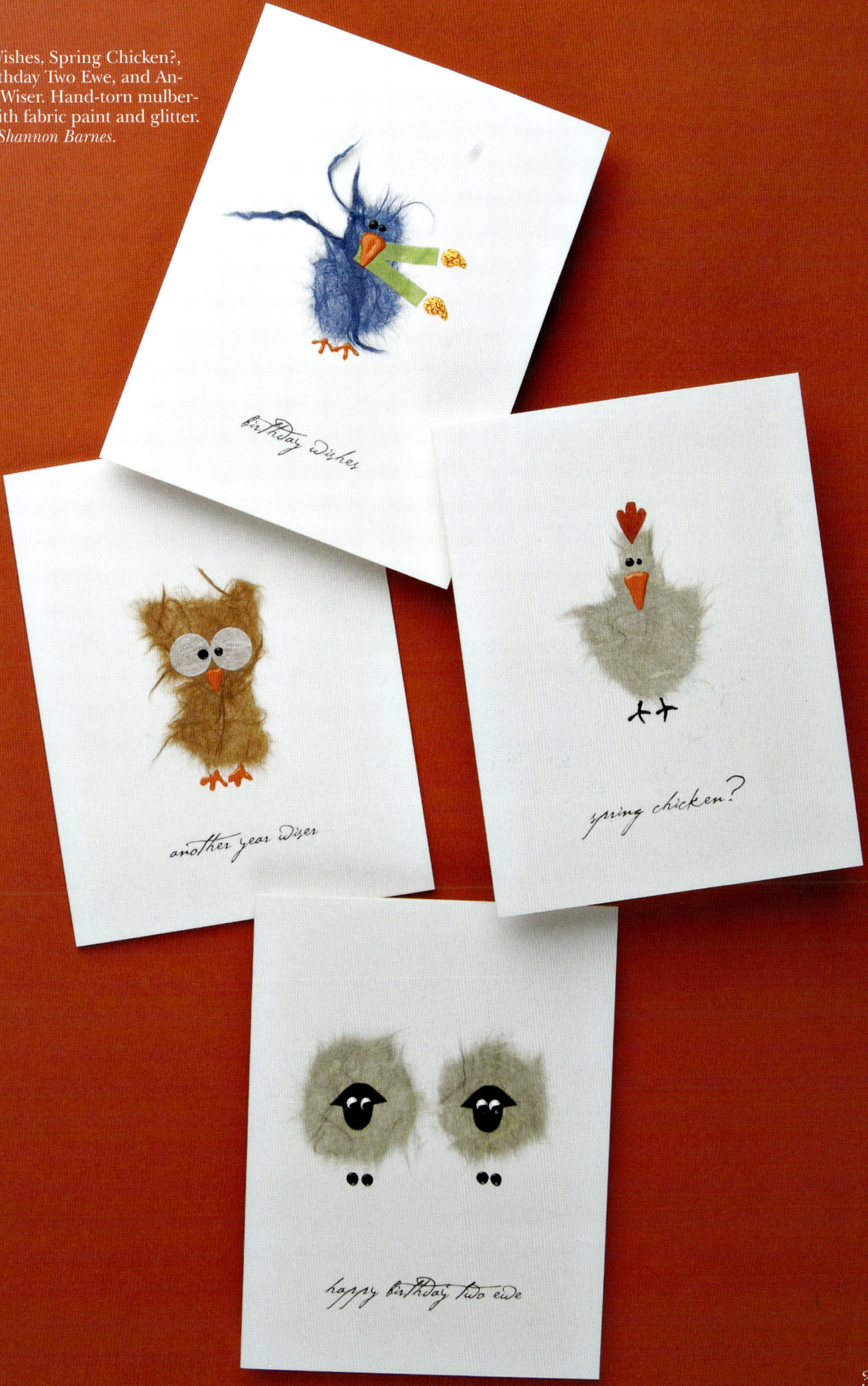

Mira Aster

www.miraaster.com

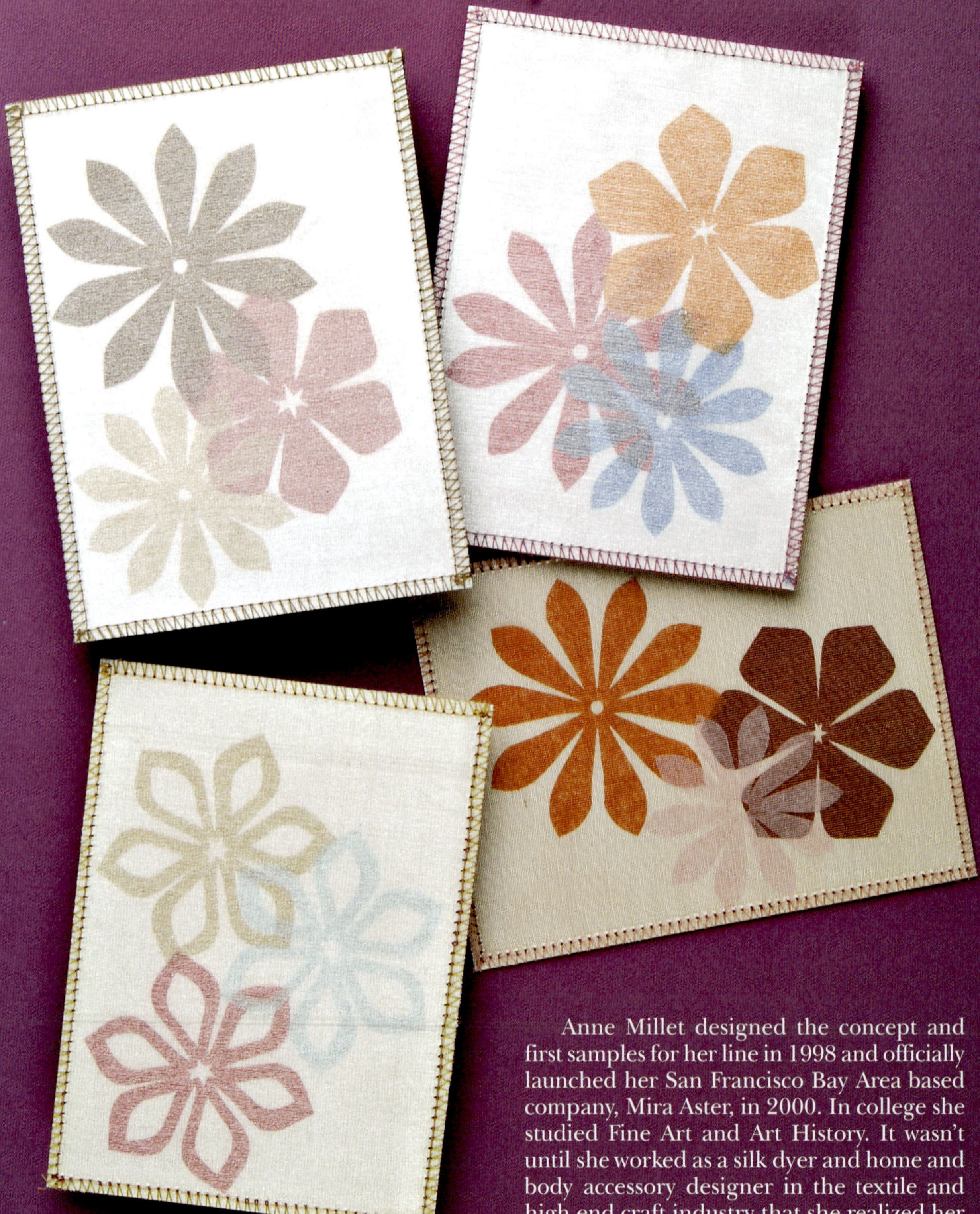

Classic Tissue Flower Cards in assorted colors. Silk organza sewn onto card stock over hand-cut tissue flowers. *Courtesy of Anne Millett.*

Anne Millet designed the concept and first samples for her line in 1998 and officially launched her San Francisco Bay Area based company, Mira Aster, in 2000. In college she studied Fine Art and Art History. It wasn't until she worked as a silk dyer and home and body accessory designer in the textile and high end craft industry that she realized her love for fabric. Her new love of fabric was a natural extension of her love for paper as she incorporates it into her card designs. Mira Aster cards can be found in the Permanent Collection of Contemporary Design at the Victoria and Albert Museum in London.

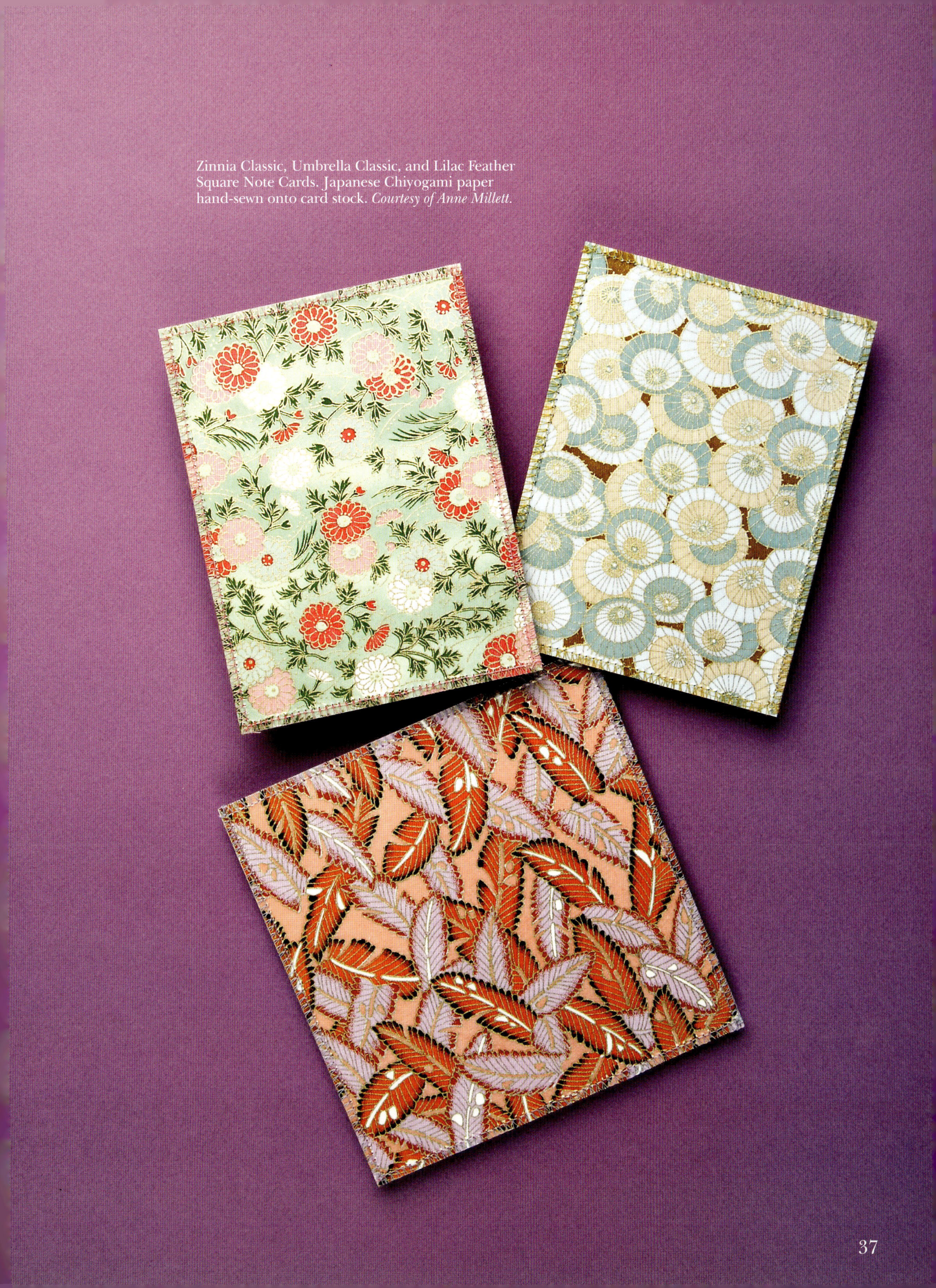

Zinnia Classic, Umbrella Classic, and Lilac Feather Square Note Cards. Japanese Chiyogami paper hand-sewn onto card stock. *Courtesy of Anne Millett.*

You Send Me

www.yousendme.com

Jenni Kelly and Karen Leeds are the creative spark behind their award winning company based in Chattanooga, Tennessee. More than just business partners, they have been good friends since eighth grade. They both went on to earn degrees in Graphic Design and collaborated over the years on different projects. They knew that they worked well together, so in February of 1998 they bit the bullet and sold some Valentines to their favorite store in Seattle.

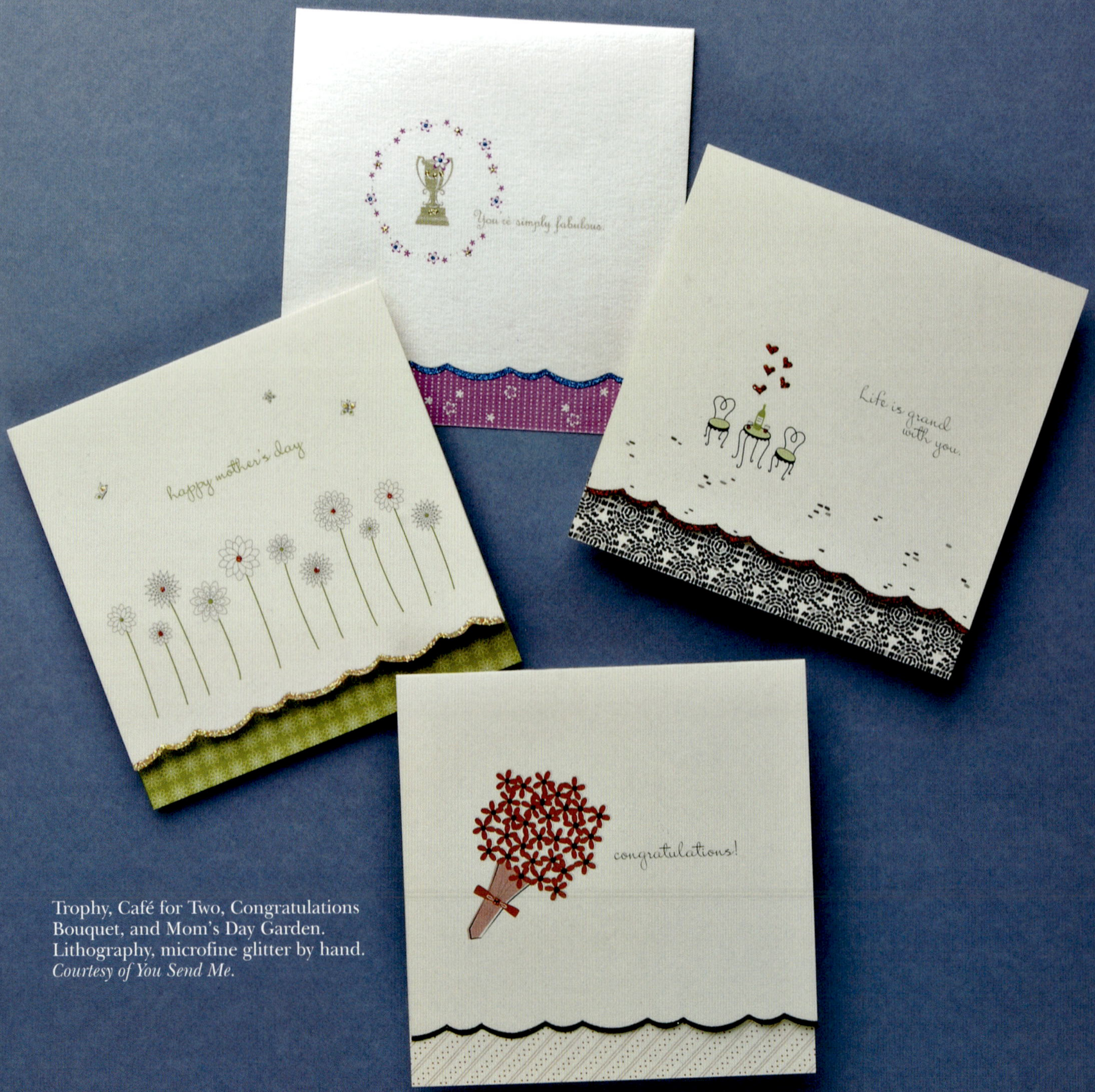

Trophy, Café for Two, Congratulations Bouquet, and Mom's Day Garden. Lithography, microfine glitter by hand. *Courtesy of You Send Me.*

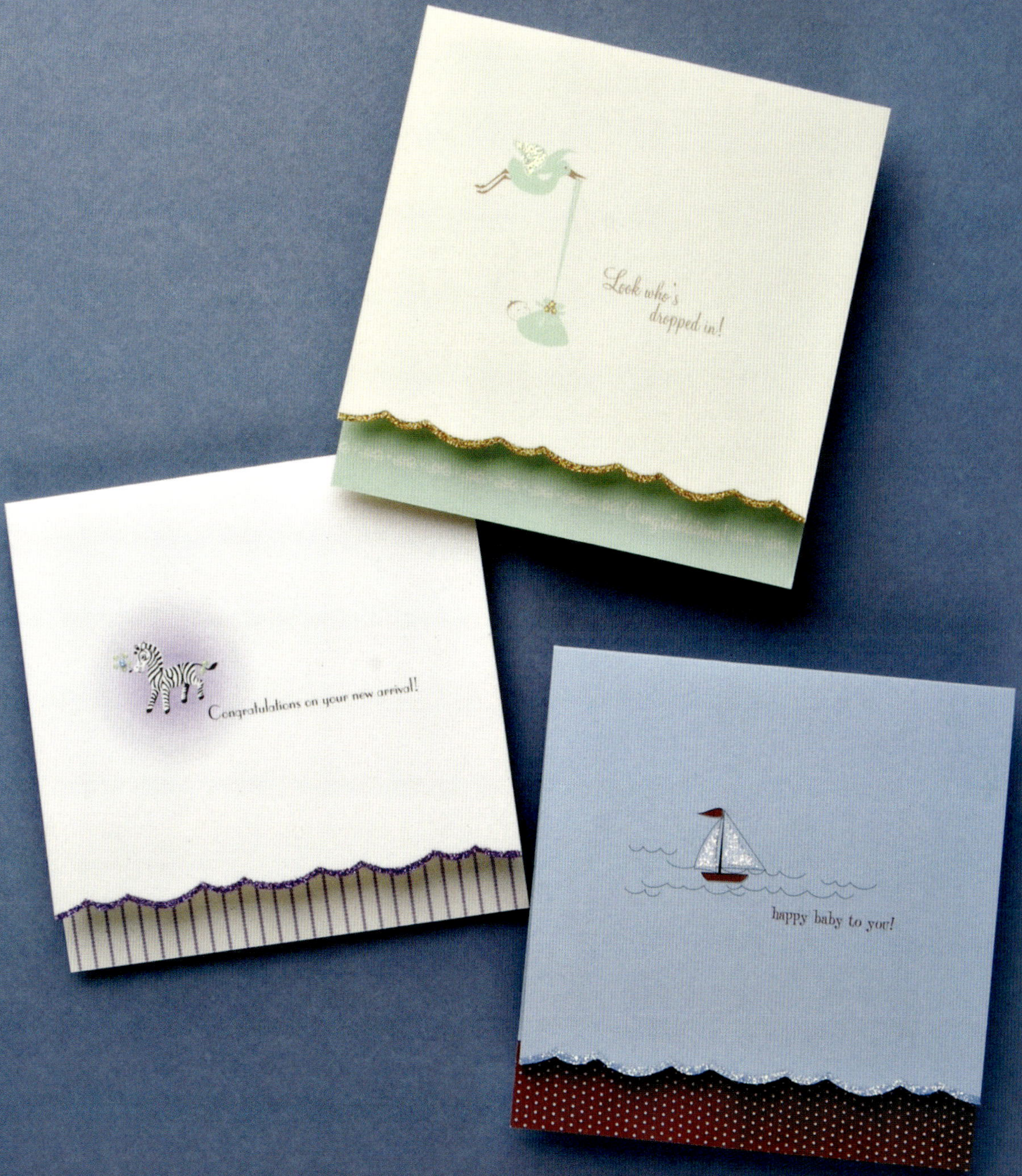

Stork, Baby Sailboat, and Baby Zebra.
Lithography, microfine glitter by hand.
Courtesy of You Send Me.

Turquoise Creative

www.turquoisecreative.com

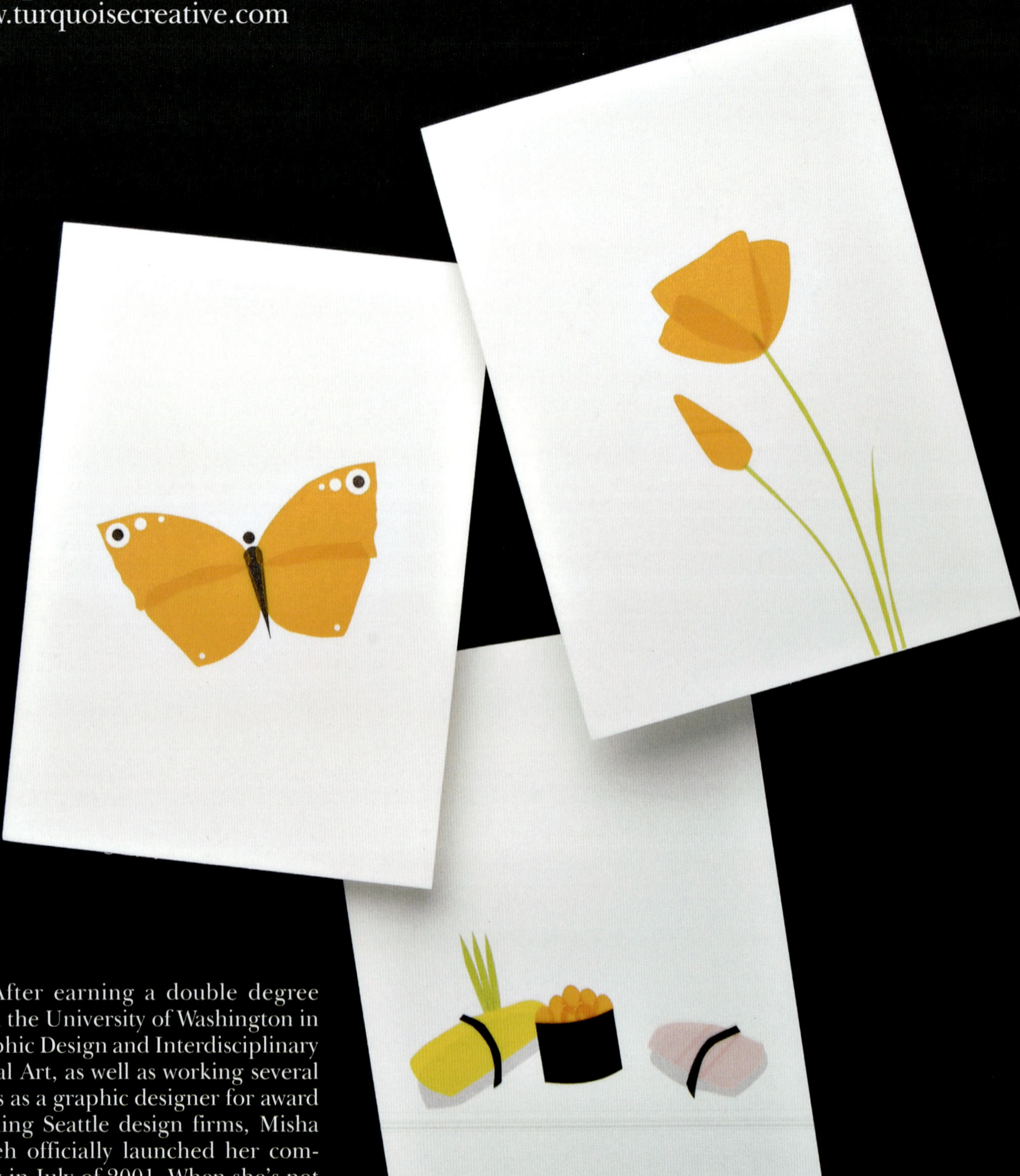

After earning a double degree from the University of Washington in Graphic Design and Interdisciplinary Visual Art, as well as working several years as a graphic designer for award winning Seattle design firms, Misha Zadeh officially launched her company in July of 2001. When she's not busy designing, Misha can be found working on "the house" with her husband Ben Graham (also a designer), taking a stroll with her two young sons, or enjoying the urban life with her eclectic mix of friends.

California Poppy, Orange Butterfly, and Sushi. Cut vellum on cardstock. *Courtesy of Turquoise Creative.*

Aqua Snail, Aqua/Lime Birds, and Aqua Lanterns. Cut vellum on cardstock. *Courtesy of Turquoise Creative*.

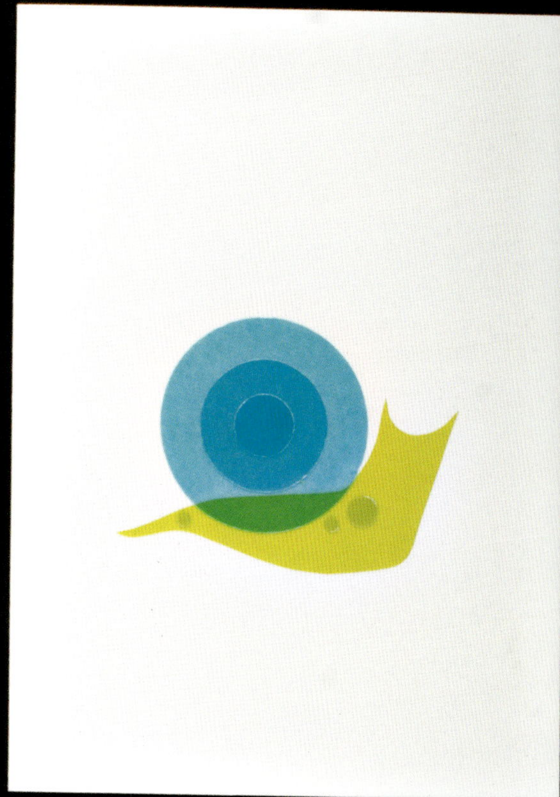

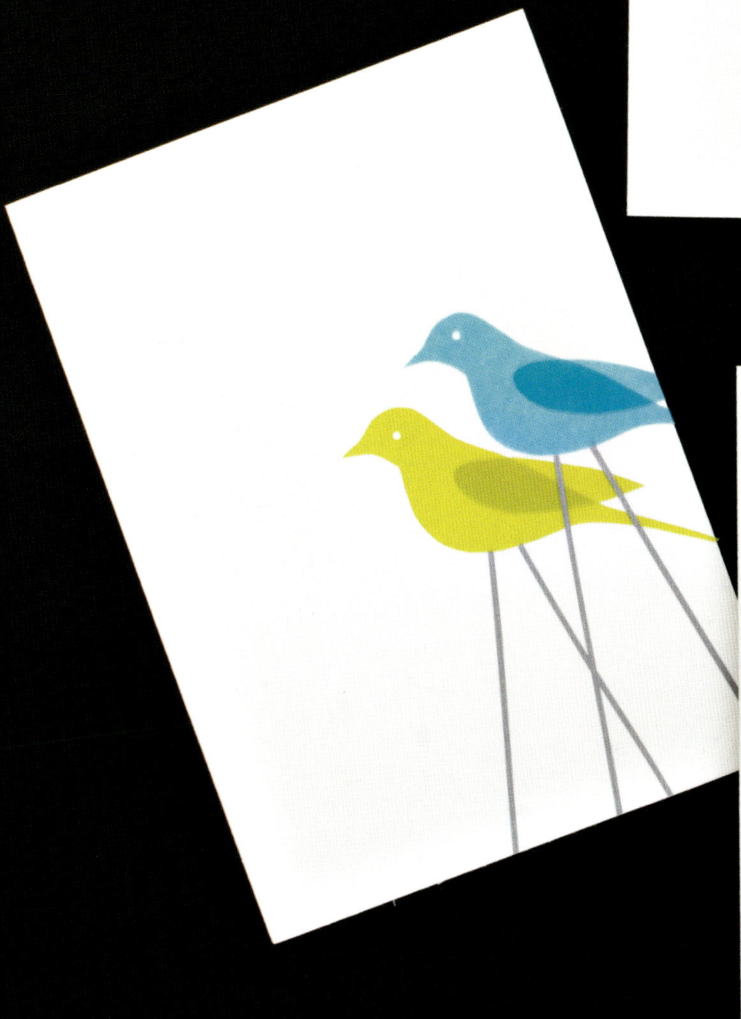

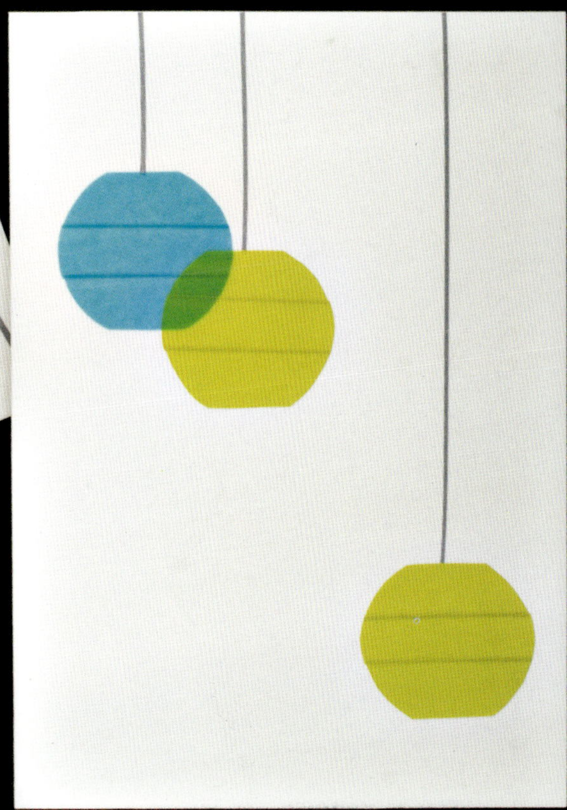

Townsend Sakai

www.townsendsakai.com

Theresa Dykes of Long Beach, California, has enjoyed journaling, drawing, sewing, and creating from an early age. She made her first greeting card for a friend fourteen years ago but officially launched her business in 2006. She is inspired by everything and anything. She loves reading, thumbing through magazines, fashion, modern design, Ray and Charles Eames, and nature. Theresa currently lives in an urban, downtown high-rise, but it is her dream to one day live in a home surrounded by trees.

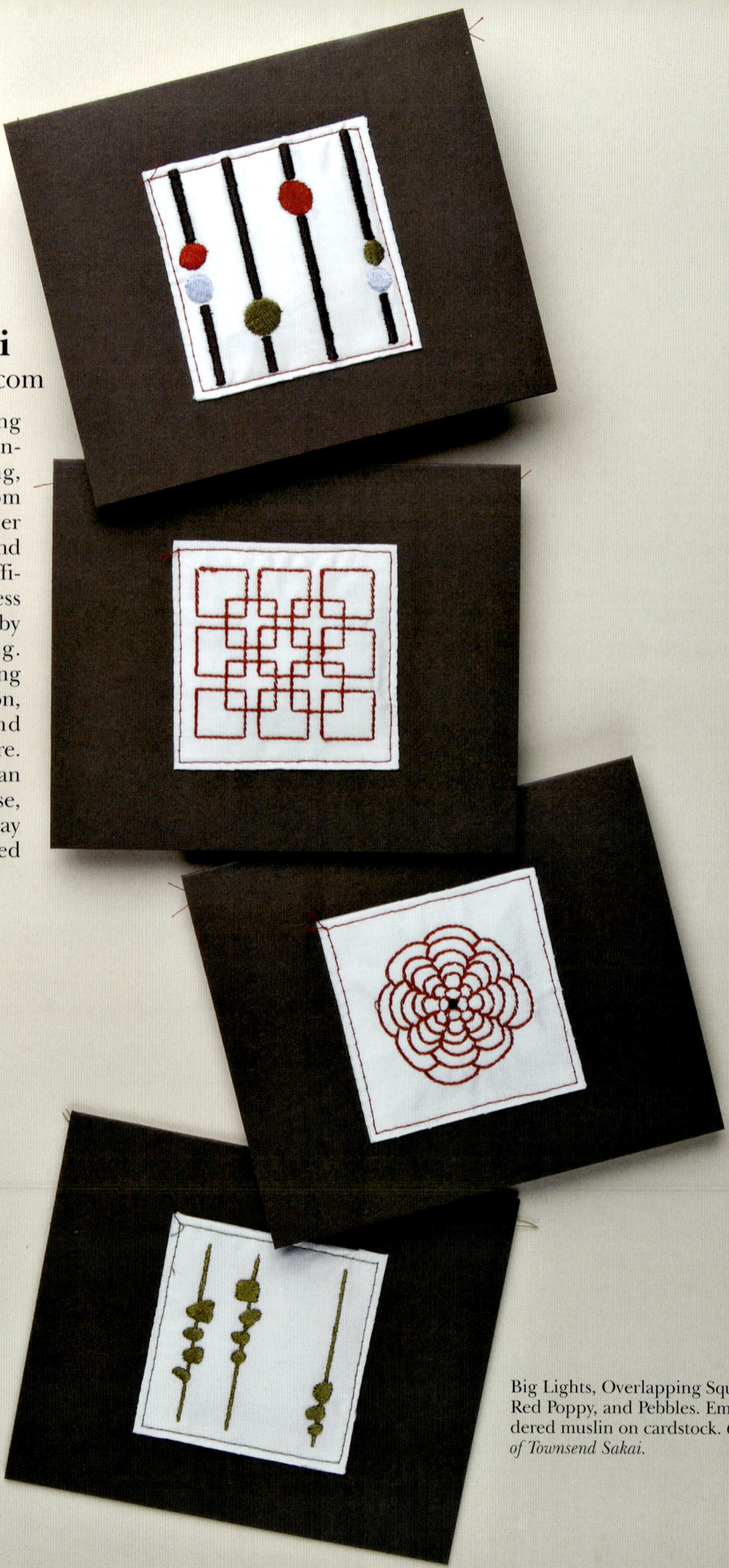

Big Lights, Overlapping Squares, Red Poppy, and Pebbles. Embroidered muslin on cardstock. *Courtesy of Townsend Sakai.*

Cherry Blossom, Bird, and Cow. Embroidered muslin on cardstock. *Courtesy of Townsend Sakai.*

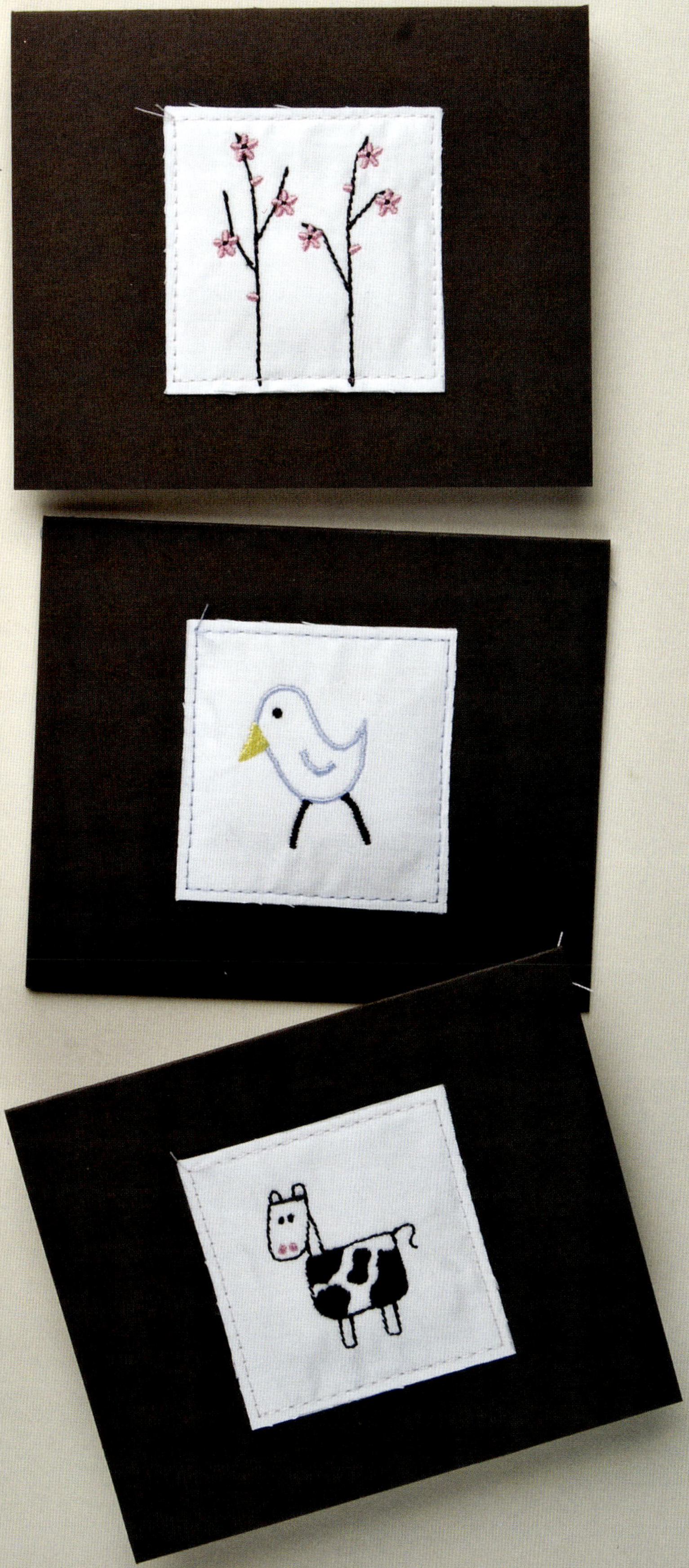

Tori Higa Stationery

www.torihiga.com

Tori Higa has worked as a starving artist, graphic design assistant, and textile designer before finding her niche as an illustrator for stationery products in 2004. She finds great inspiration in vintage design by taking something old and making it new with an unexpected twist. Her cherished family and friends also inspire her. She enjoys living in Southern California with her business partner husband, Branden, and baby boy.

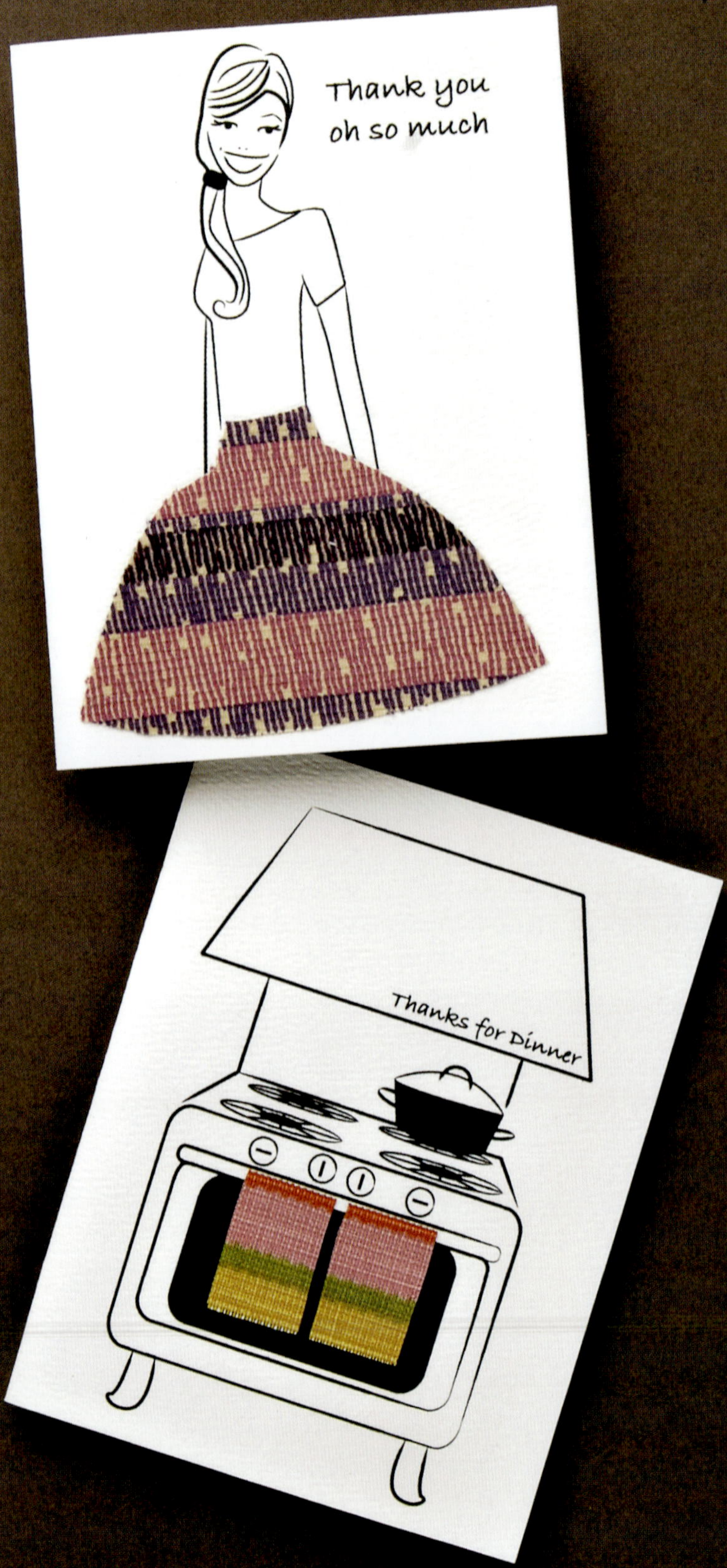

Thank You Oh So Much and Thanks for Dinner. Handmade with vintage fabric. *Courtesy of Tori Higa Stationery.*

Coffee is Fun, Purses are Fun, and Mail is Fun. Handmade with vintage fabric. *Courtesy of Tori Higa Stationery.*

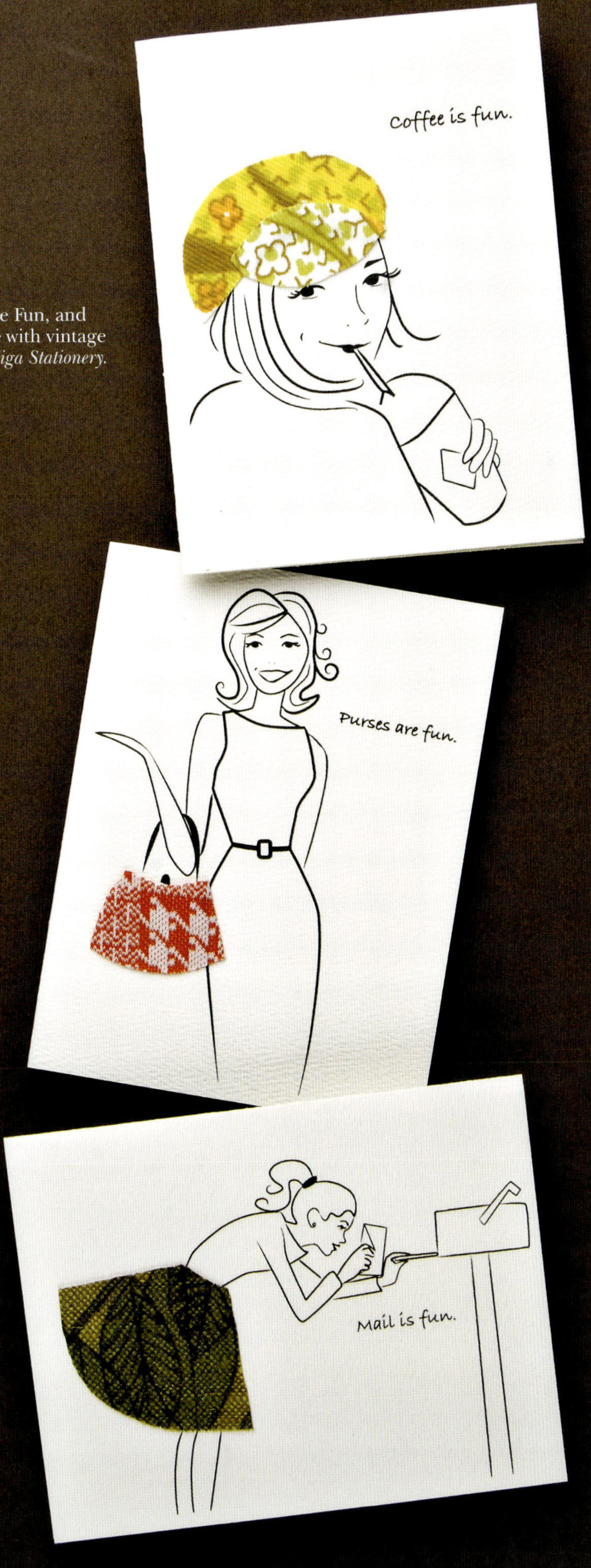

Unique Artistry
www.uniqueartistry.com

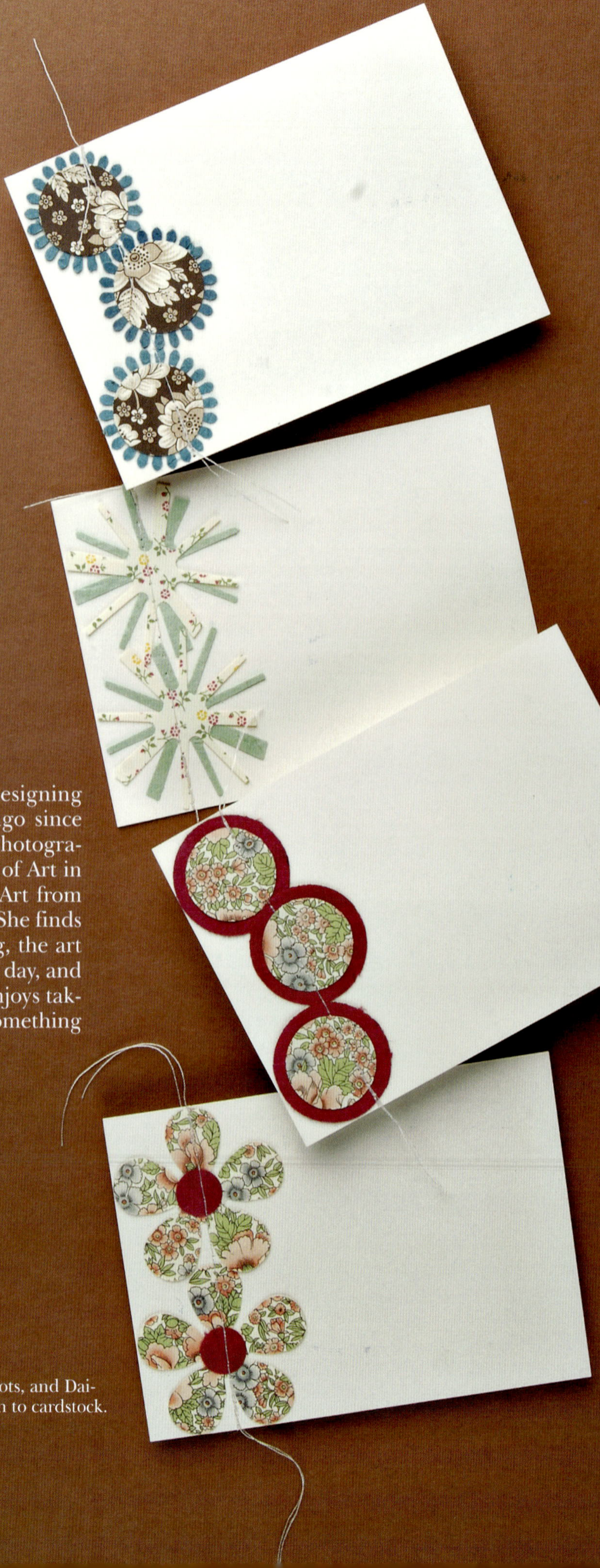

Andrea Grage has been designing her handmade cards in Chicago since 1996. She holds an MFA in Photography from Cranbrook Academy of Art in Michigan and a BA in Studio Art from St. Olaf College in Minnesota. She finds inspiration in quilting, knitting, the art of making, being creative every day, and her studio environment. She enjoys taking the ordinary and making something extraordinary.

Sunflowers, Starbursts, Dots, and Daisies. Cut paper hand sewn to cardstock. *Courtesy of Andrea Grage.*

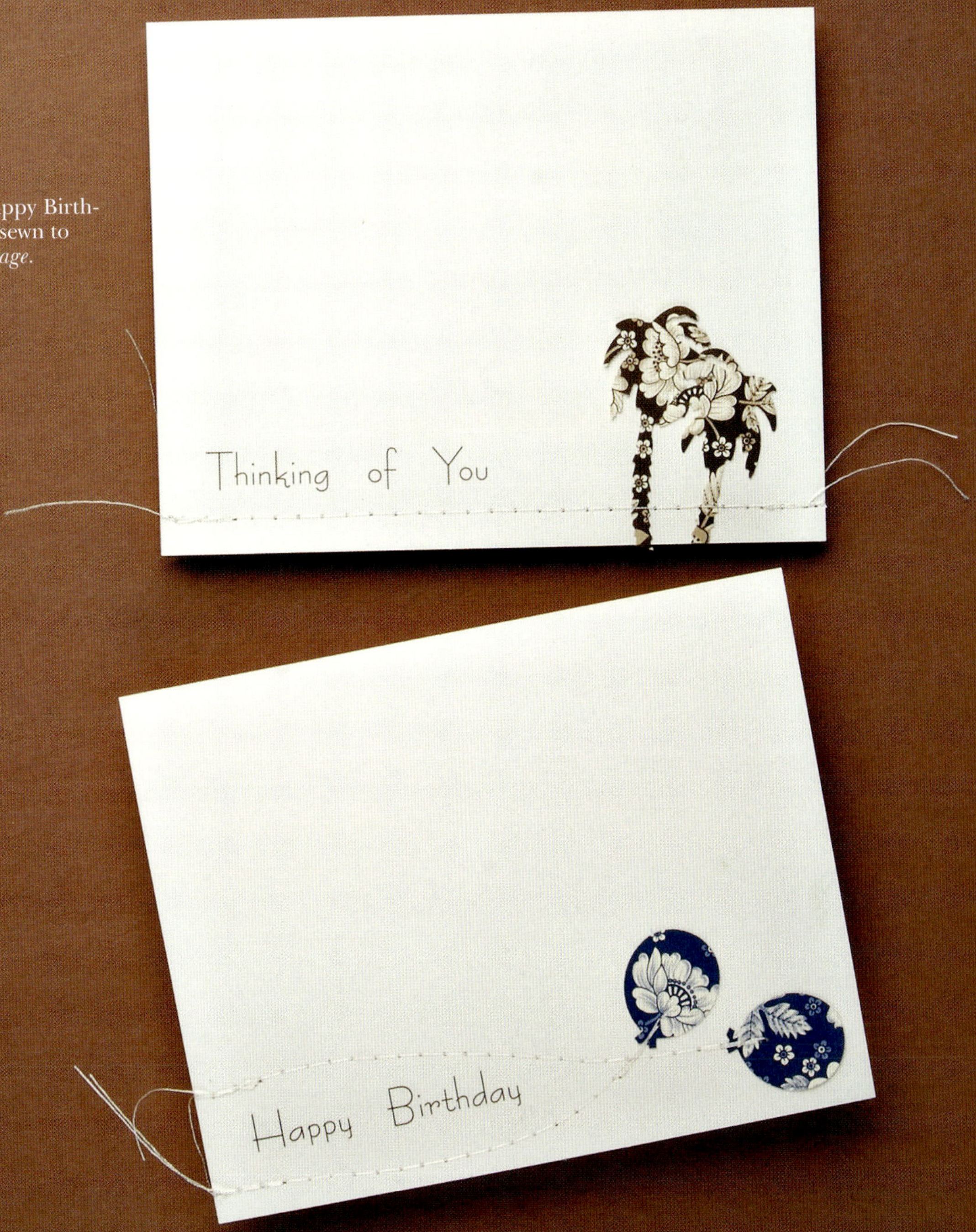

Thinking of You Palms and Happy Birthday Balloons. Cut paper hand sewn to cardstock. *Courtesy of Andrea Grage.*

Spotbear Productions

www.spotbear.com

After Lynne Willis earned her Master's Degree in Biology, she decided to focus on her creative talents by studying textile design. She went on to design fabrics for Knoll Textiles and DesignTex with impressive clients like Nike, Gap, Disney, and AT&T. She ended up starting her own company in 2001 and is settled down in San Francisco. She draws her design inspiration from medieval illuminated manuscripts, Victorian architecture, Art Nouveau, Art Deco, and textile prints from the 1940s.

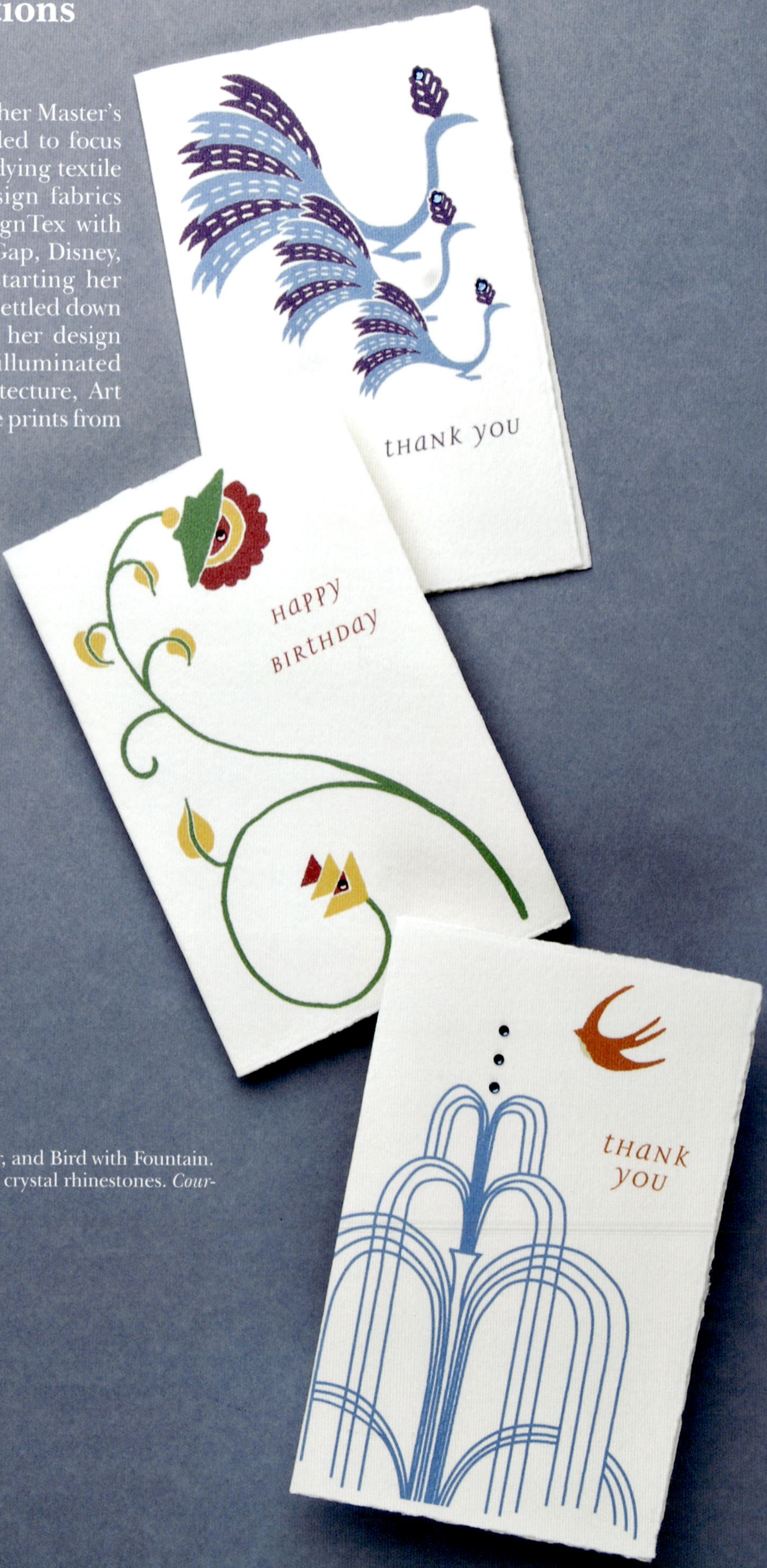

Three Peacocks, Art Deco Flower, and Bird with Fountain. Hand embellished with Austrian crystal rhinestones. *Courtesy of Spotbear Productions.*

Thank You Flowers, Bouquet, Floral, and Congratulations. Hand embellished with Austrian crystal rhinestones. *Courtesy of Spotbear Productions.*

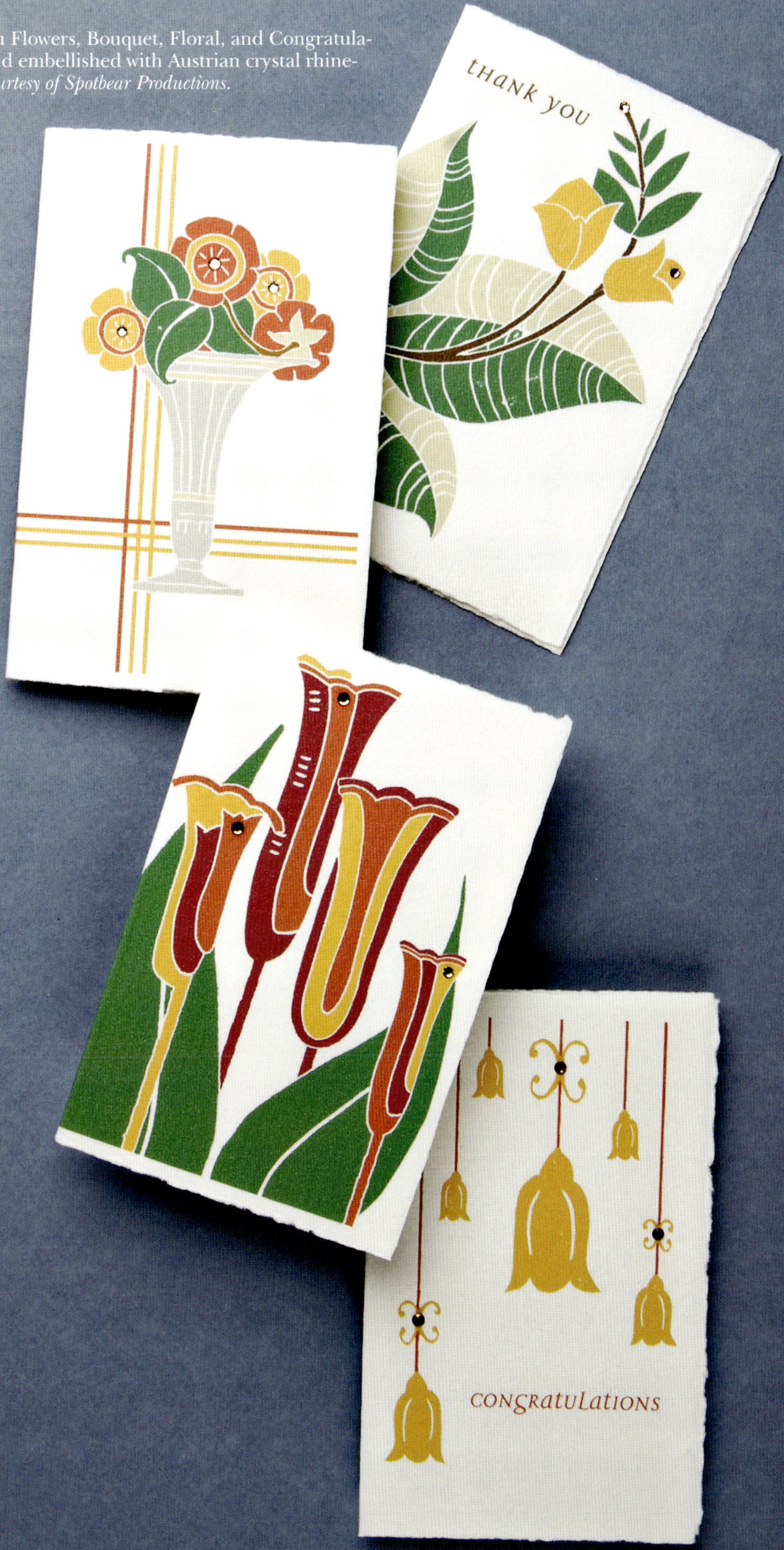

Laboratory 5
www.laboratory5.com

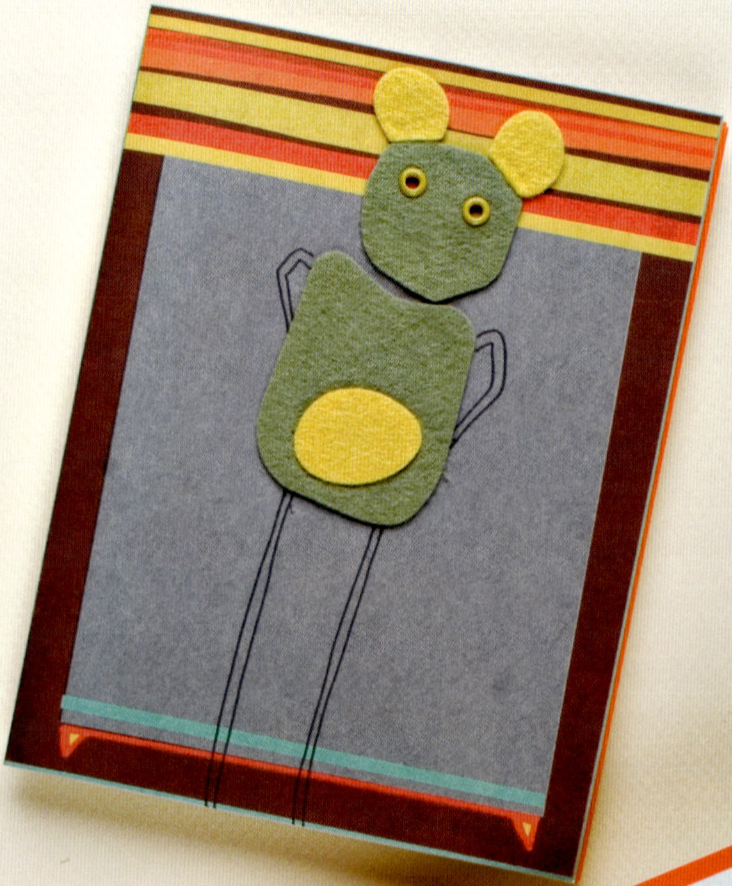

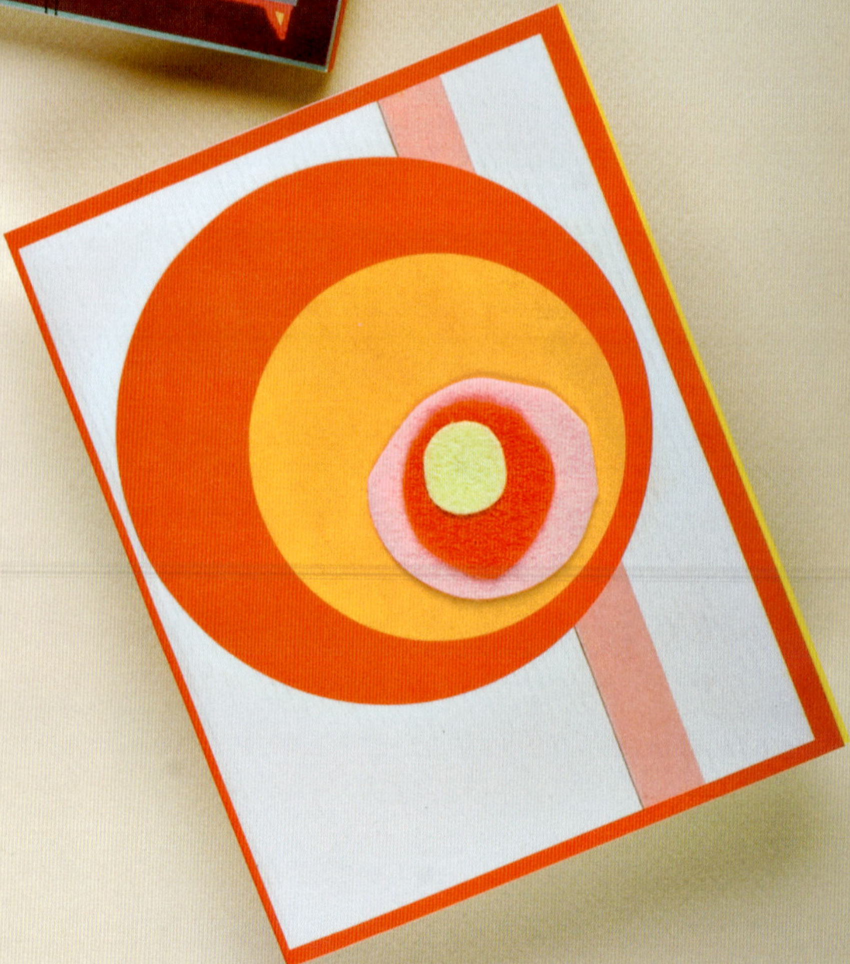

Green Critter and Orange Graphic Circles. Hand cut felt on paper. *Courtesy of Cyndi Coon of Laboratory 5.*

Wedding Rings and Pink Birthday Cake. Hand cut felt on paper. *Courtesy of Cyndi Coon of Laboratory 5.*

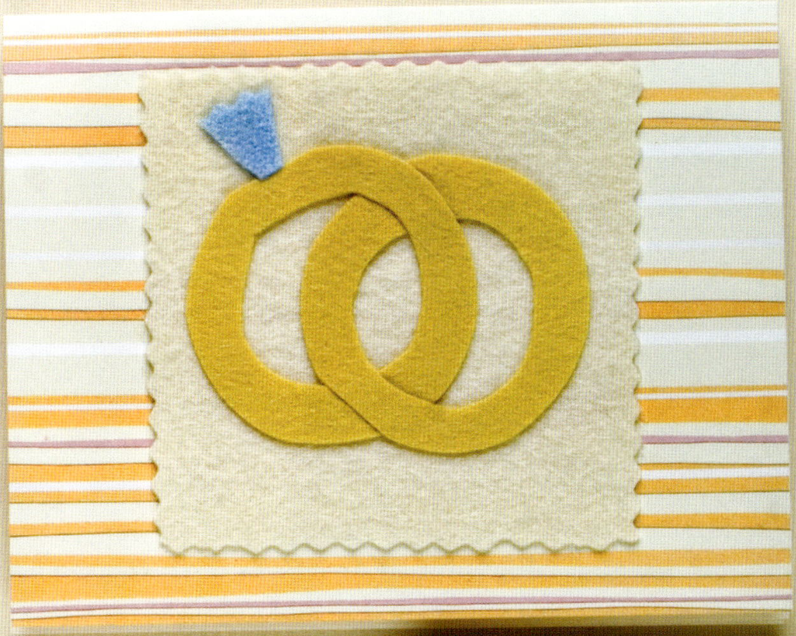

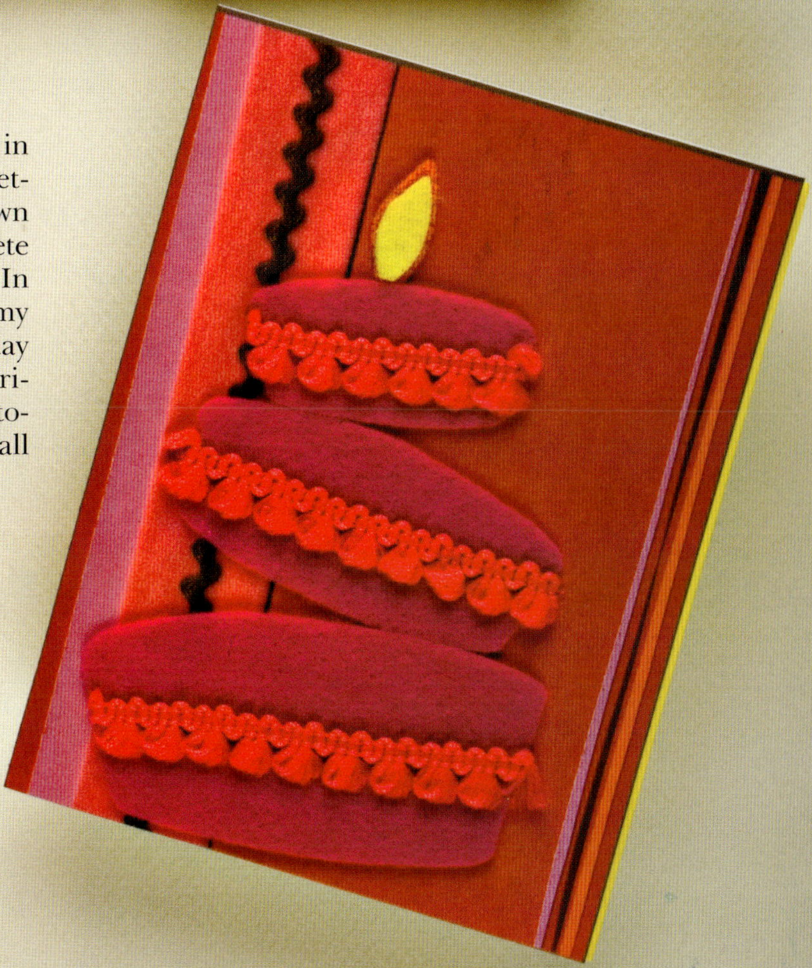

Cyndi Coon holds a BFA and MFA in Fine Art and has always had a love for greeting card design. She even started her own card "company" at age four or five, complete with her own logo and original designs. In 2001, together with her husband, Jeremy Briddell, she launched Laboratory 5. Today the creative couple lives in Phoenix, Arizona, where they enjoy an artistic lifestyle together. Cyndi is currently launching a small works/child accessible line of paintings.

Ess & Jae

www.essandjae.com

Ess & Jae is a collaboration between two friends, Sierra Christensen and Jillian Waters. The two Cal Poly, San Luis Obispo alumni started their company in 2004 after spending their early post graduate years in the graphic design field. They are currently happily living in Paso Robles, California, with their winemaking (slightly neglected) husbands.

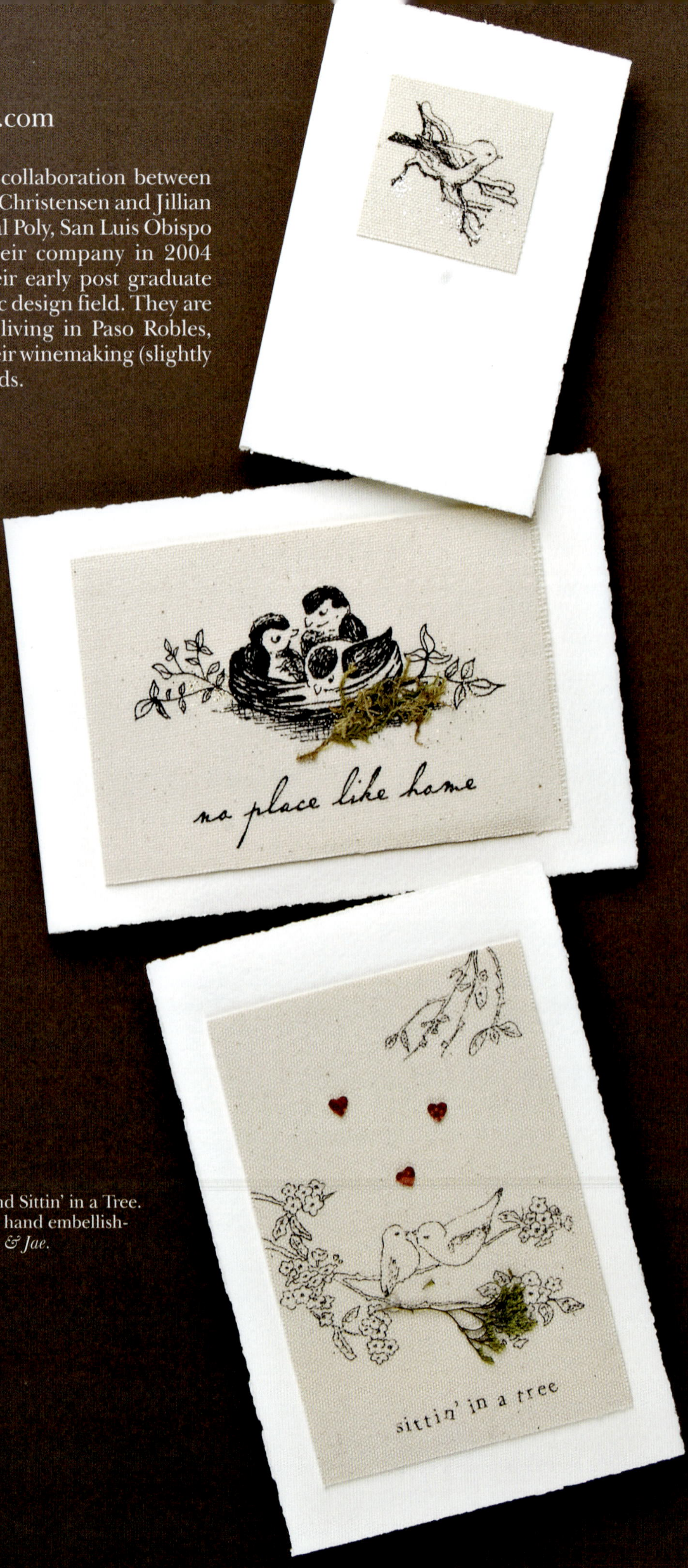

Winter Bird, Nest, and Sittin' in a Tree. Fabric on paper with hand embellishments. *Courtesy of Ess & Jae.*

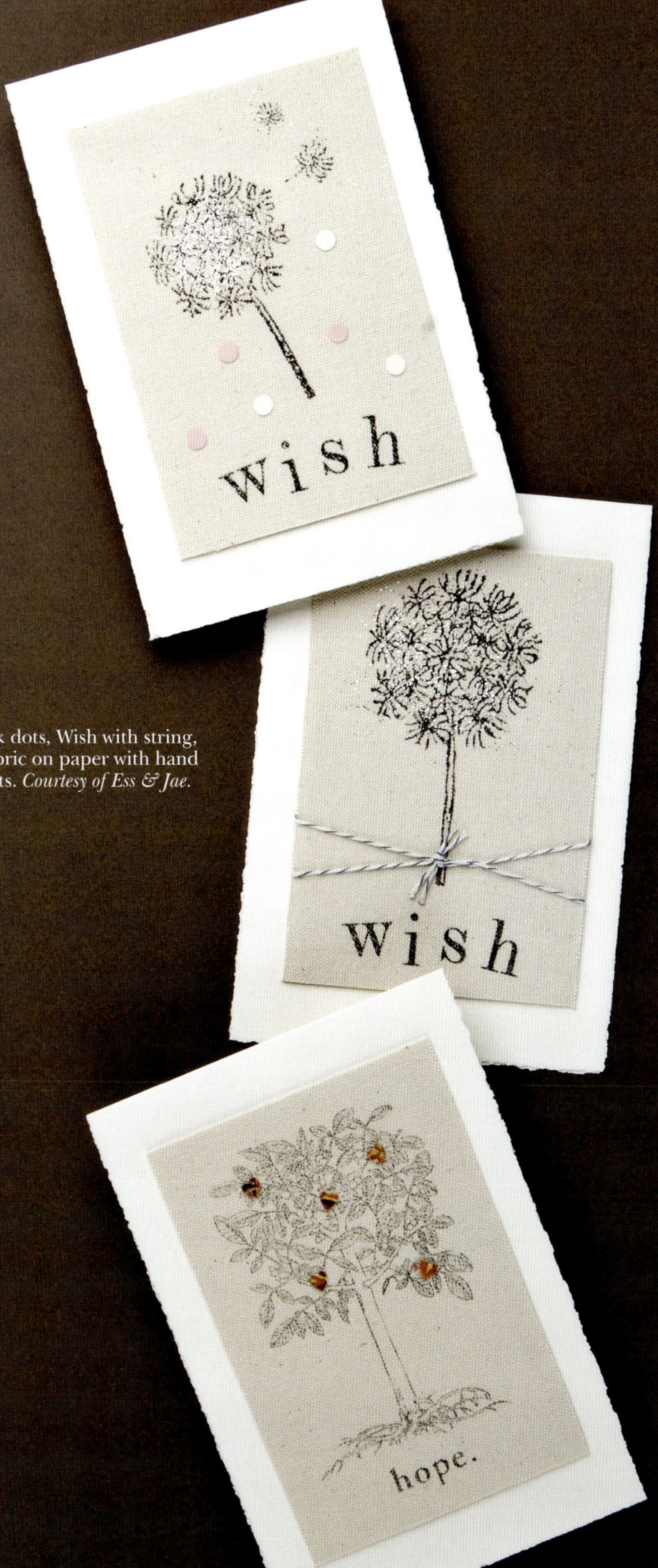

Wish with pink dots, Wish with string, and Hope. Fabric on paper with hand embellishments. *Courtesy of Ess & Jae.*

Driscoll Design

www.driscolldesign.com

Angela Driscoll launched Driscoll Design together with her husband, Charlie Driscoll, in 2004. She holds a BFA in Graphic Design and has since worked for several leading design firms in Seattle with high profile clients such as Starbucks, Microsoft, and Wells Fargo. She also licenses exclusive stationery designs to Madison Park Greetings. Her biggest inspirations are her German mother, family traditions, the many charming Seattle boutiques, arts and lifestyle, interior design, nostalgia, and her husband.

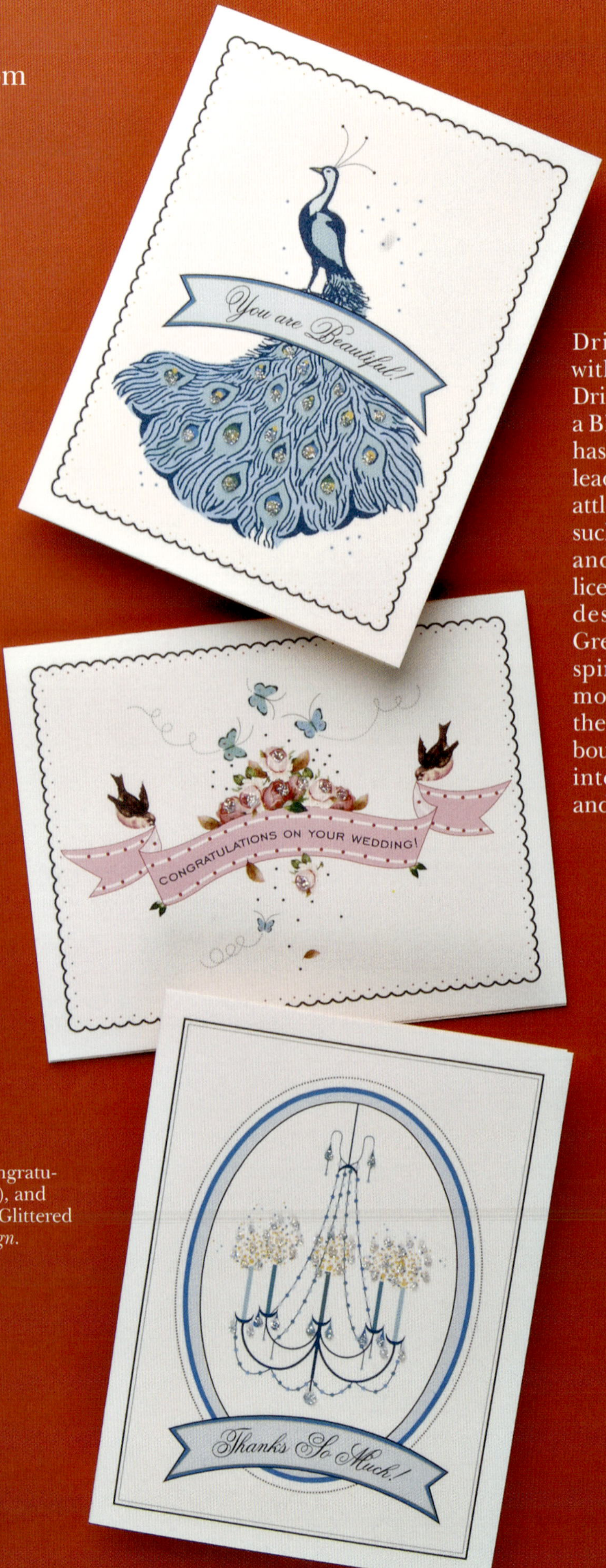

You are Beautiful (Peacock), Congratulations Wedding (Floral Banner), and Thanks So Much (Chandelier). Glittered by hand. *Courtesy of Driscoll Design.*

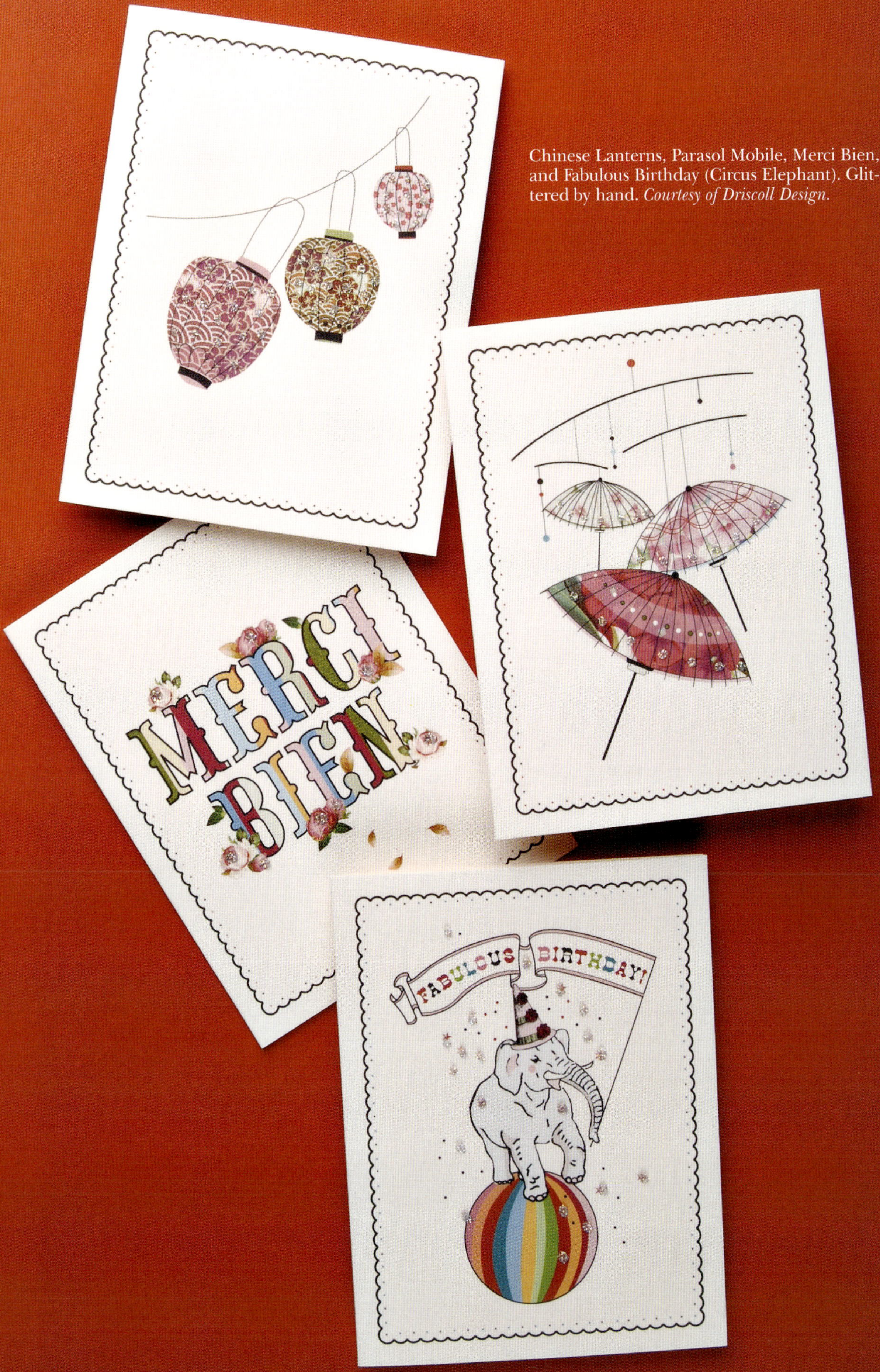

Chinese Lanterns, Parasol Mobile, Merci Bien, and Fabulous Birthday (Circus Elephant). Glittered by hand. *Courtesy of Driscoll Design.*

Chapter Three
Letterpress

Letterpress printing has been used to communicate for over 500 years. Throughout the centuries, letterpress eventually became obsolete because of the cost, time, and newer, more efficient methods for mass printing. In recent years innovative companies such as *Snow and Graham, Elum Designs,* and *Egg Press* have since revived the art form within the stationery industry. Melissa Foster, president and founder of *Elum Designs,* notes "just a few years ago the bulk of letterpress stationery in the marketplace consisted of antique motifs. When we launched our first collection, we surprised the industry by pairing the antiquated art form of letterpress with the use of bold modern design."

The stationery industry is now filled with letterpress companies and its popularity in the marketplace continues to grow. This section profiles a few of the most unique and creative talents in the industry. They focus on design, craftsmanship, and a love for letterpress.

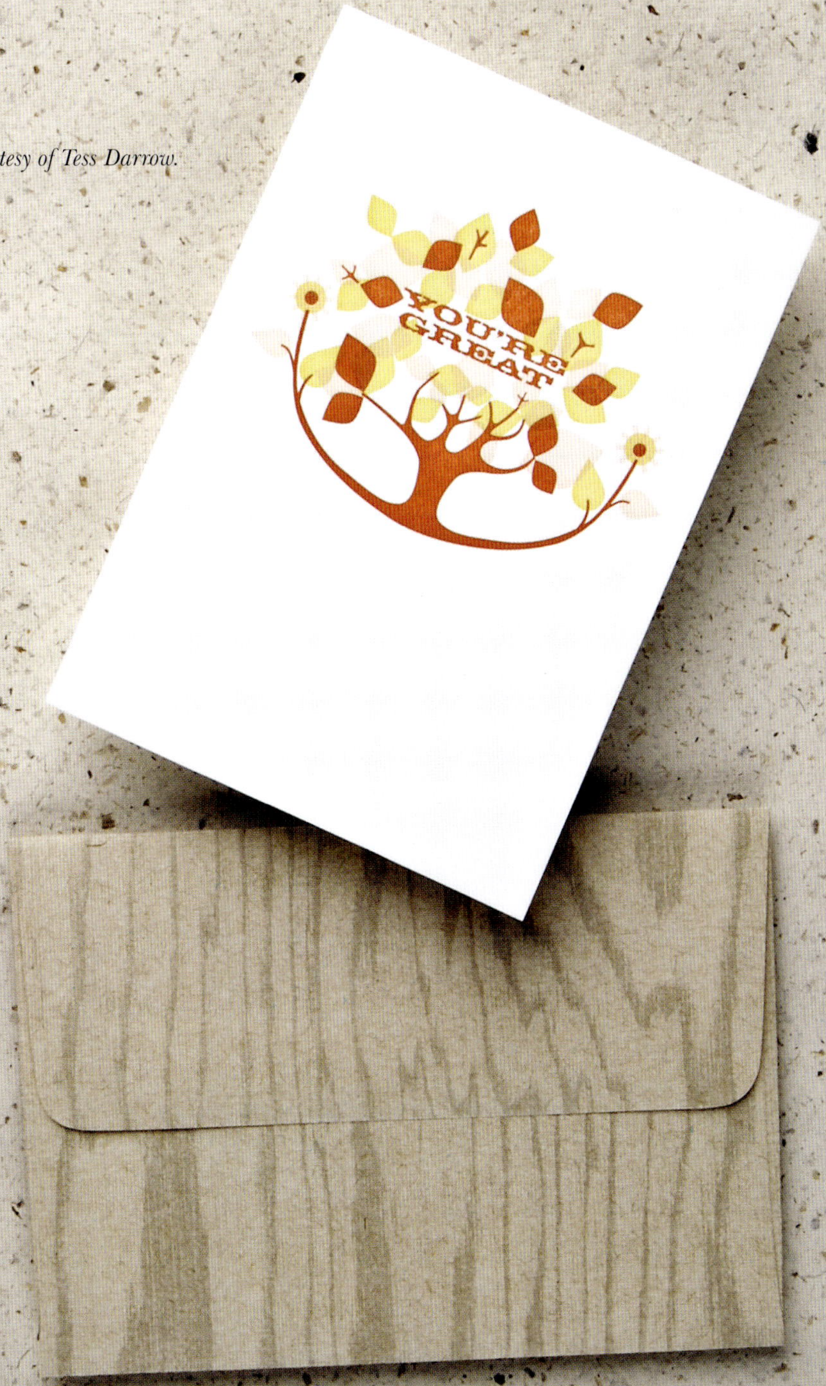

You're Great Tree. *Courtesy of Tess Darrow.*

Egg Press

www.eggpress.com

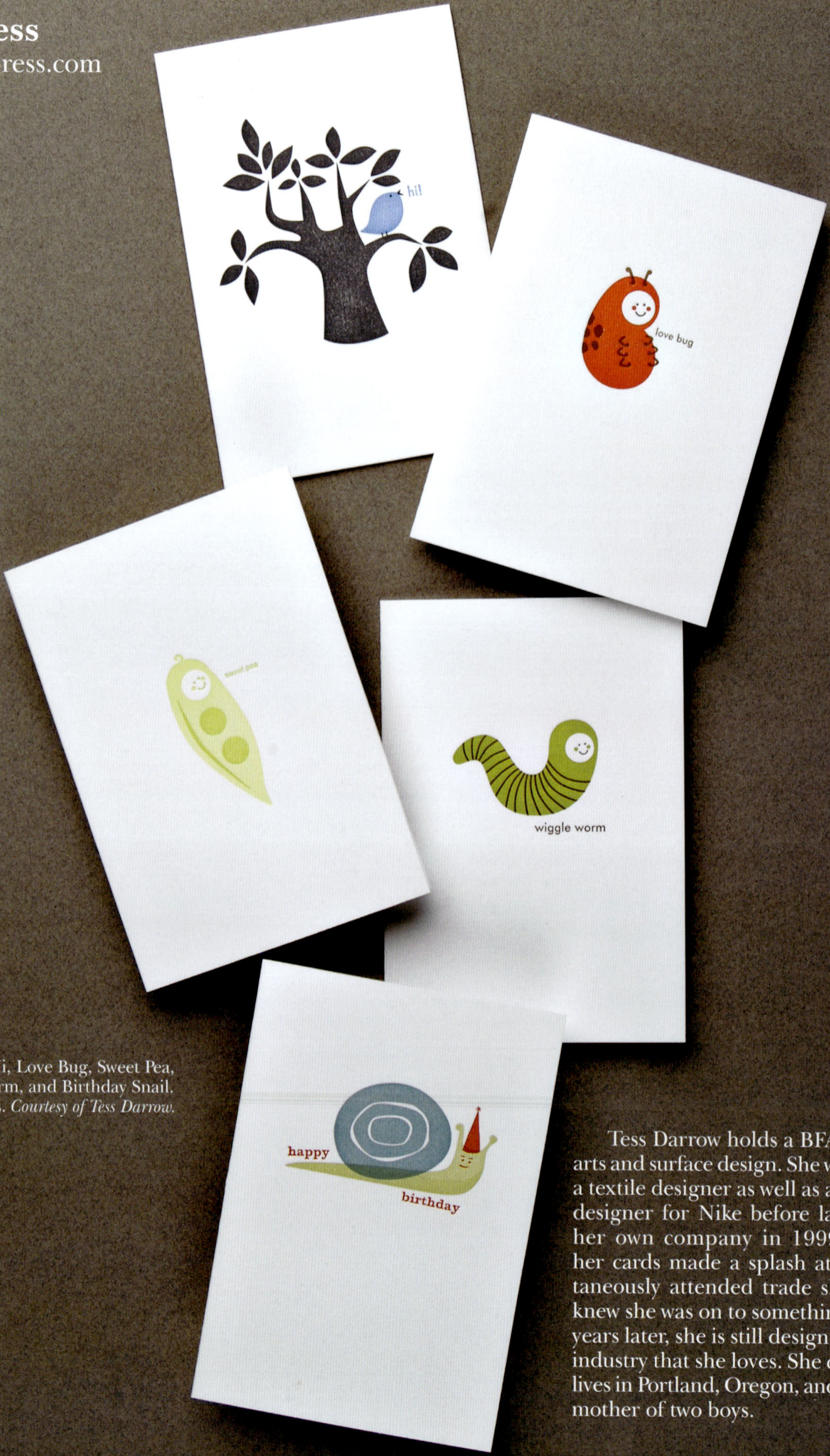

Bluebird Hi, Love Bug, Sweet Pea, Wiggle Worm, and Birthday Snail. Letterpress. *Courtesy of Tess Darrow.*

Tess Darrow holds a BFA in fiber arts and surface design. She worked as a textile designer as well as a graphic designer for Nike before launching her own company in 1999. When her cards made a splash at a spontaneously attended trade show, she knew she was on to something. Eight years later, she is still designing in an industry that she loves. She currently lives in Portland, Oregon, and is a new mother of two boys.

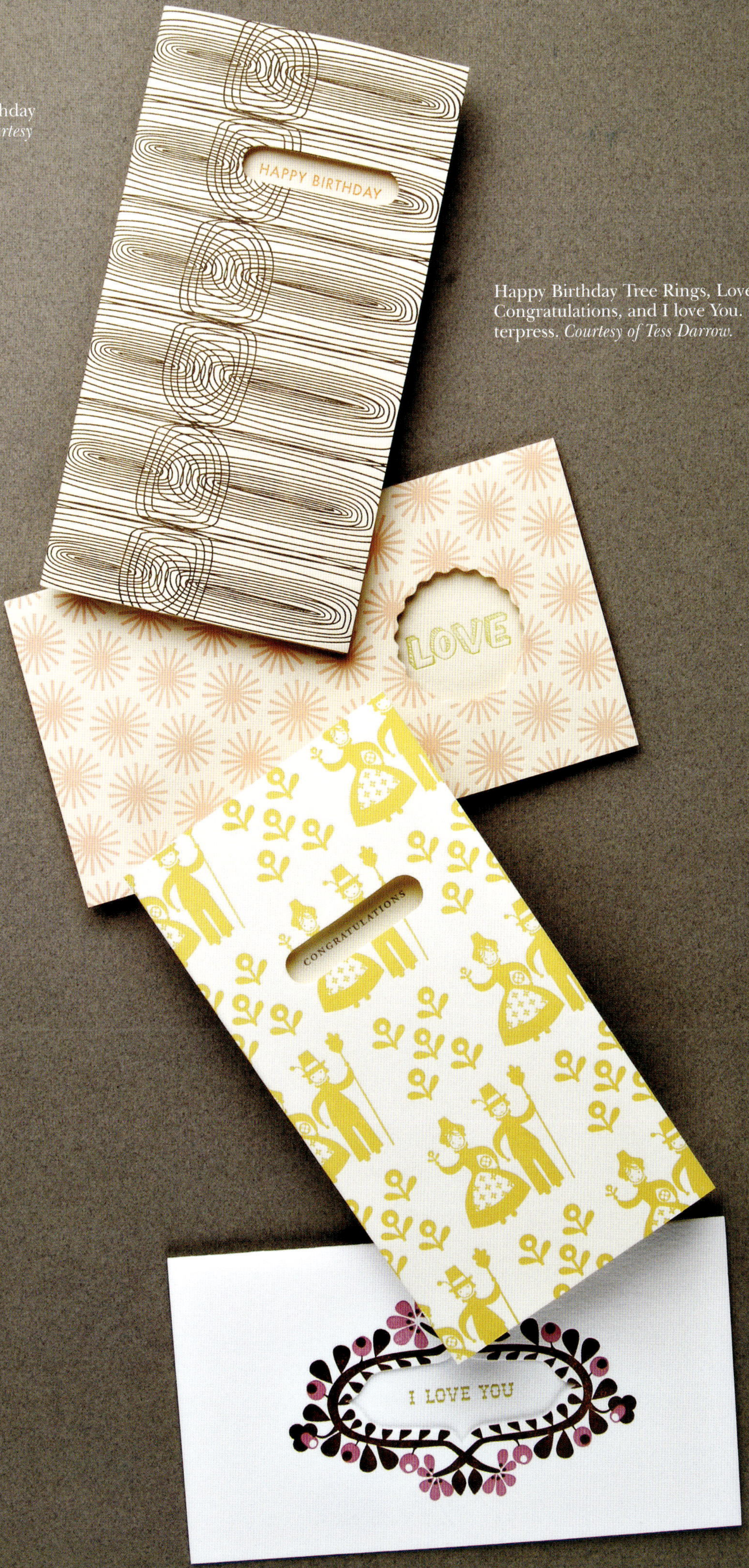

Birthday Raccoon and Birthday Tweetings. Letterpress. *Courtesy of Tess Darrow.*

Happy Birthday Tree Rings, Love, Congratulations, and I love You. Letterpress. *Courtesy of Tess Darrow.*

Snow and Graham

www.snowandgraham.com

Snow and Graham has been delighting stationery lovers since 1997. Ebony Snow Chafey is the talented artist behind the Chicago based company. She holds a BFA from the School of Art Institute of Chicago. While in school, she focused on sculpture and worked in the metals foundry. Ebony says that, "If I could do anything else I would bake cakes and arrange flowers for a living…for now, I draw pictures."

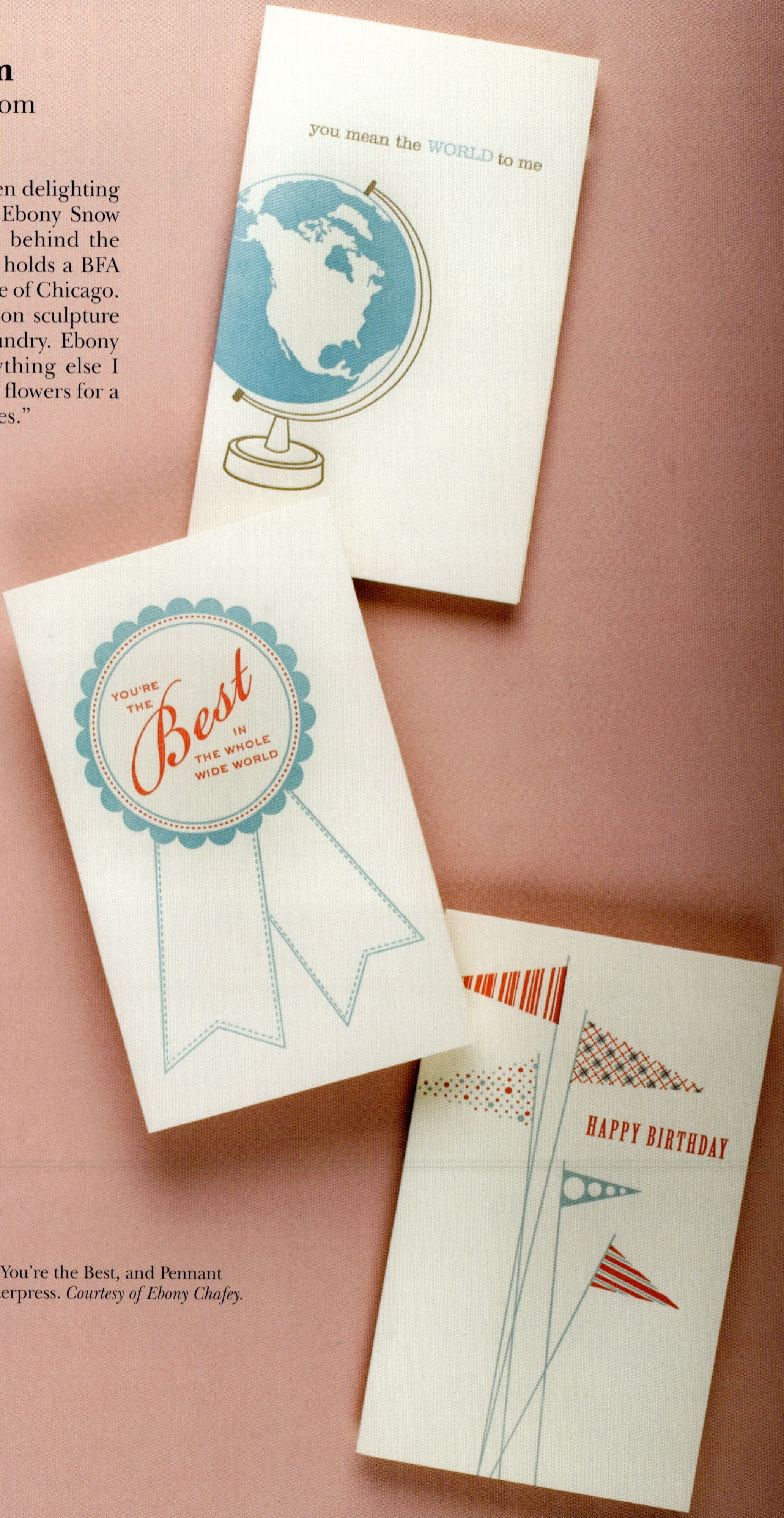

World to Me, You're the Best, and Pennant Birthday. Letterpress. *Courtesy of Ebony Chafey.*

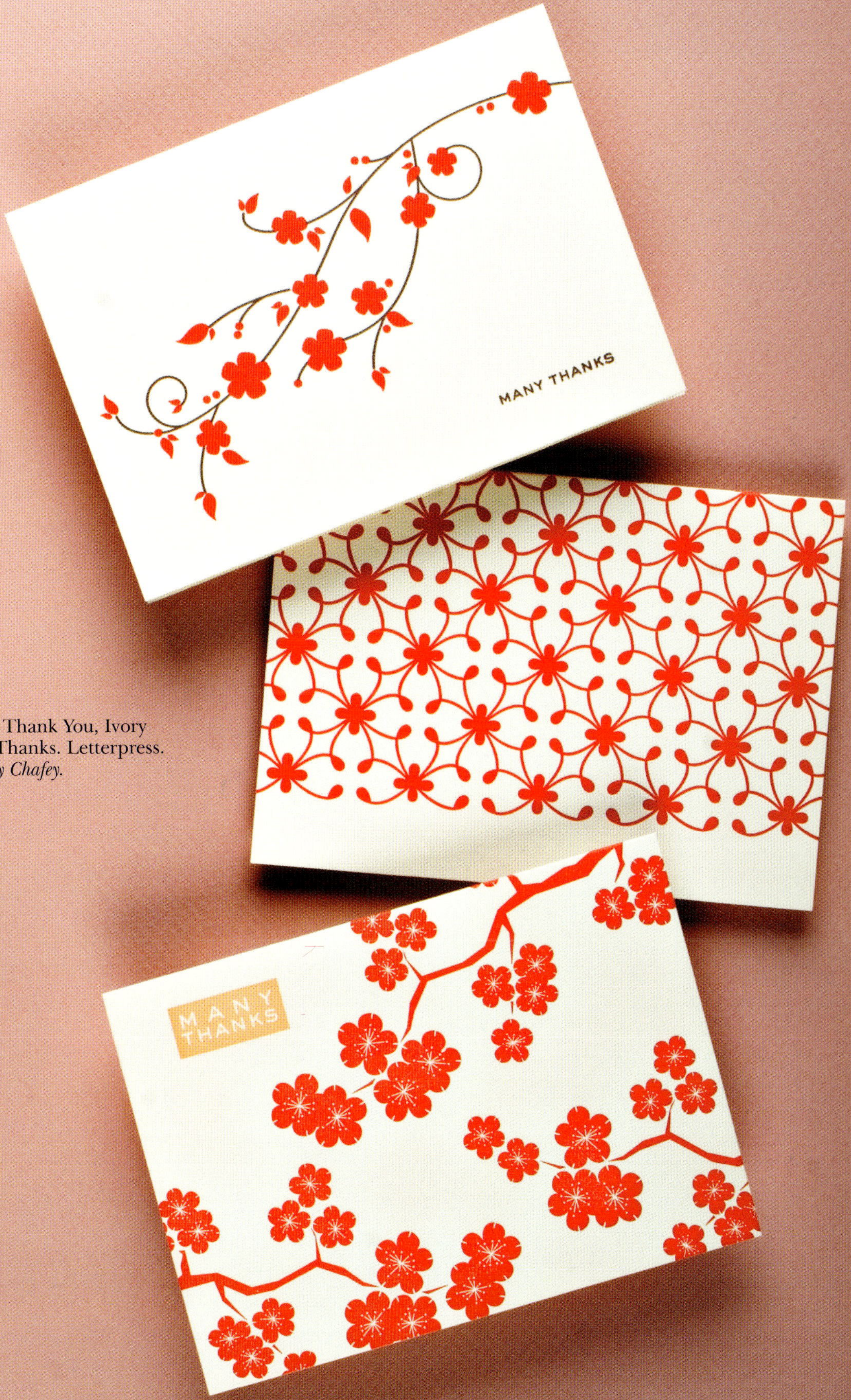

Flowering Vine Thank You, Ivory Pattern, Many Thanks. Letterpress. *Courtesy of Ebony Chafey.*

Louella Press

www.louellapress.com

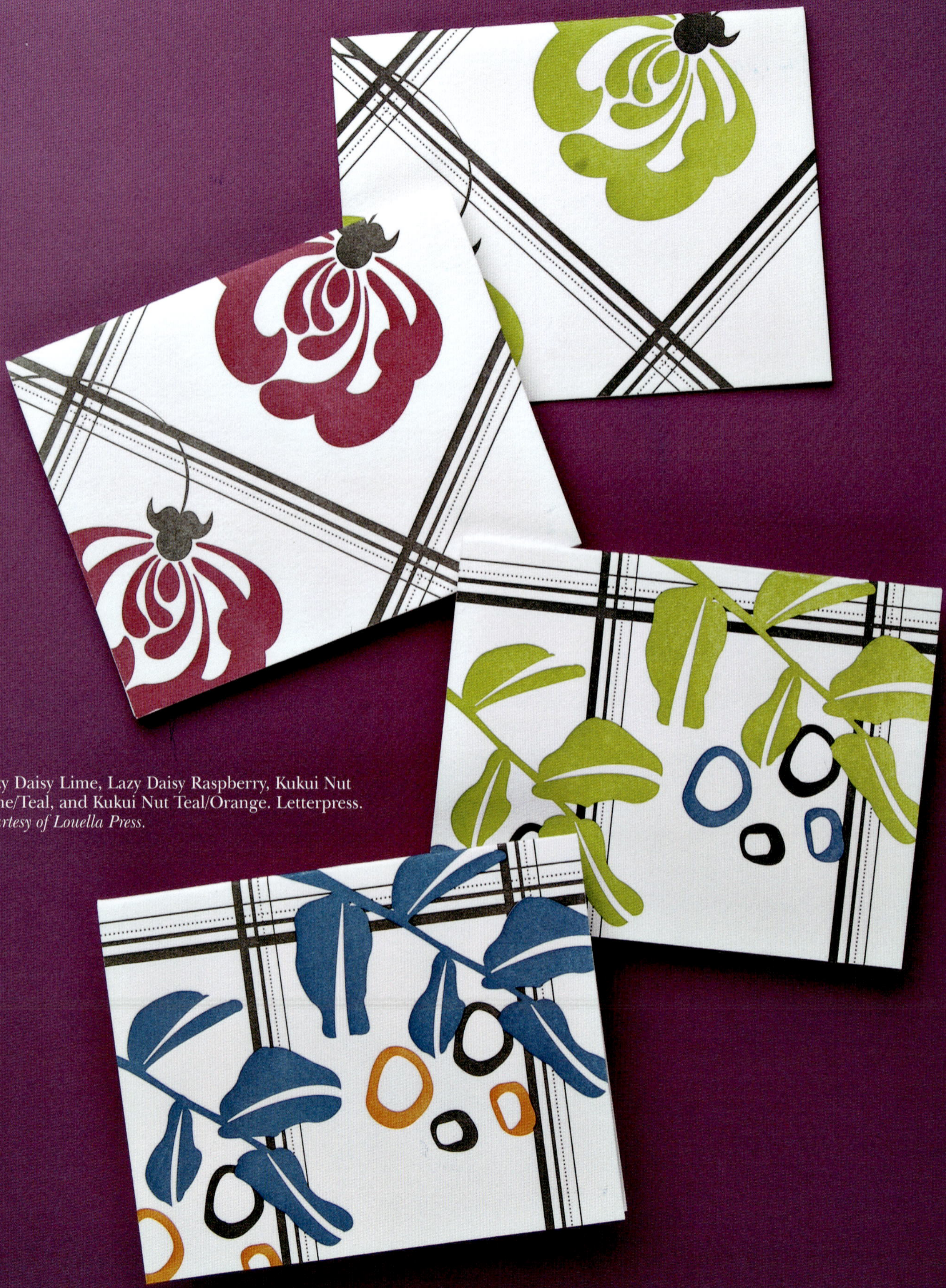

Lazy Daisy Lime, Lazy Daisy Raspberry, Kukui Nut Lime/Teal, and Kukui Nut Teal/Orange. Letterpress. *Courtesy of Louella Press.*

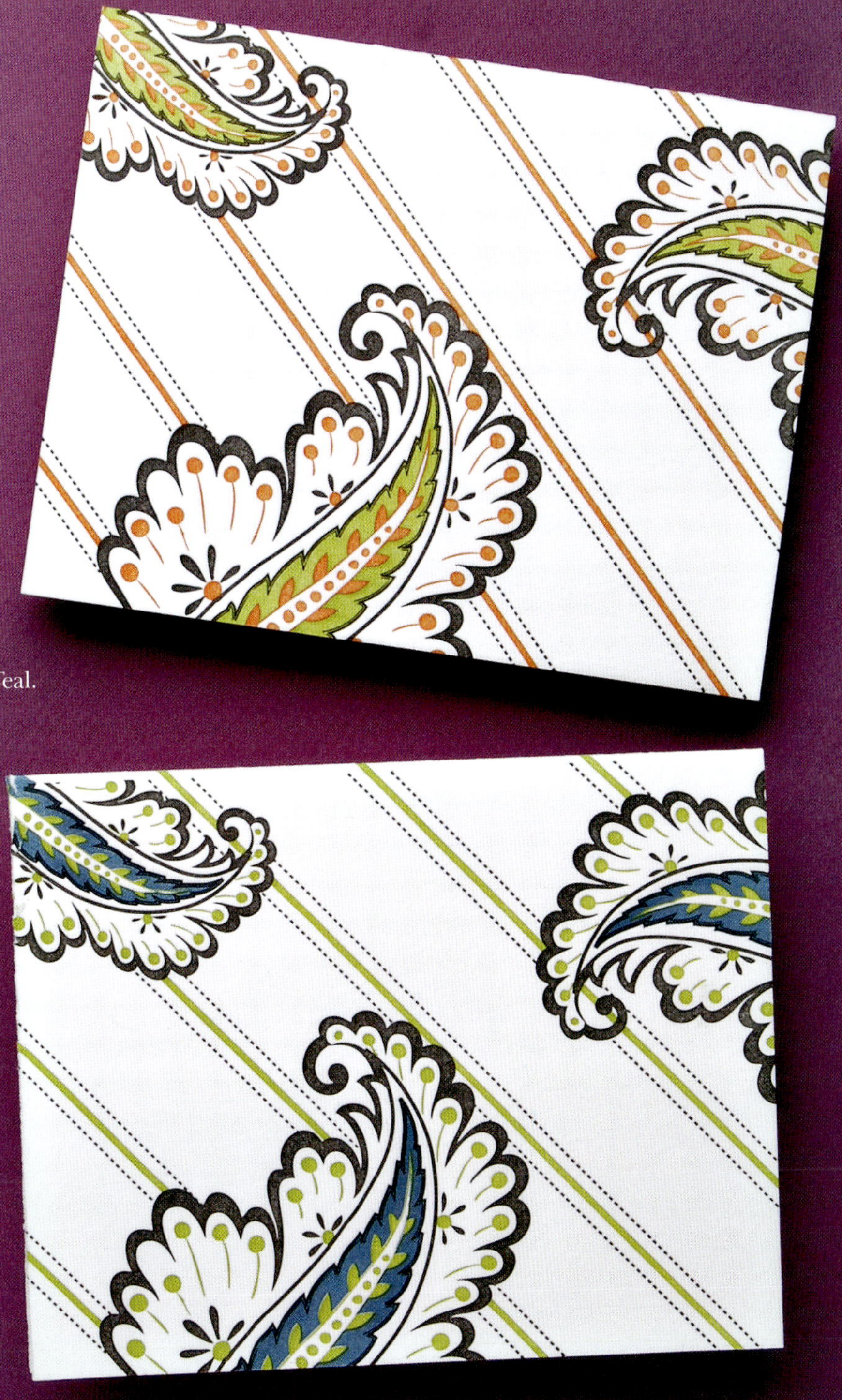

Paisley Orange/Lime and Paisley Lime/Teal. Letterpress. *Courtesy of Louella Press.*

In 2006, Vanessa Kreckel introduced Louella Press, a sister company of Philadelphia-based custom design studio Two Paperdolls. Featuring a hand engraved invitation album and a juicy line of letterpress note cards, Louella Press was inspired by Kreckel's love of textured printing and bold design. She and her talented staff of "dolls" continue to bring new and exciting designs to the world of stationery and paper goods. Kreckel is an alumnus of both Cedar Crest College and Moore College of Art and Design, and has a soft spot for vintage fabric, sunny days at the beach and all things chocolate.

Peculiar Pair Press

www.peculiarpairpress.com

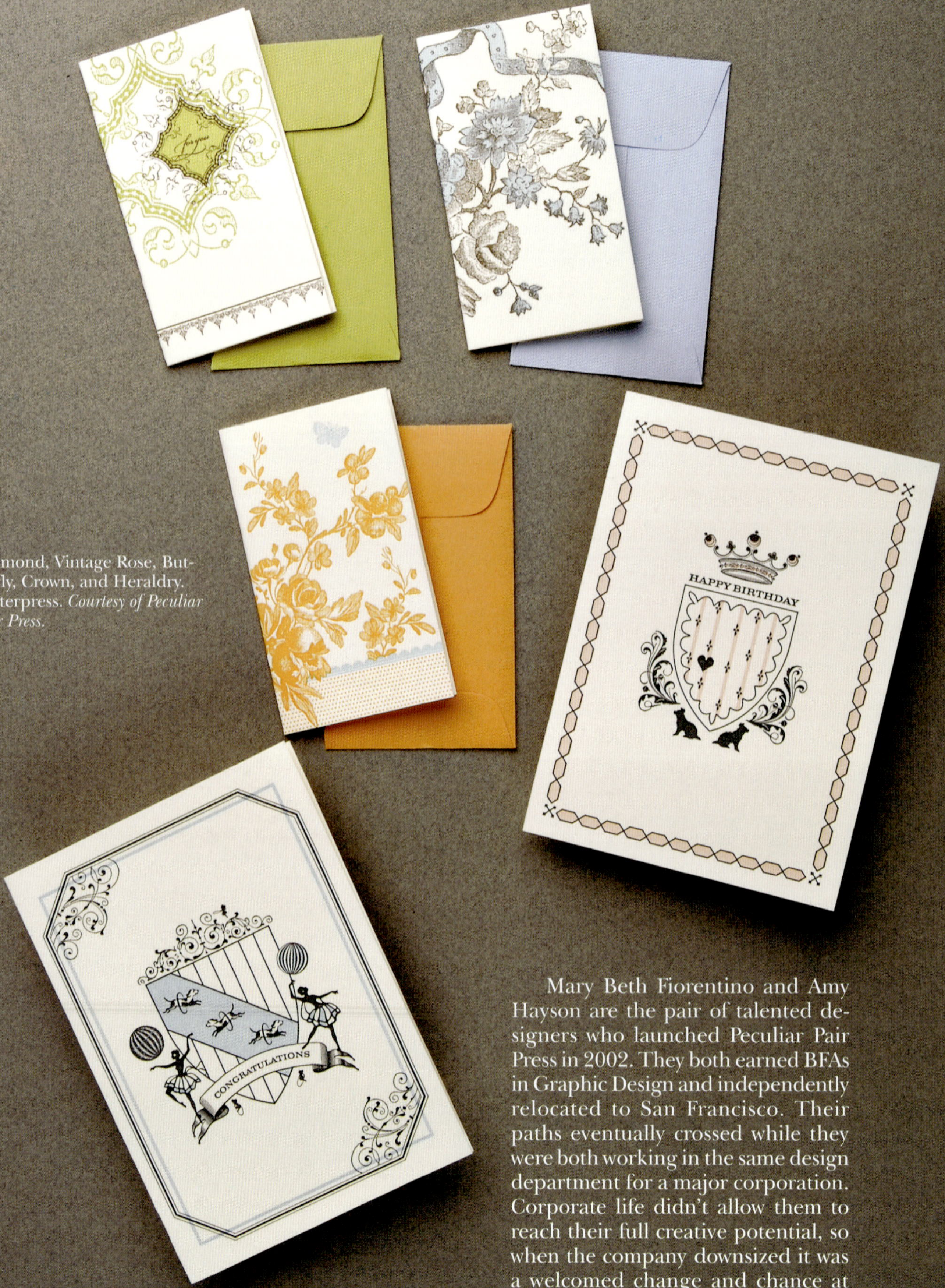

Diamond, Vintage Rose, Butterfly, Crown, and Heraldry. Letterpress. *Courtesy of Peculiar Pair Press.*

Mary Beth Fiorentino and Amy Hayson are the pair of talented designers who launched Peculiar Pair Press in 2002. They both earned BFAs in Graphic Design and independently relocated to San Francisco. Their paths eventually crossed while they were both working in the same design department for a major corporation. Corporate life didn't allow them to reach their full creative potential, so when the company downsized it was a welcomed change and chance at creative freedom.

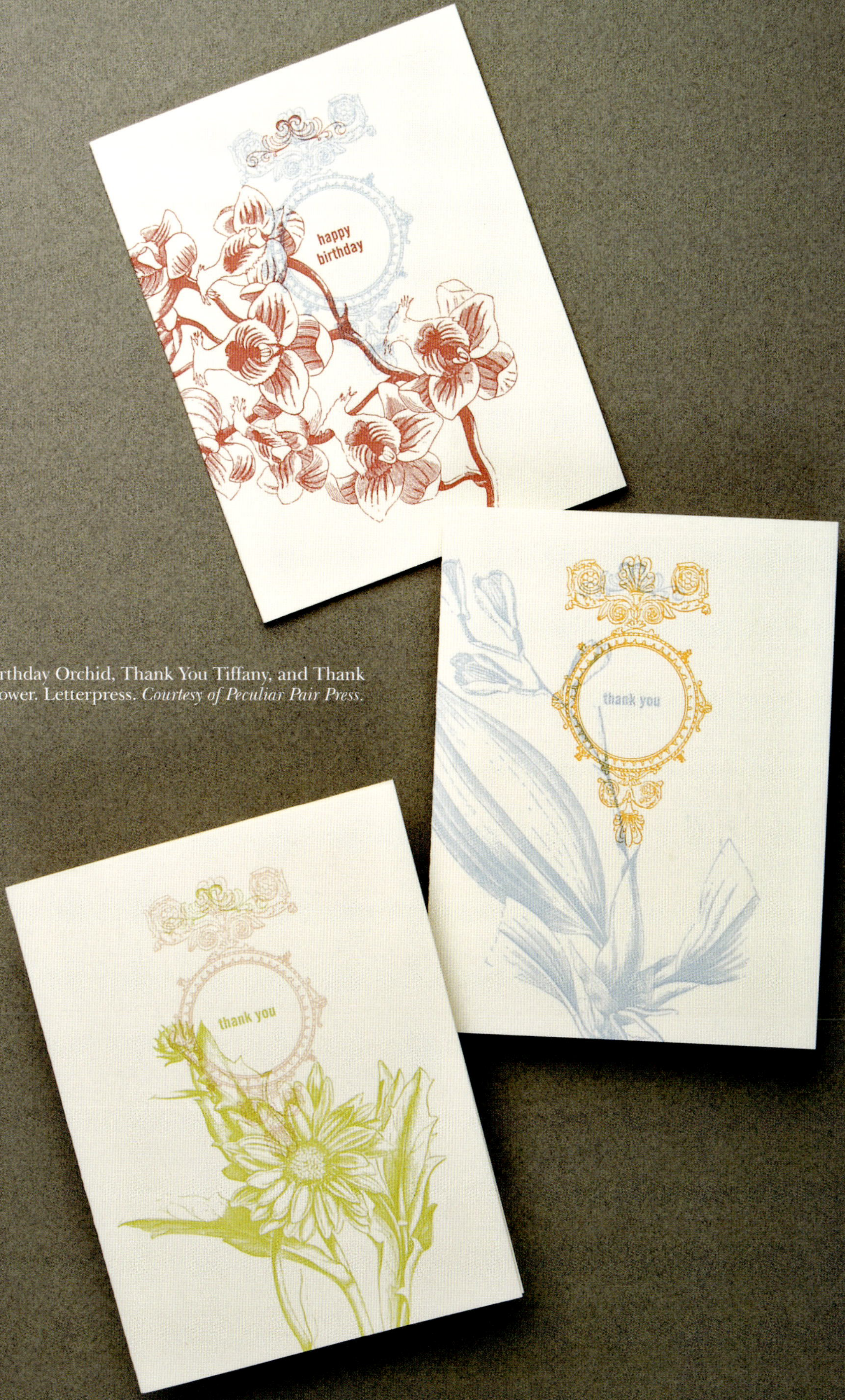

Happy Birthday Orchid, Thank You Tiffany, and Thank You Sunflower. Letterpress. *Courtesy of Peculiar Pair Press.*

Paper + Cup Design

www.papercupdesign.com

Minhee Park began her company in 2003 and currently resides in Brooklyn, New York. She has a BA in fine art from UCLA and a second BA in graphic design from the School of Visual Arts in New York. She loves vintage stationery, fabric, wallpaper, furniture, walking around the city, flea markets, cupcakes, Stephan Chow movies, collecting postcards, making collages, painting, riddles and brainteasers, anything to do with time travel, and attempting to do a crossword puzzle with her husband on Sunday afternoons with a fresh hot cup of coffee.

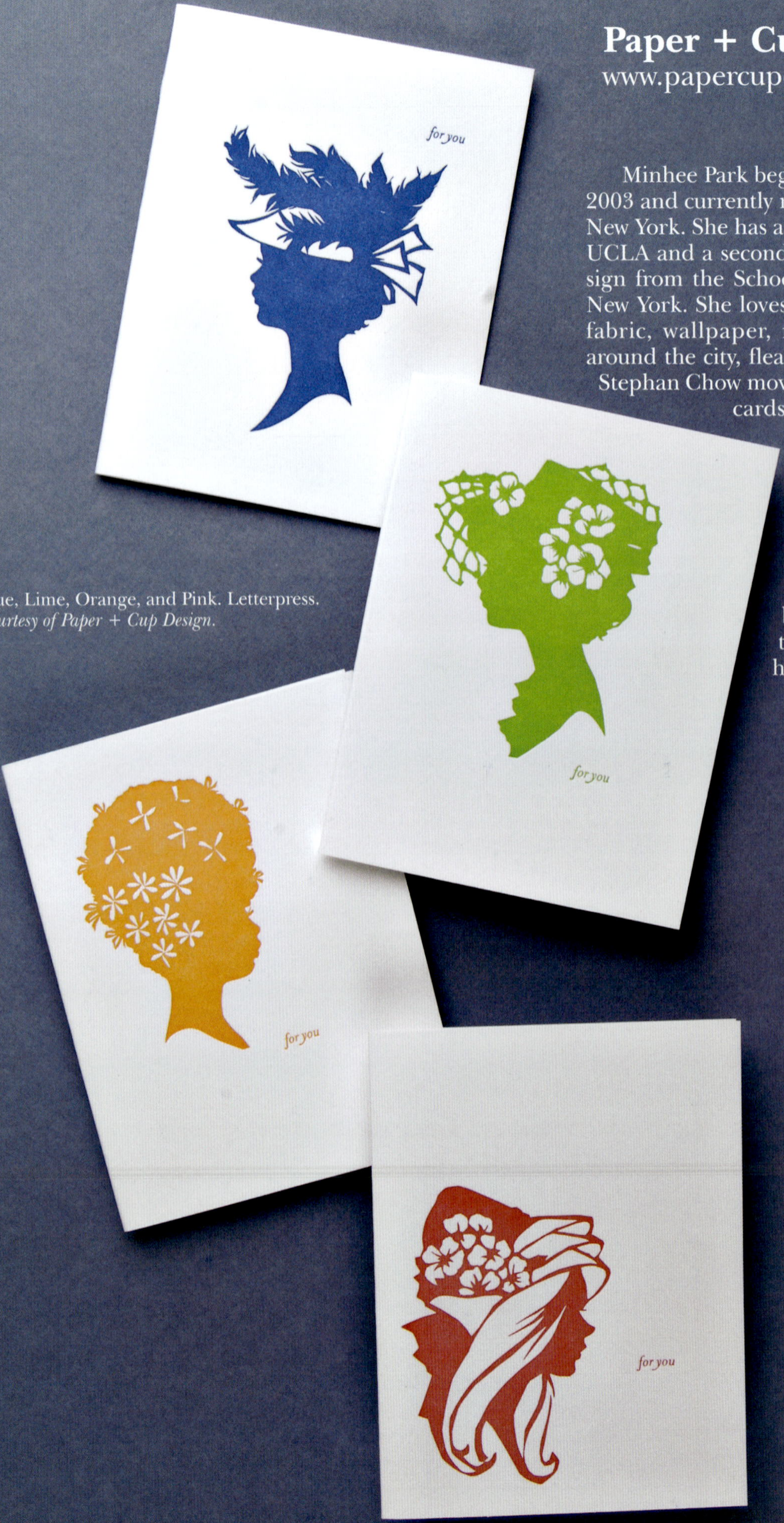

Blue, Lime, Orange, and Pink. Letterpress.
Courtesy of Paper + Cup Design.

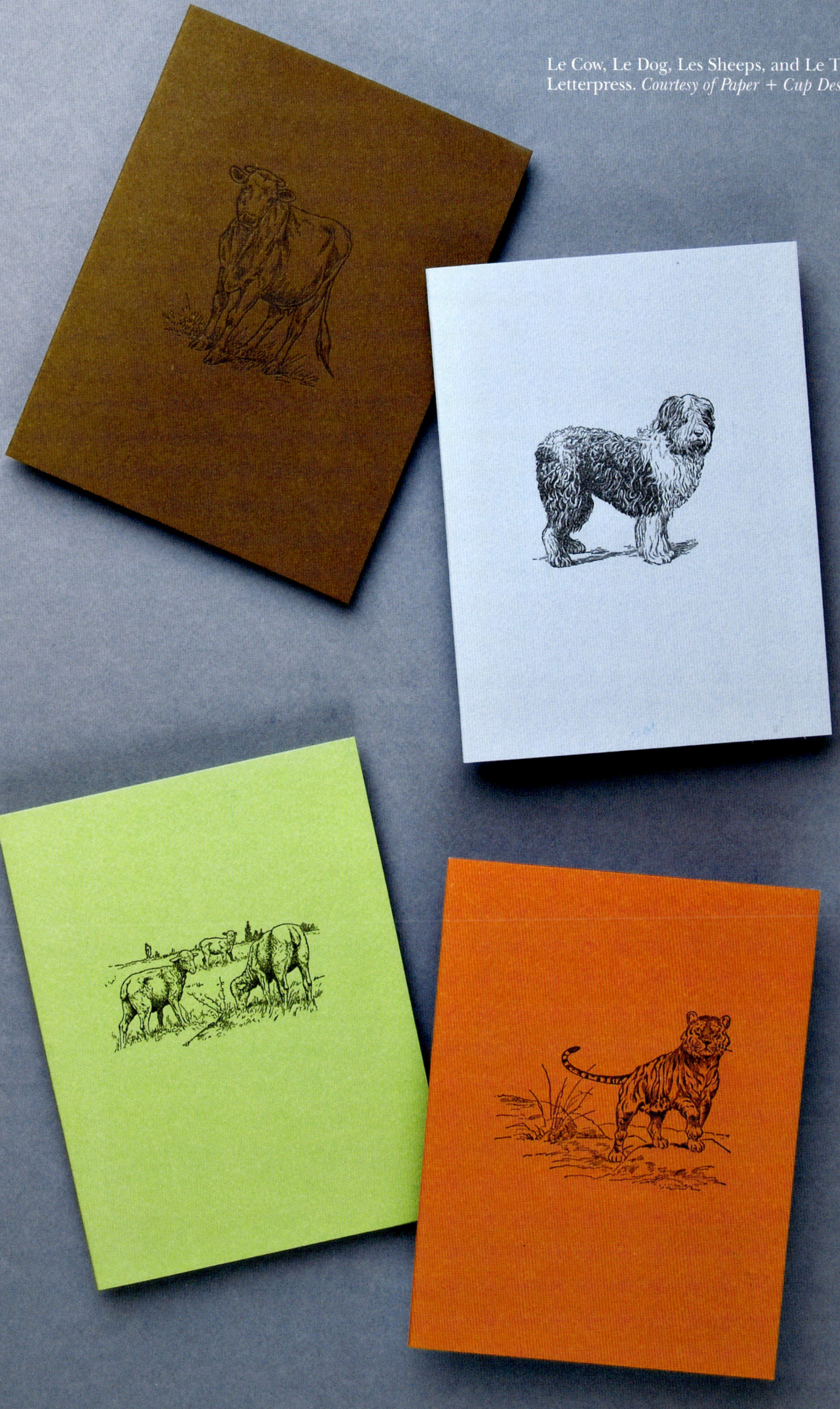

Le Cow, Le Dog, Les Sheeps, and Le Tiger. Letterpress. *Courtesy of Paper + Cup Design.*

Hammerpress

www.hammerpress.net

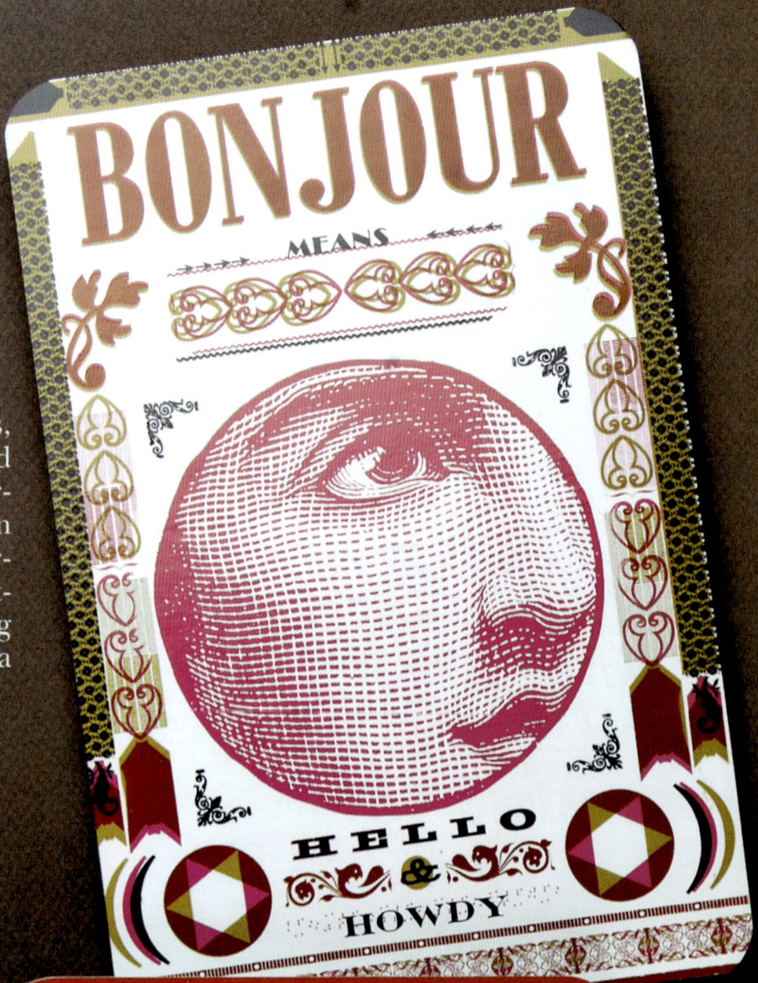

Brady Vest, Lindsay Laricks, and Matt McNary are the talented artists who make up the Hammerpress crew. Established in 1994 in Kansas City, Missouri, Hammerpress has been creating unique letterpress designs as well as providing graphic design services for over a decade.

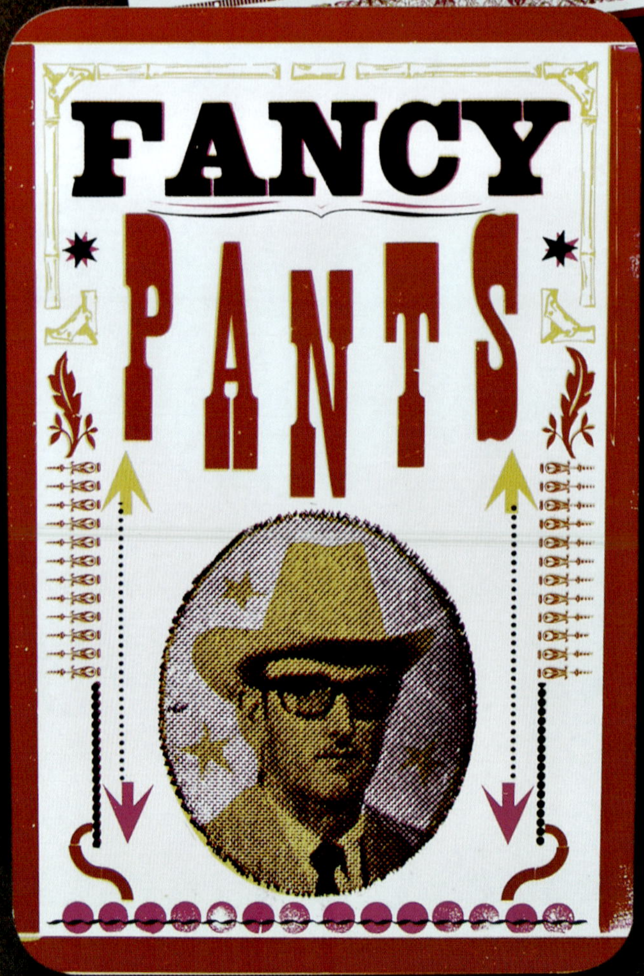

Bonjour Postcard Gigantique and Fancy Pants Postcard Gigantique. Letterpress. *Courtesy of Hammerpress.*

Sombrero Postcard, Turban Postcard, Derby Postcard, and Fez Postcard. Letterpress. *Courtesy of Hammerpress.*

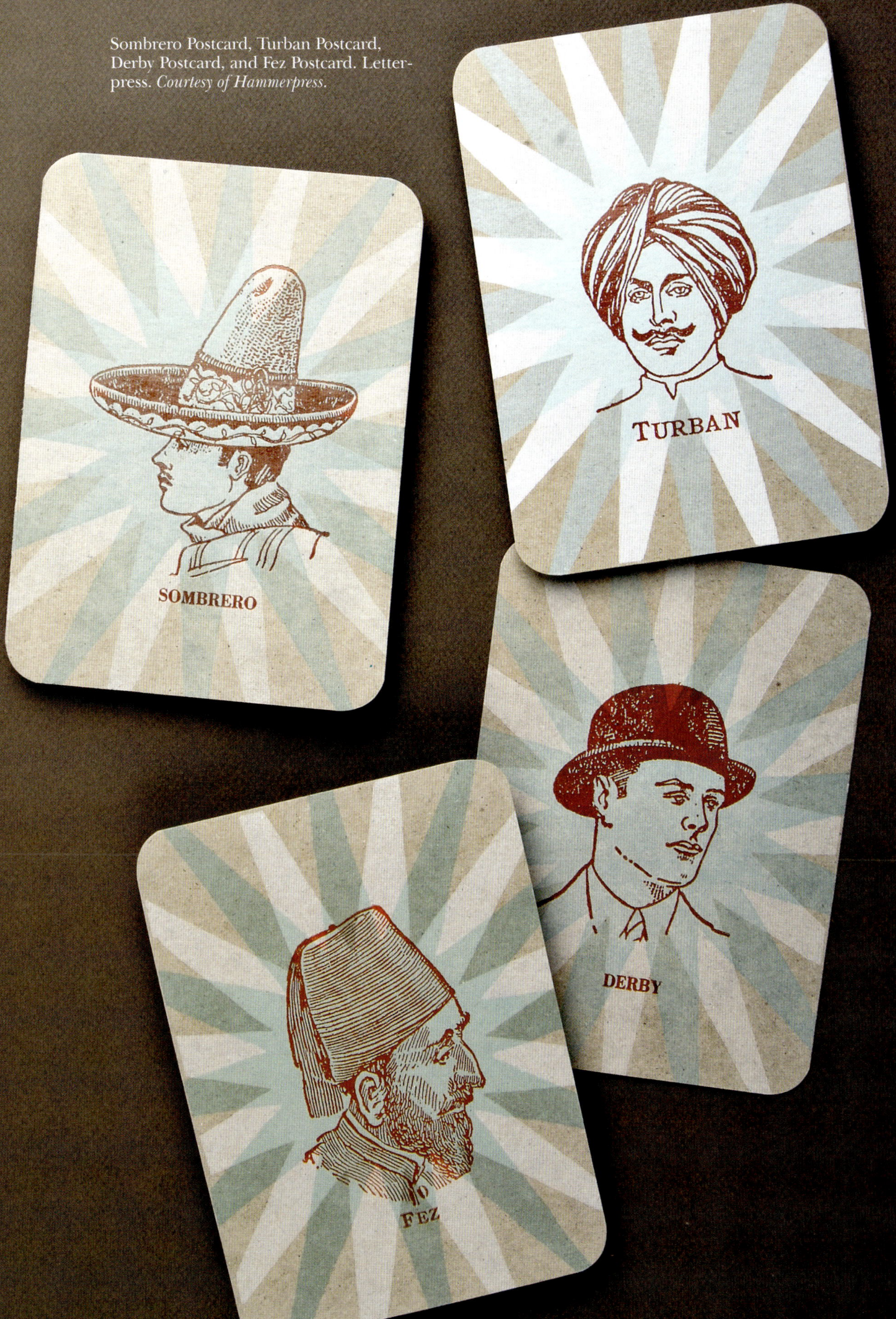

Hello!Lucky

www.hellolucky.com

Founded in 2003 in San Francisco, Hello!Lucky is the creation of two sisters, Eunice Moyle and Sabrina Moyle. Both sisters are artists, but bring different strengths to their company. Sabrina holds a degree from Stanford Business School and has always wanted to start a creative business. Eunice started out designing invitations and announcements for friends and family on her antique Vandercook press. On a whim, she sent her cards to Kate's Paperie in New York, and they immediately placed a large order.

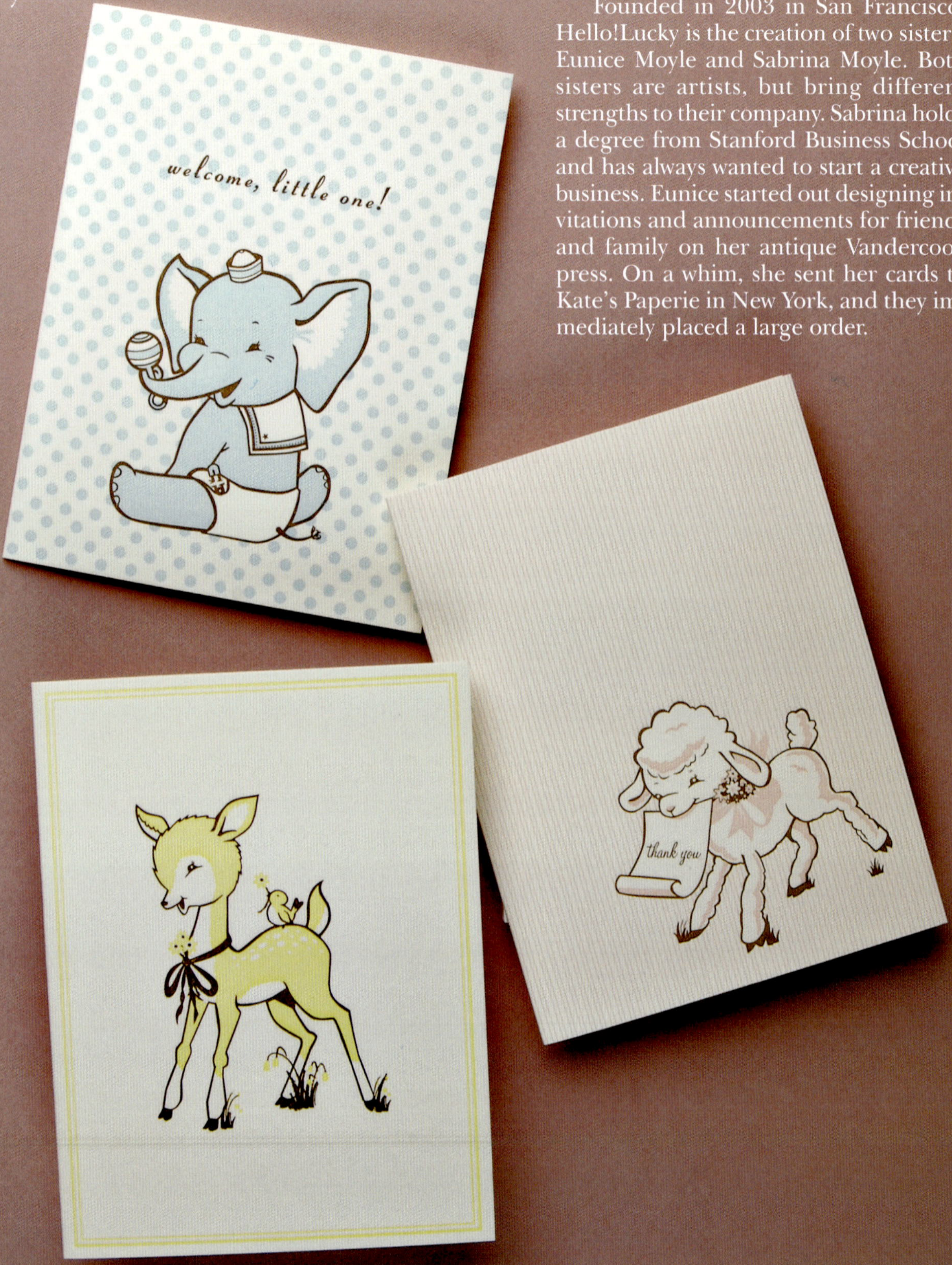

Diapered Elephant, Lambie, and Darling Fawn. Letterpress. *Courtesy of Hello!Lucky.*

Fashionista Terrier and Fashionista Scottie. Letterpress. *Courtesy of Hello!Lucky.*

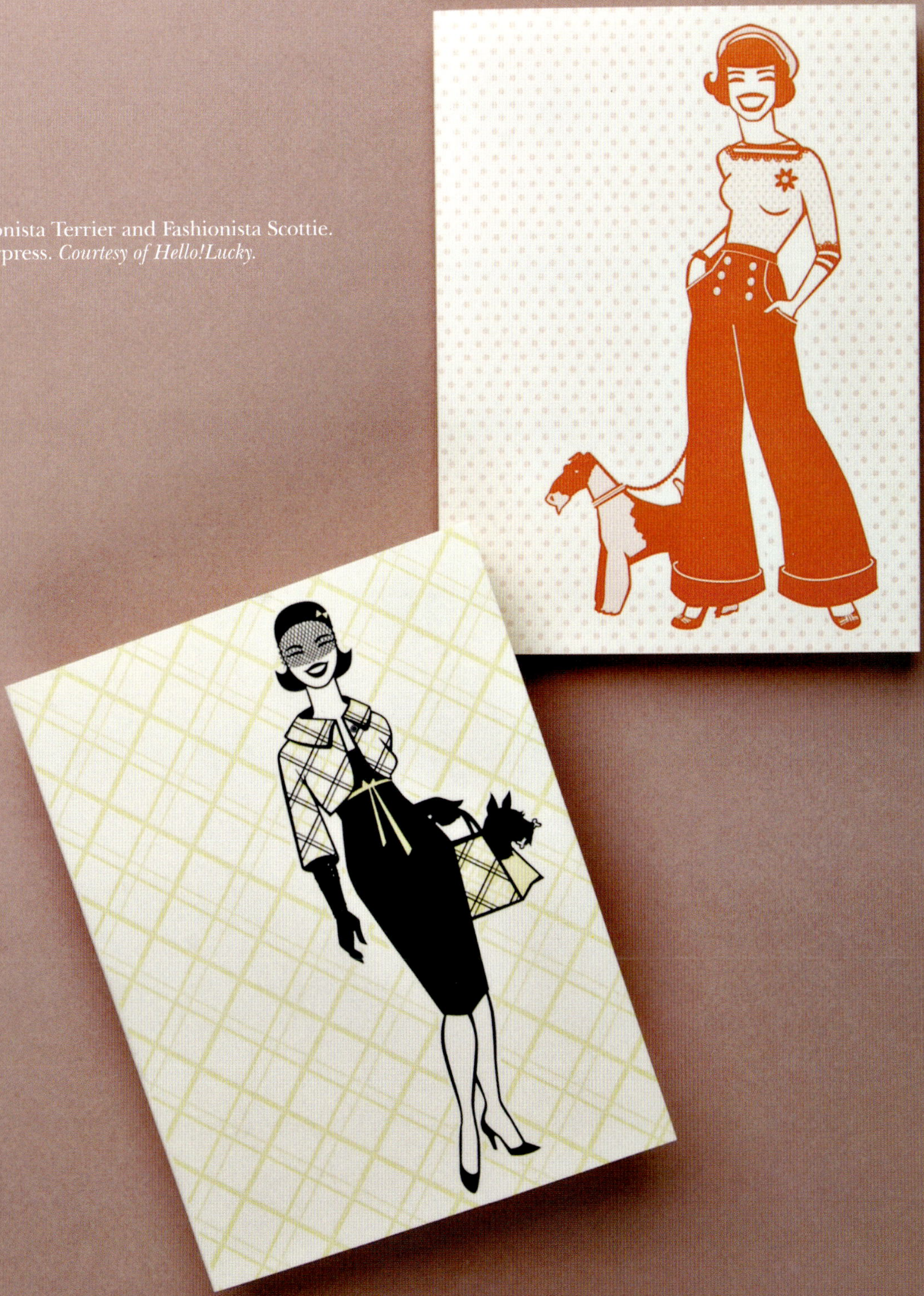

Smudge Ink

www.smudgeink.com

Smudge Ink consists of three different talented designers: Kate Saliba, Deb Lavoie, and Erin Dillow. Kate and Deb work out of Boston, Massachusetts, while Erin works out of Fort Worth, Texas. Both Kate and Deb have taken a lifetime of art courses. Kate learned the art of letterpress printing through two apprenticeships. Deb has a background in historic preservation of architecture. Erin holds a BFA in design from the University of Texas and enjoys reading, painting, and refinishing old furniture. All three designers love being outdoors and feel that weekends are sacred.

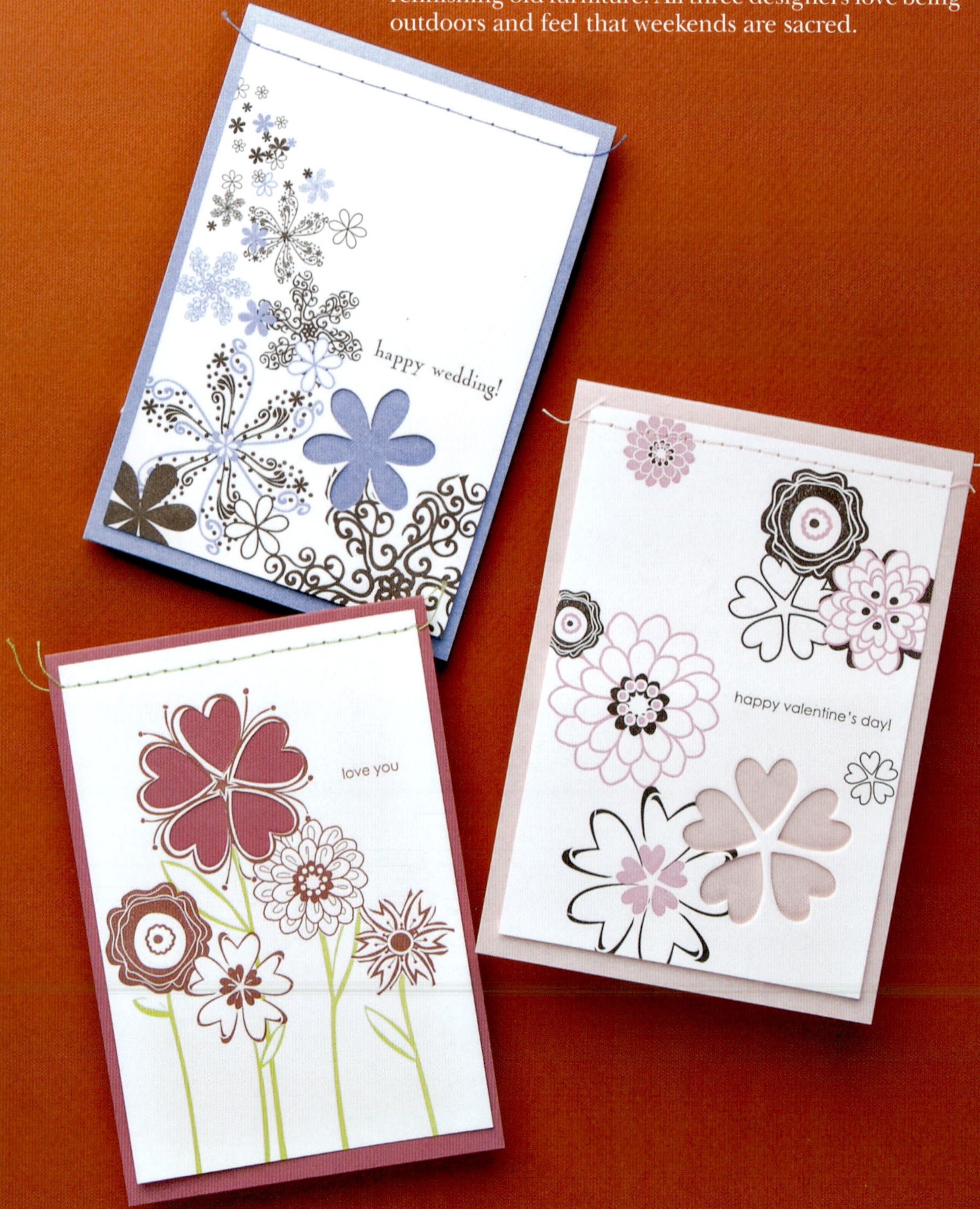

Happy Wedding Flower Confetti, Love You Heart Flower Garden, and Valentine's Day Floating Heart Flowers. Letterpress. *Courtesy of Smudge Ink.*

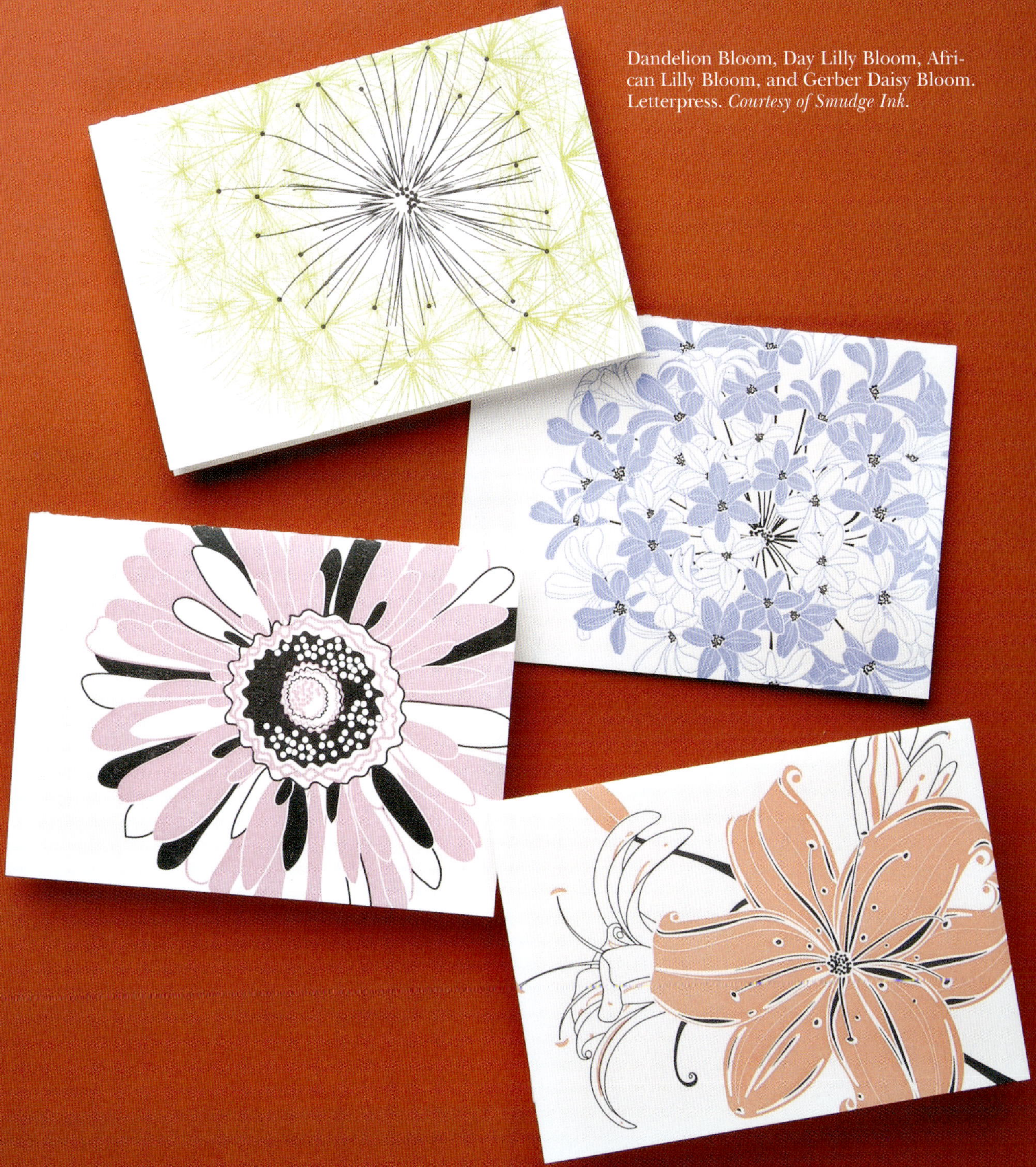

Dandelion Bloom, Day Lilly Bloom, African Lilly Bloom, and Gerber Daisy Bloom. Letterpress. *Courtesy of Smudge Ink.*

Pancake & Franks

www.pancakeandfranks.com

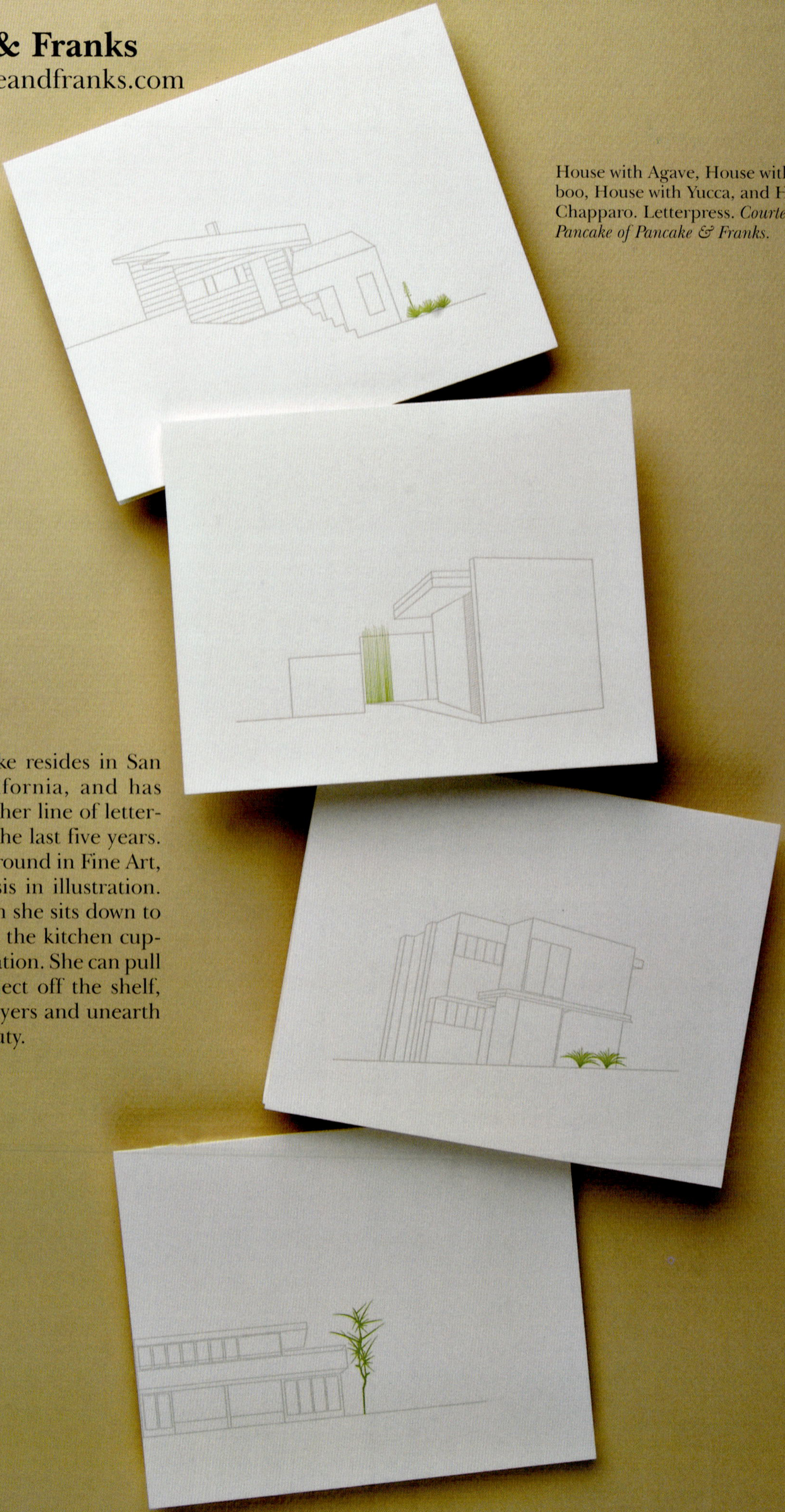

House with Agave, House with Bamboo, House with Yucca, and House with Chapparo. Letterpress. *Courtesy of Stacy Pancake of Pancake & Franks.*

Stacy Pancake resides in San Francisco, California, and has been designing her line of letterpress cards for the last five years. She has a background in Fine Art, with an emphasis in illustration. Sometimes when she sits down to draw, she opens the kitchen cupboard for inspiration. She can pull an everyday object off the shelf, chip away the layers and unearth its essential beauty.

Horse, Chicken, Pig, and Cow. Letterpress. *Courtesy of Stacy Pancake of Pancake and Franks.*

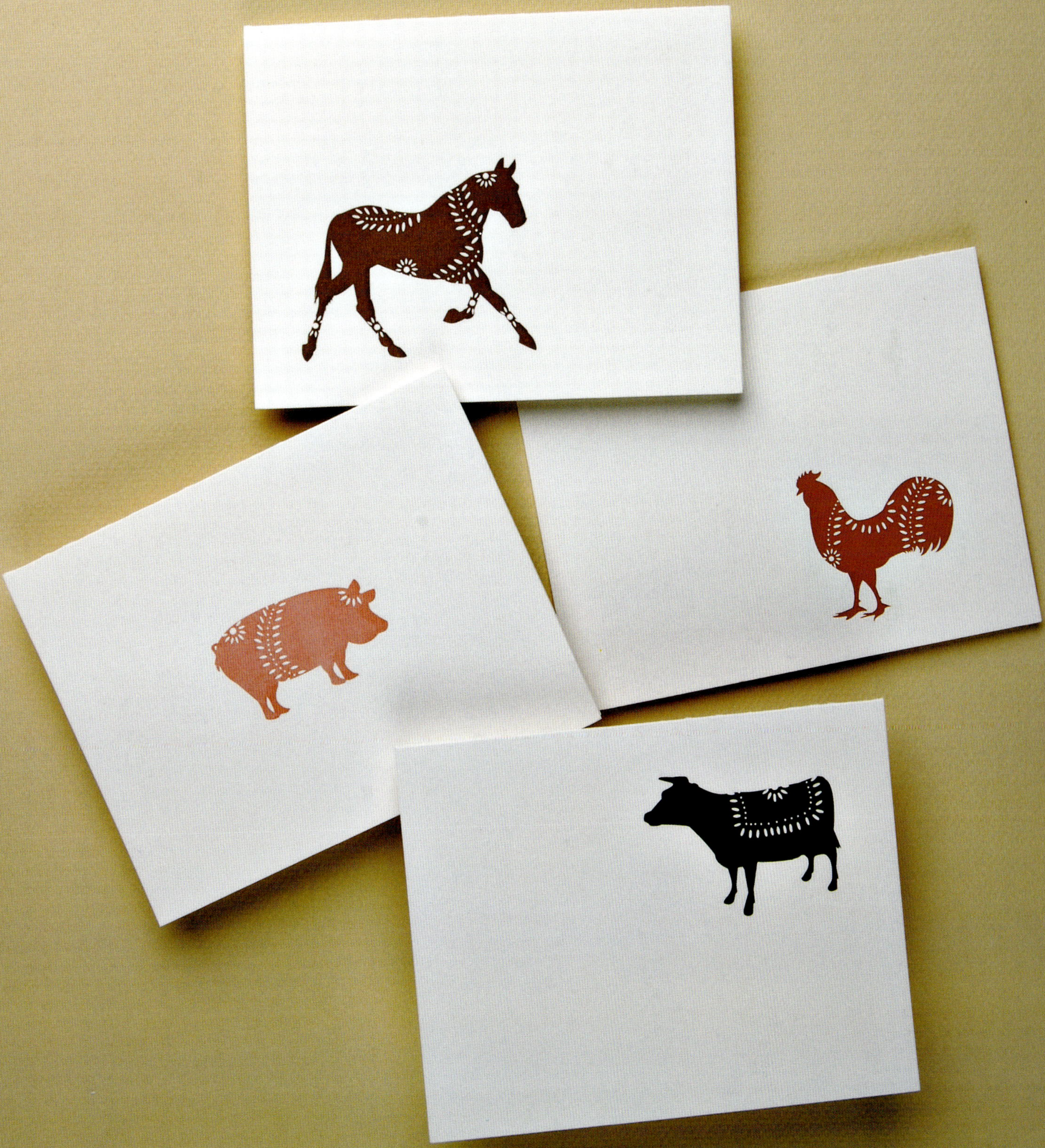

Two Piglets/Century Guild Press

www.twopiglets.com

Jesse Ellico of Monrovia, California, is the man behind Two Piglets/Century Guild Press. Century Guild has been designing award-winning invitations since 1995. Karen and Hiroshi Beard started Two Piglets in 2002. Jesse graduated with a degree in Mechanical Design from the University of Southern California and is a member of the Industrial Design Faculty at Art Center College of Design and Otis College of Art and Design in Los Angeles. Jesse always looks at the lighter side and tends to not take himself too seriously…hence the silly topics of most of the card designs.

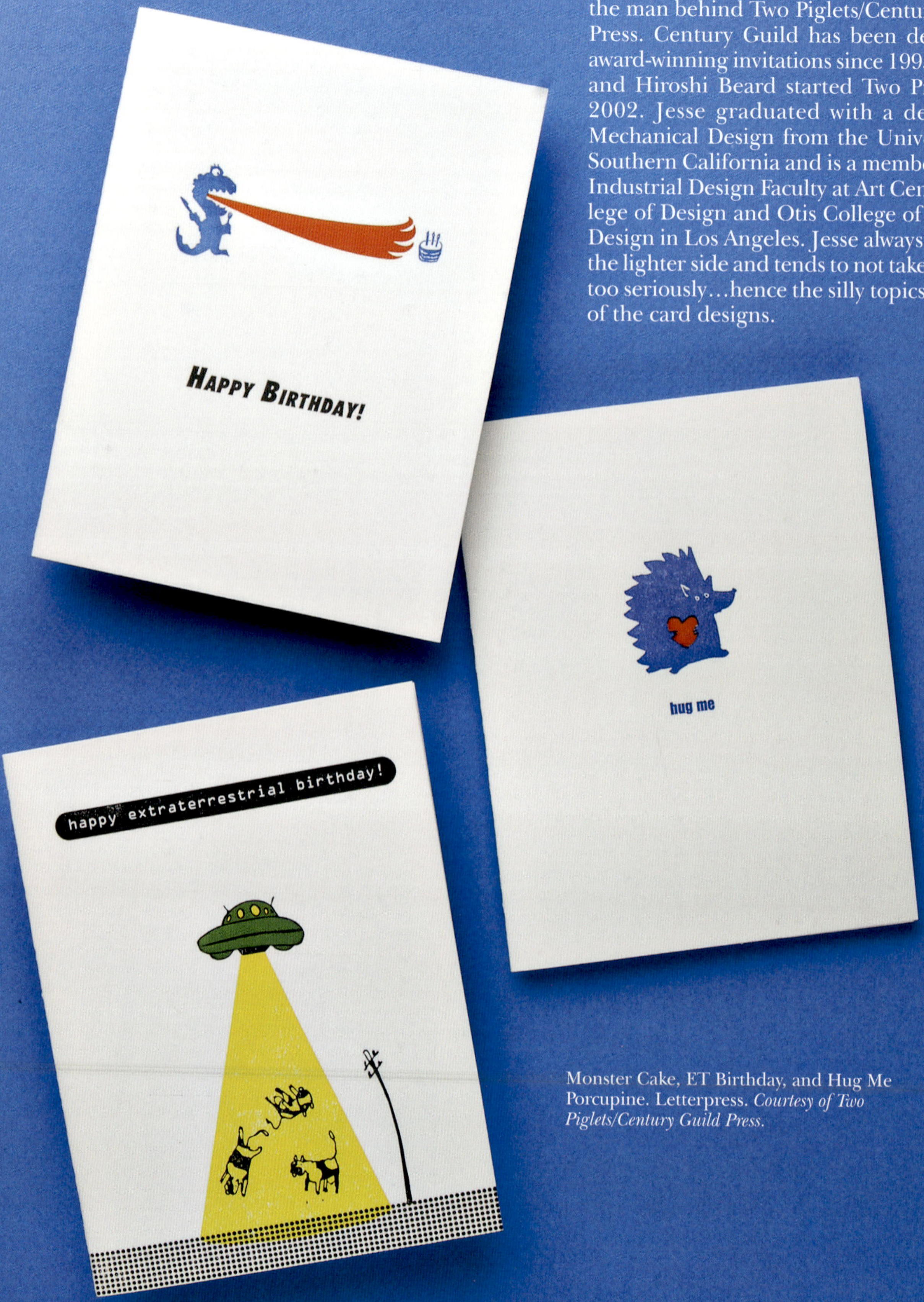

Monster Cake, ET Birthday, and Hug Me Porcupine. Letterpress. *Courtesy of Two Piglets/Century Guild Press.*

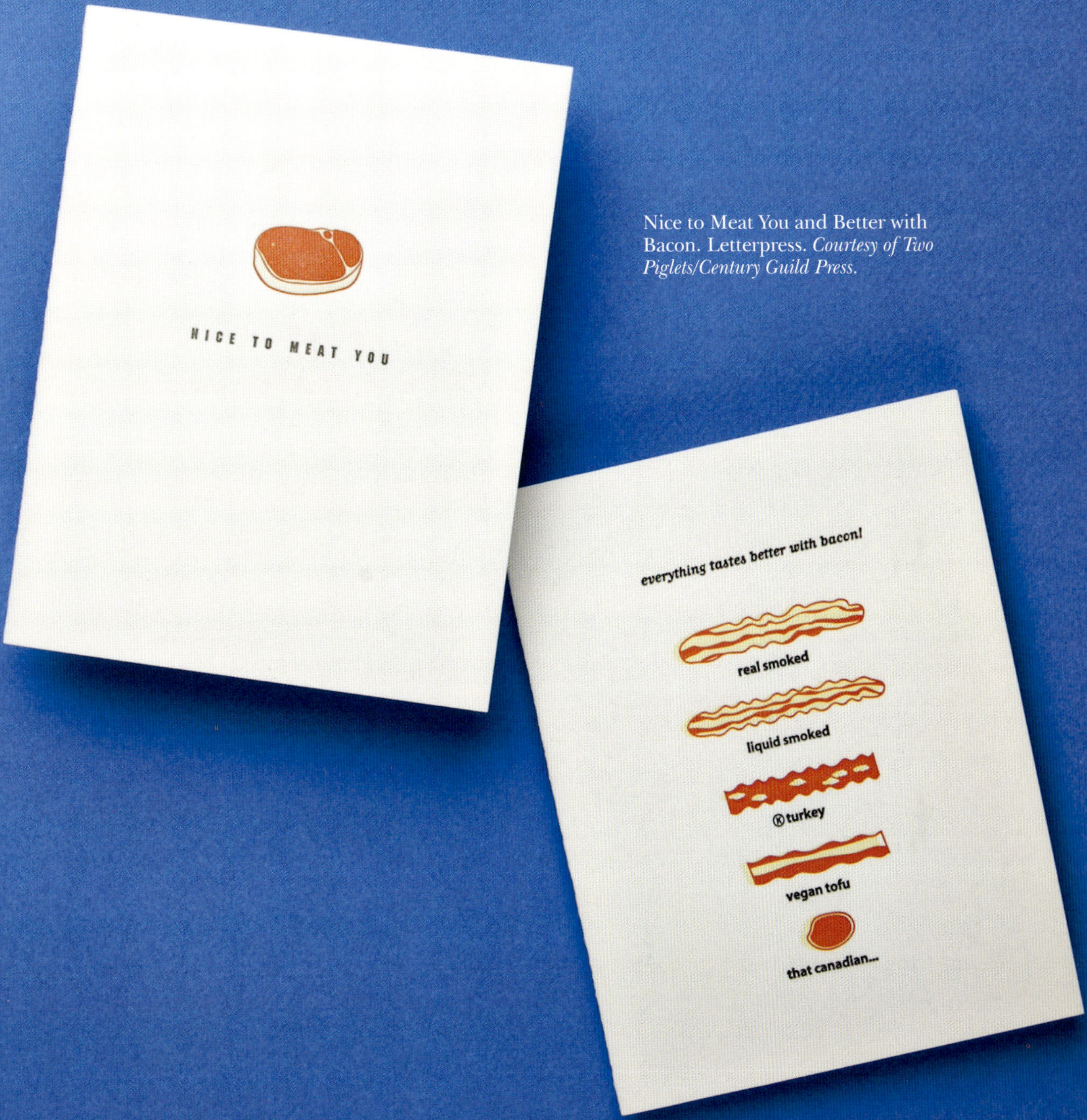

Nice to Meat You and Better with Bacon. Letterpress. *Courtesy of Two Piglets/Century Guild Press.*

Elum Designs

www.elumdesigns.com

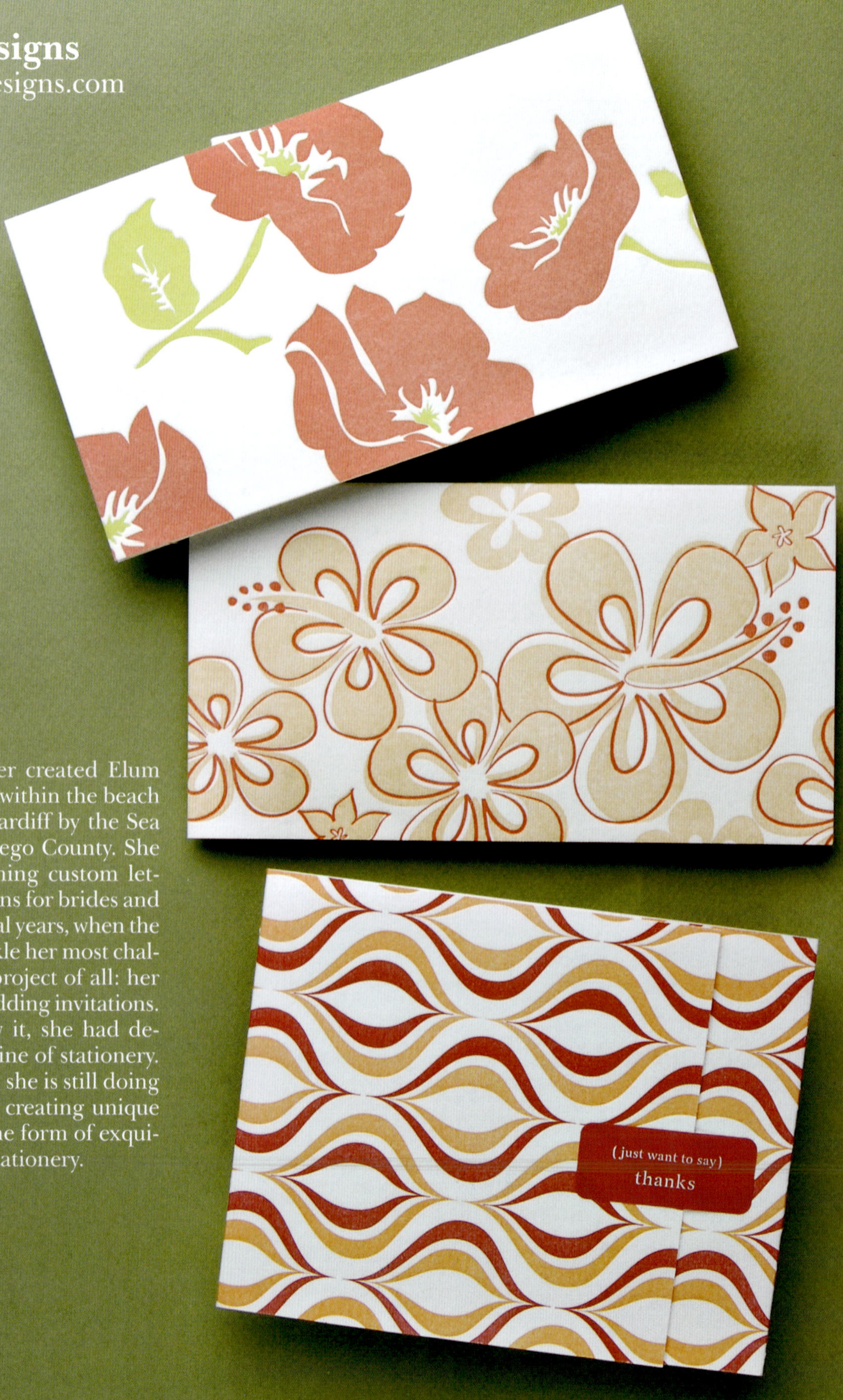

Melissa Foster created Elum Designs in 2002 within the beach community of Cardiff by the Sea in North San Diego County. She had been designing custom letterpress invitations for brides and grooms for several years, when the time came to tackle her most challenging design project of all: her own personal wedding invitations. Before she knew it, she had designed her first line of stationery. Many years later, she is still doing what she loves – creating unique works of art in the form of exquisite letterpress stationery.

Magnolias, Surfer Girl, and Lips. Letterpress.
Courtesy of Elum Designs.

Empress Green, Empress Pink, Greyhound Gray, and Greyhound Pink. Letterpress. *Courtesy of Elum Designs.*

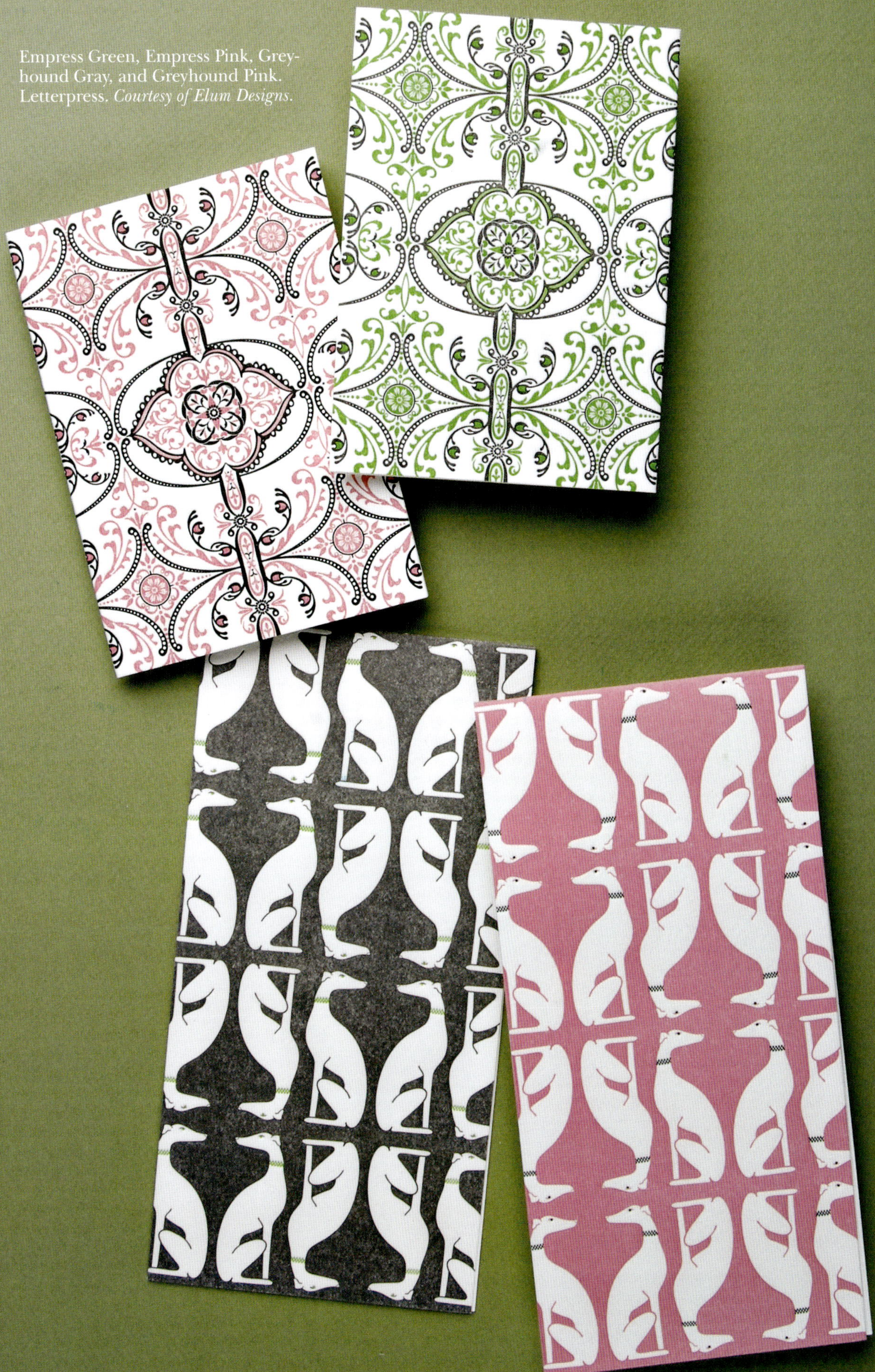

Yee-Haw Industries

www.yeehawindustries.com

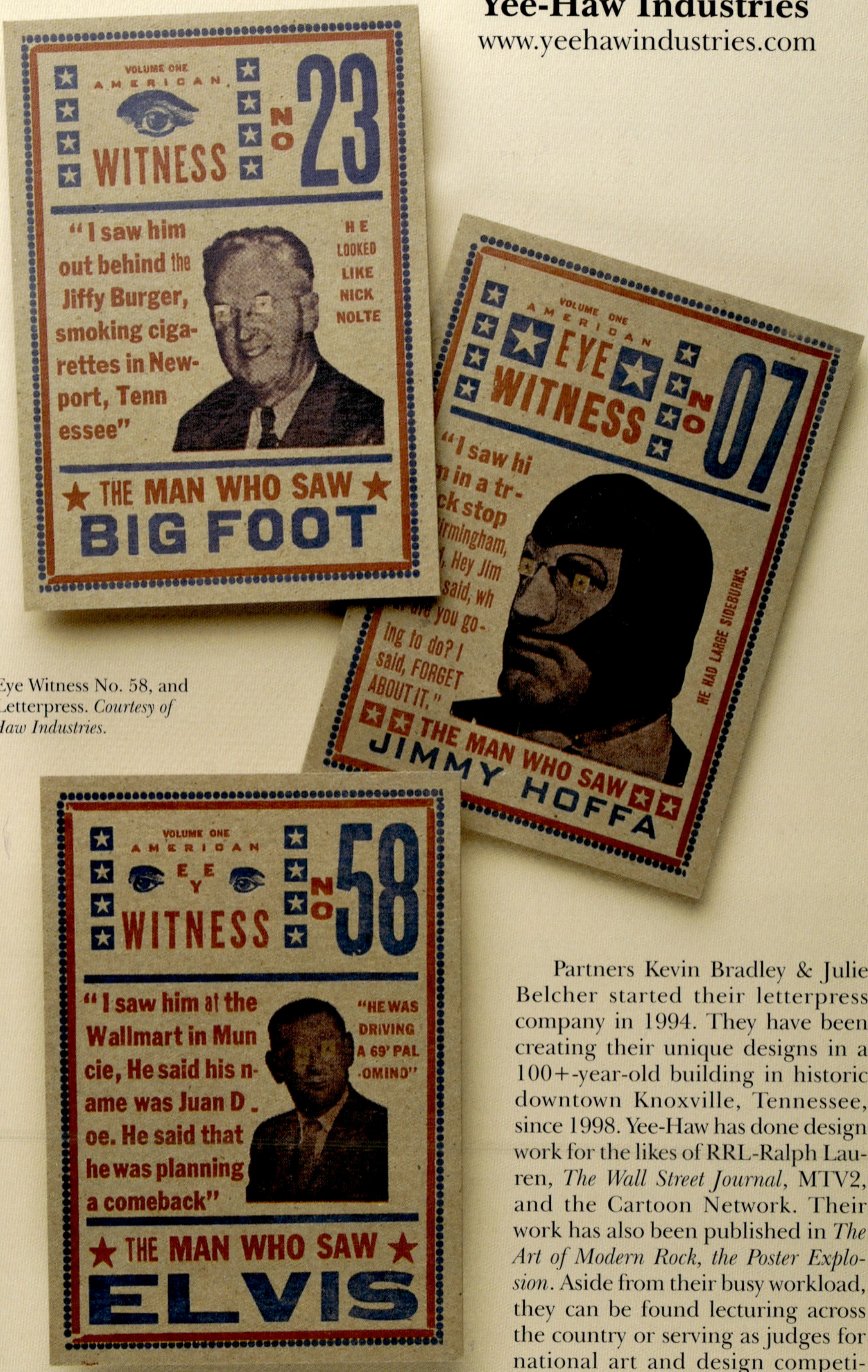

Eye Witness No. 07, Eye Witness No. 58, and Eye Witness No. 23. Letterpress. *Courtesy of Kevin Bradley for Yee-Haw Industries.*

Partners Kevin Bradley & Julie Belcher started their letterpress company in 1994. They have been creating their unique designs in a 100+-year-old building in historic downtown Knoxville, Tennessee, since 1998. Yee-Haw has done design work for the likes of RRL-Ralph Lauren, *The Wall Street Journal*, MTV2, and the Cartoon Network. Their work has also been published in *The Art of Modern Rock, the Poster Explosion*. Aside from their busy workload, they can be found lecturing across the country or serving as judges for national art and design competitions.

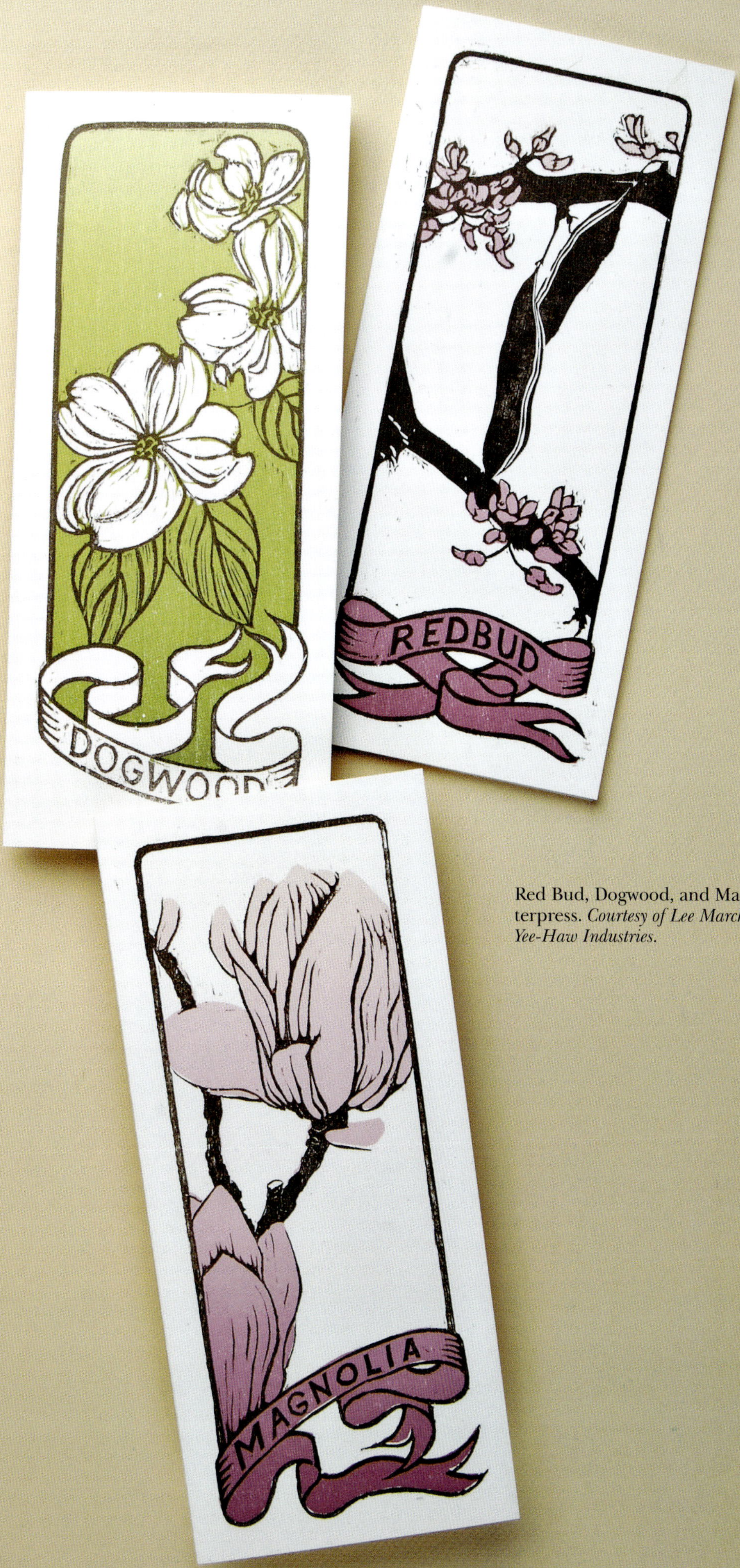

Red Bud, Dogwood, and Magnolia. Letterpress. *Courtesy of Lee Marchalonis for Yee-Haw Industries.*

Chapter Four Illustration

Some of today's top illustrators create beautiful artwork for the greeting card industry. In addition to illustrating for greeting cards and stationery, many of the artists profiled in this section are professional freelance artists whose work can be found on apparel and bed sheets (*Masha D'yans Design*), book covers (*Red Cap Cards*), canvas (*Curly Girl Design*), and a variety of giftware items (*Waghappy*).

Many illustrators license their work out to large greeting card publishers, while others choose to self publish their work.

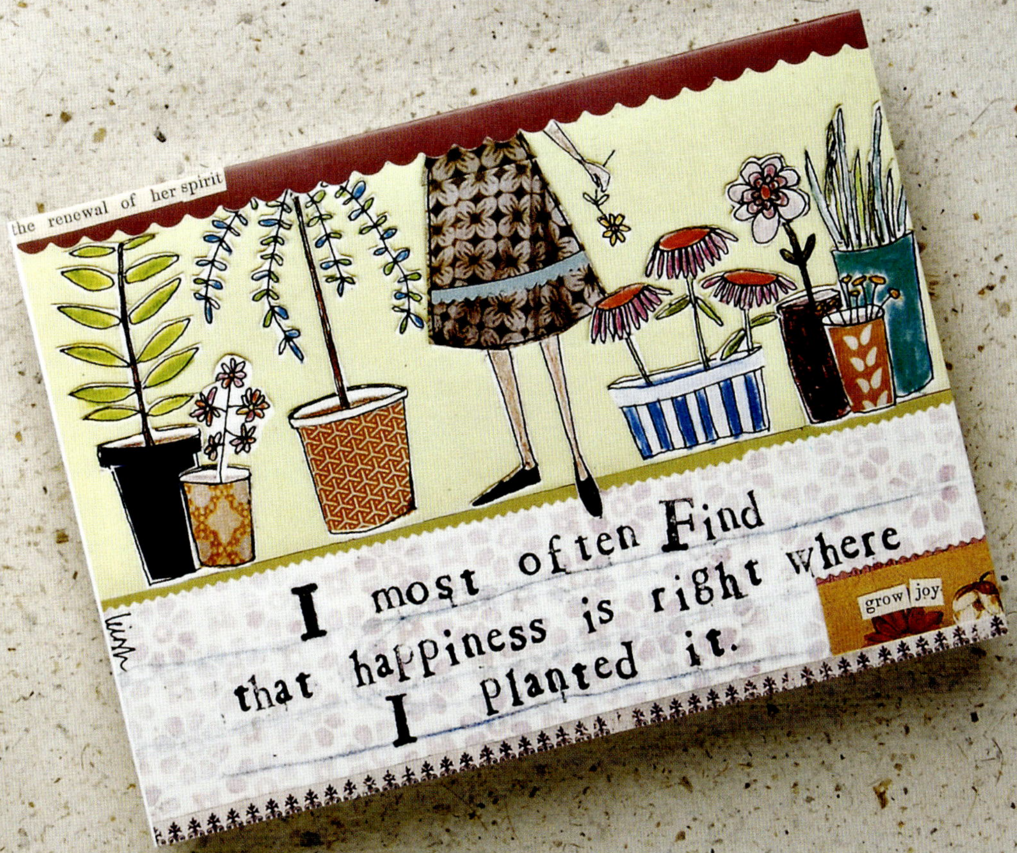

Plant Happy. Offset printed. *Courtesy of Leigh Standley of Curlygirl Design.*

Curly Girl Design

www.curlygirldesign.com

Leigh Standley began designing in seventh grade, where she got poor marks in math class for doodling. She went on to attend the University of Kansas School of Design and holds a BFA in Visual Communications. She began her award winning company in 2003 and continues to find inspiration from her incredible friends and family. Leigh has lived in Boston for six years and likes it so much that she only occasionally wishes it were Paris.

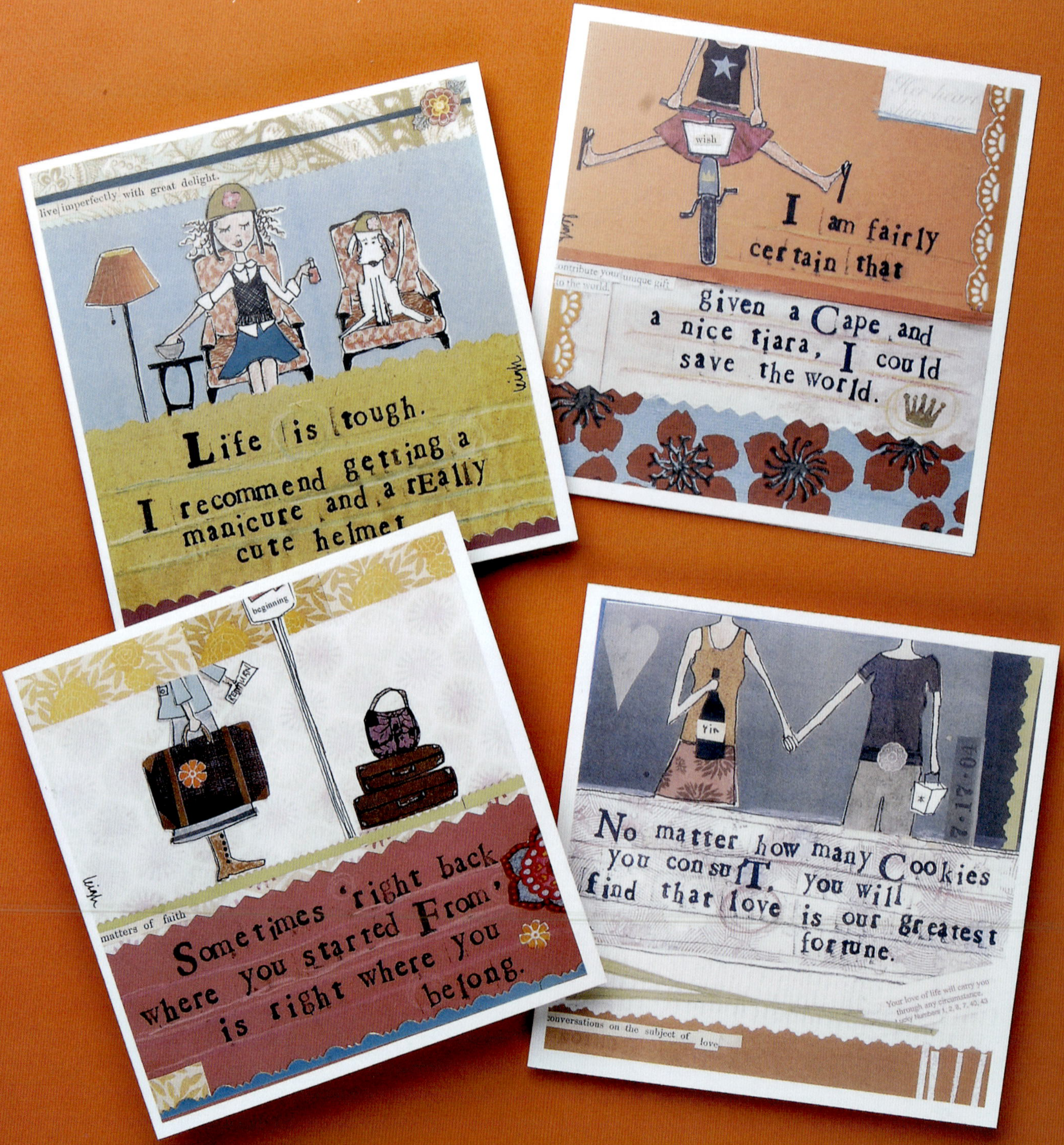

Life is Tough, Tiara, Right Back Where You Belong, and Fortune. Offset printed. *Courtesy of Leigh Standley of Curly Girl Design.*

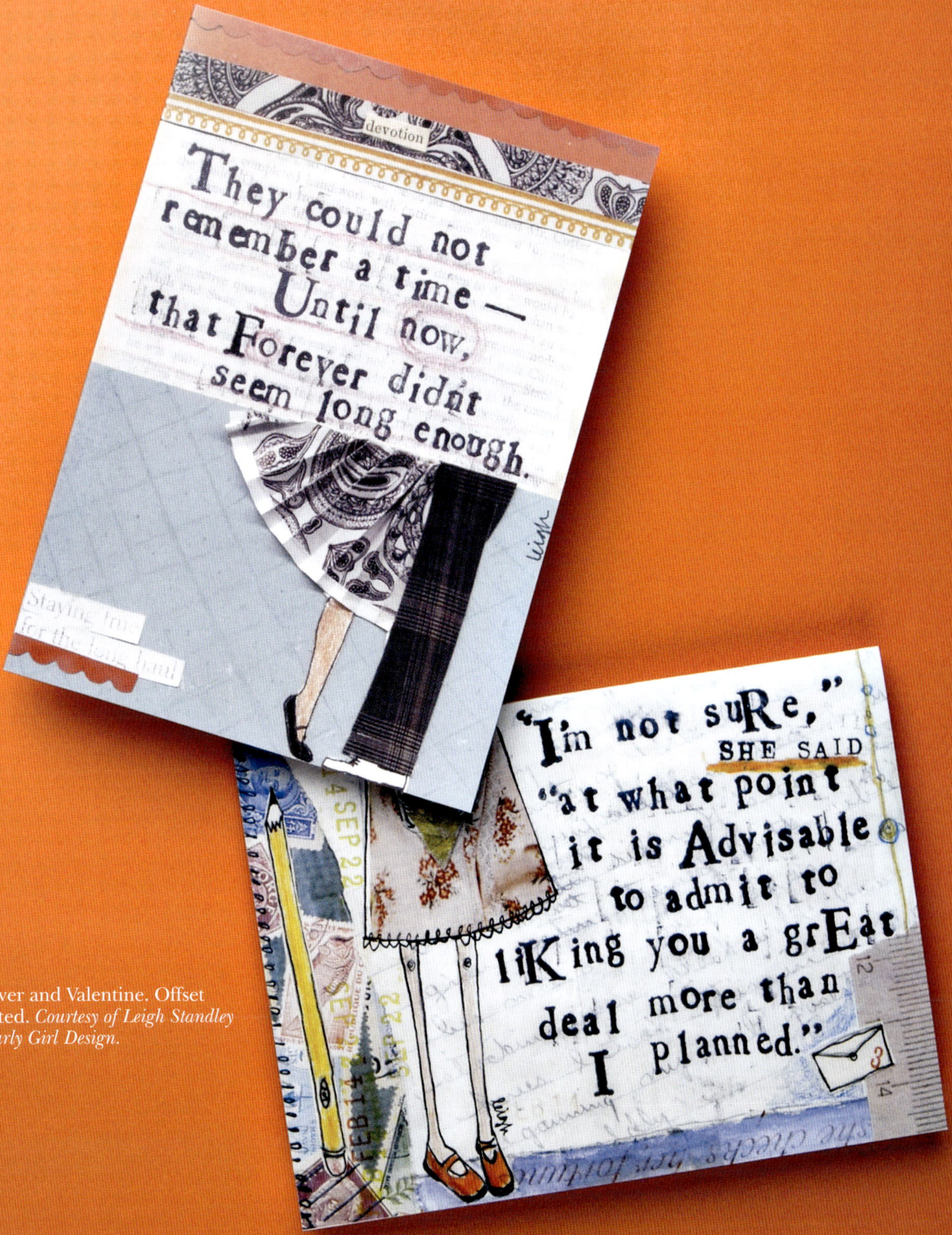

Forever and Valentine. Offset printed. *Courtesy of Leigh Standley of Curly Girl Design.*

Red Cap Cards

www.redcapcards.com

Carrie Gifford established her company in 2004, along with her husband, Hal Mertz. As a native Californian she has been directing and teaching children's theatre for eight years at South Coast Repertory. She has since illustrated book covers for Bloomsbury Publishing, and is currently illustrating her first children's book based upon one of the characters from Red Cap Cards, named Apple Moshberry.

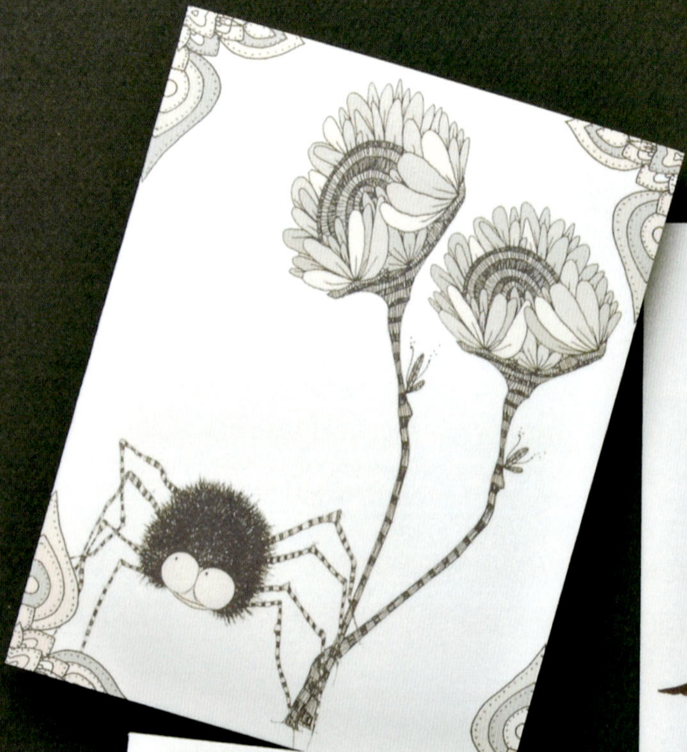

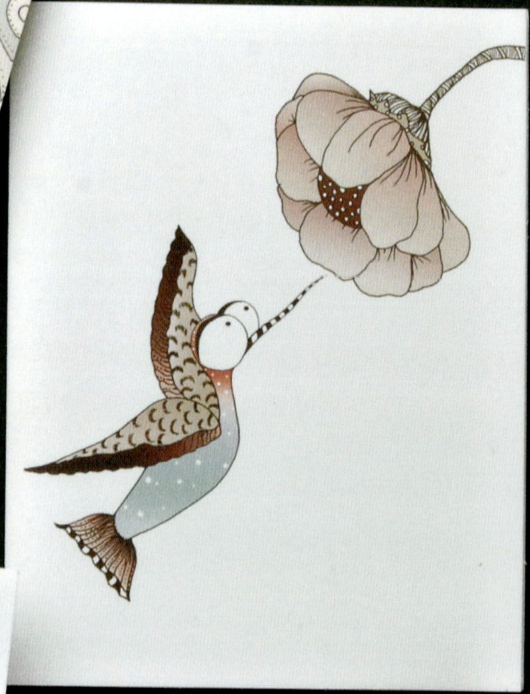

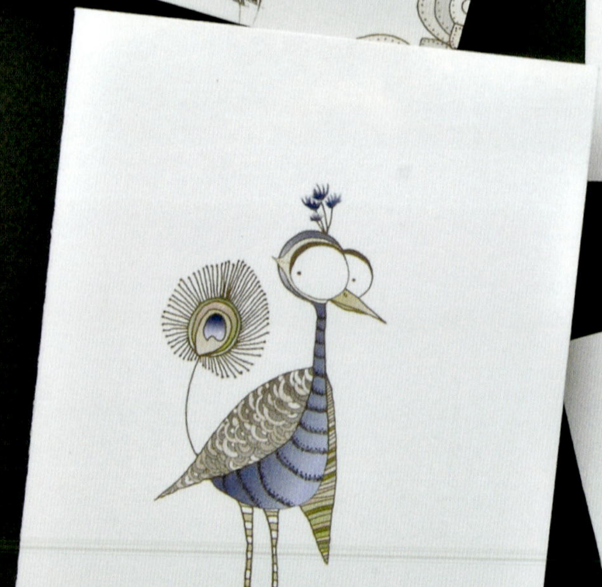

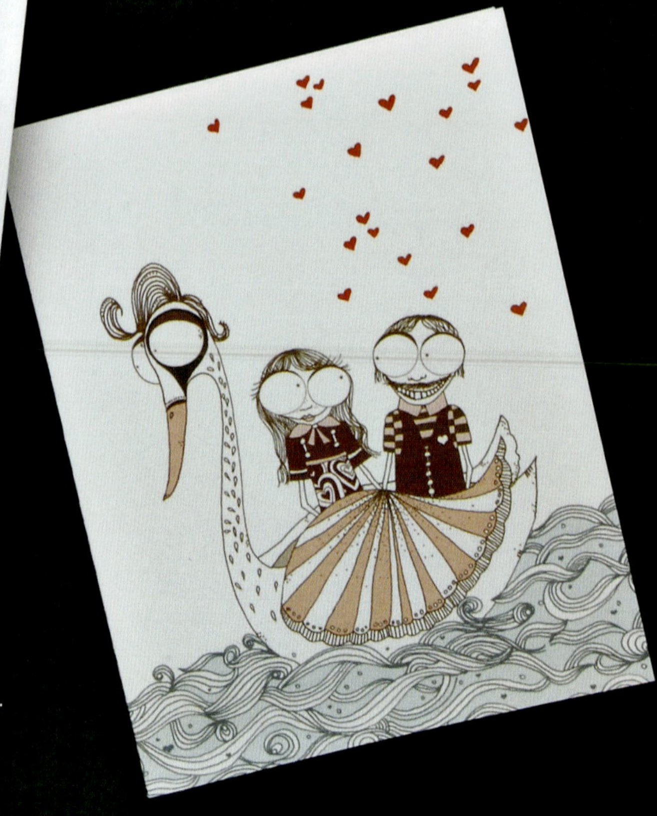

Leonard Spider, Eunice the Hummingbird, Perry the One Feathered Peacock, and The Lovers Traveled by Sea Swan. Offset printed. *Courtesy of Red Cap Cards.*

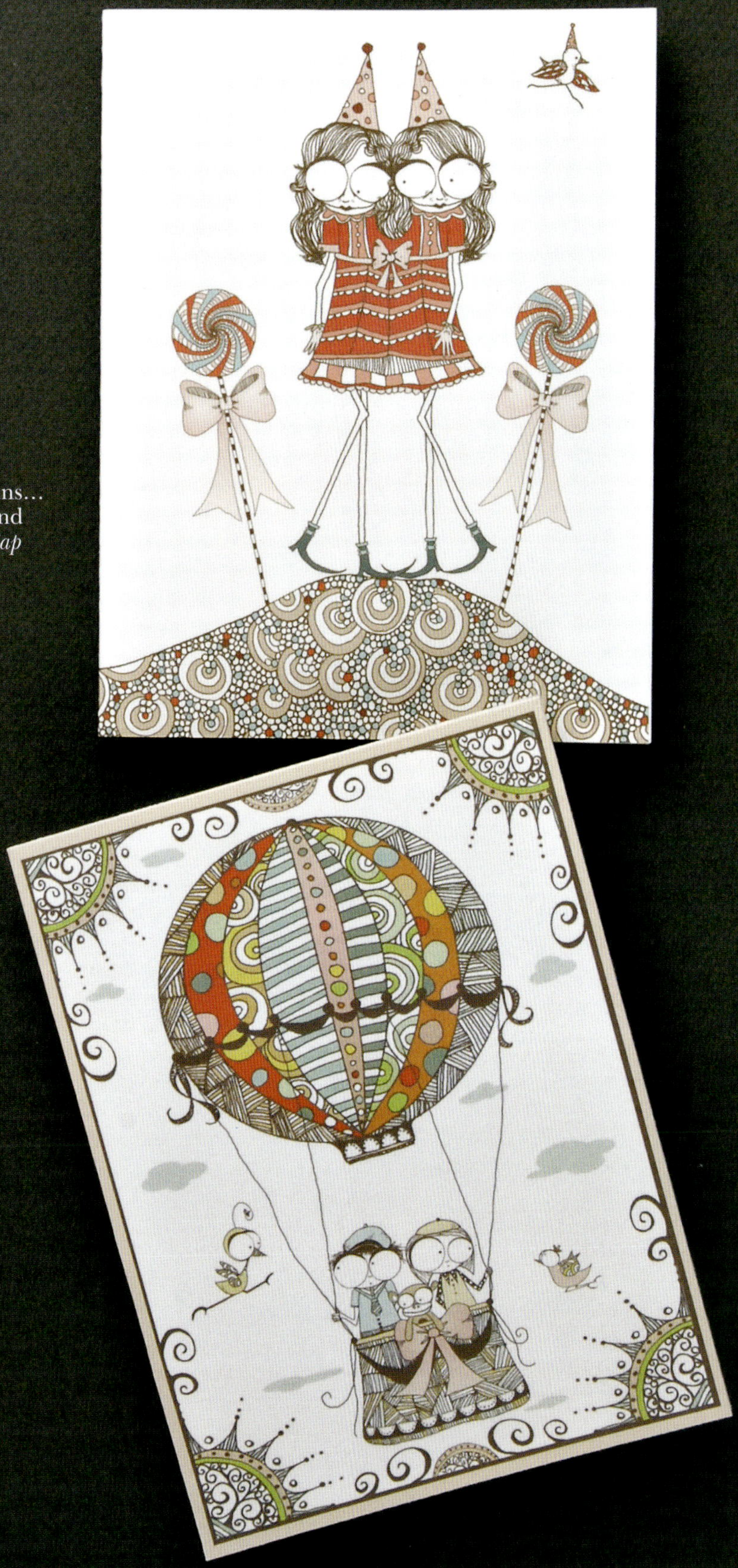

They Called Themselves the Sugar Twins... Sweet Indeed They Were and Amous and Apple. Offset printed. *Courtesy of Red Cap Cards.*

Seltzer

www.seltzergoods.com

Seltzer was launched in 2005 and is located in Astoria, New York. Gay Lam and Brian Gold are the designing duo behind the cards. Gay has a background in painting and has always had a knack for product design. Brian is an award winning creative director and self-taught designer/illustrator. They find inspiration in everyday life, candy wrappers, Philip Guston, nature, New York City, coffee, and twentieth century illustrators who wore thick glasses and sat at drafting tables.

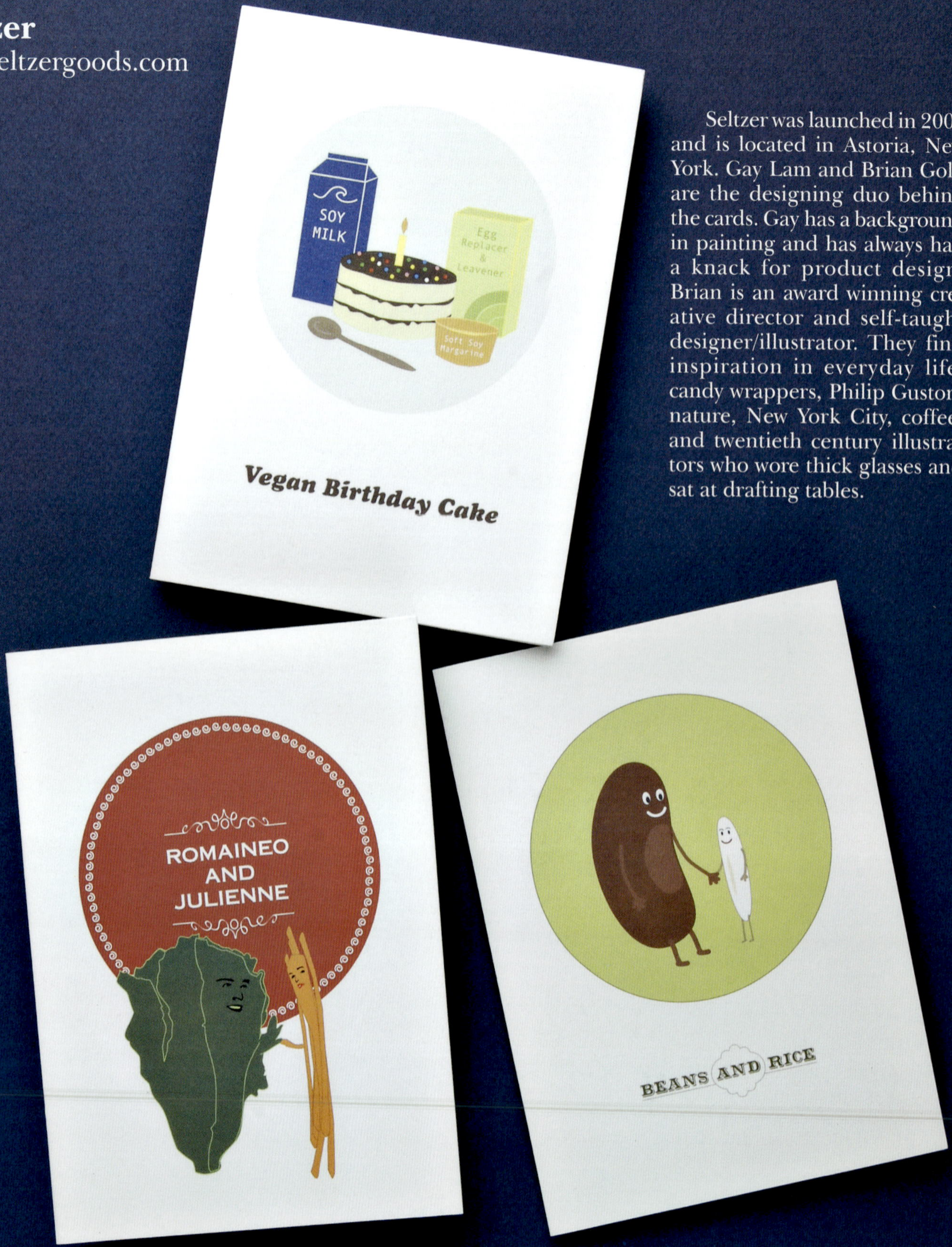

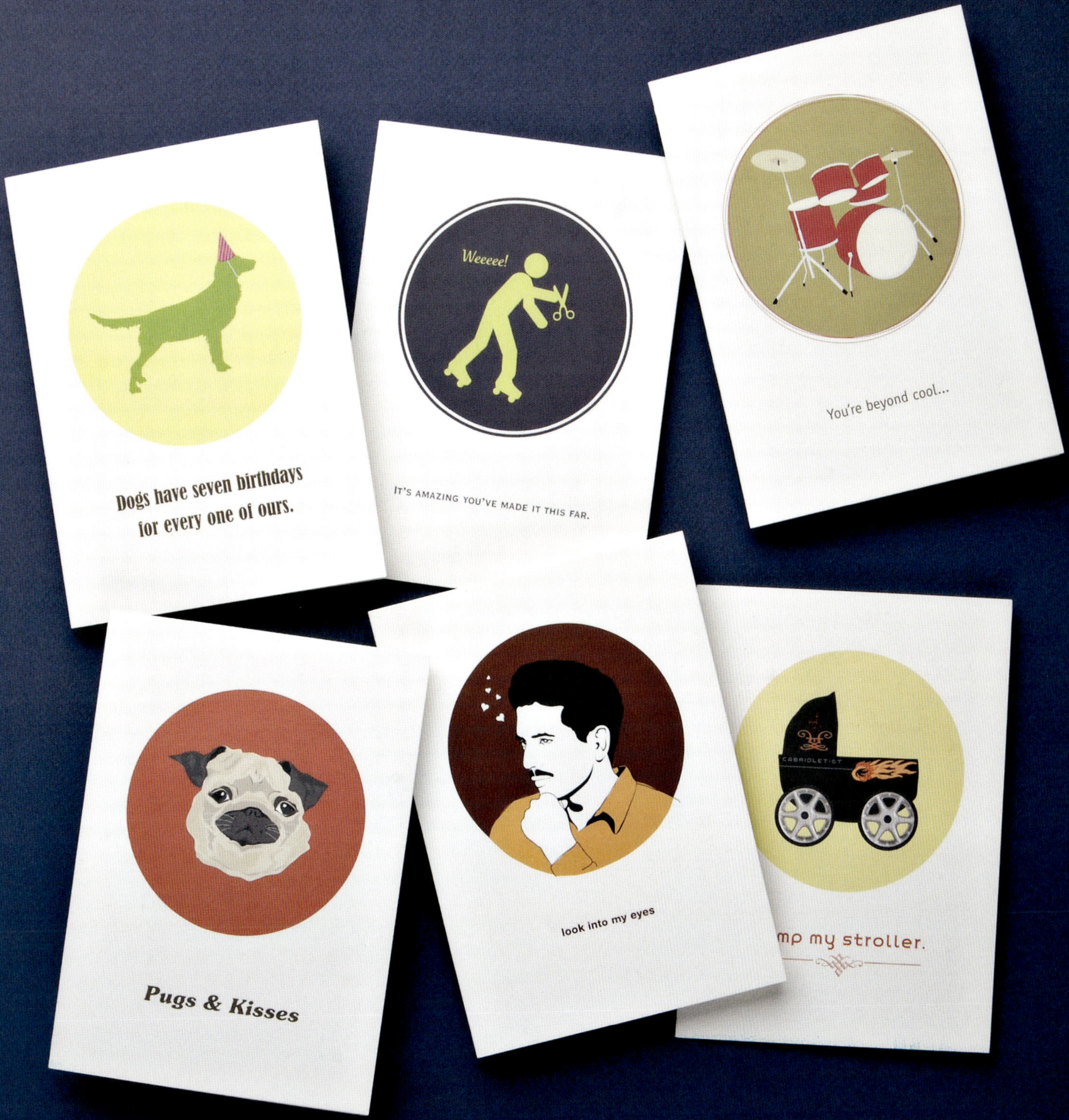

Dog Years, Scissors, Drums, Pugs and Kisses, Suave, and Stroller-Yellow. Offset lithography with vegetable based ink. *Courtesy of Seltzer.*

Good On Paper

www.goodonpaperdesign.com

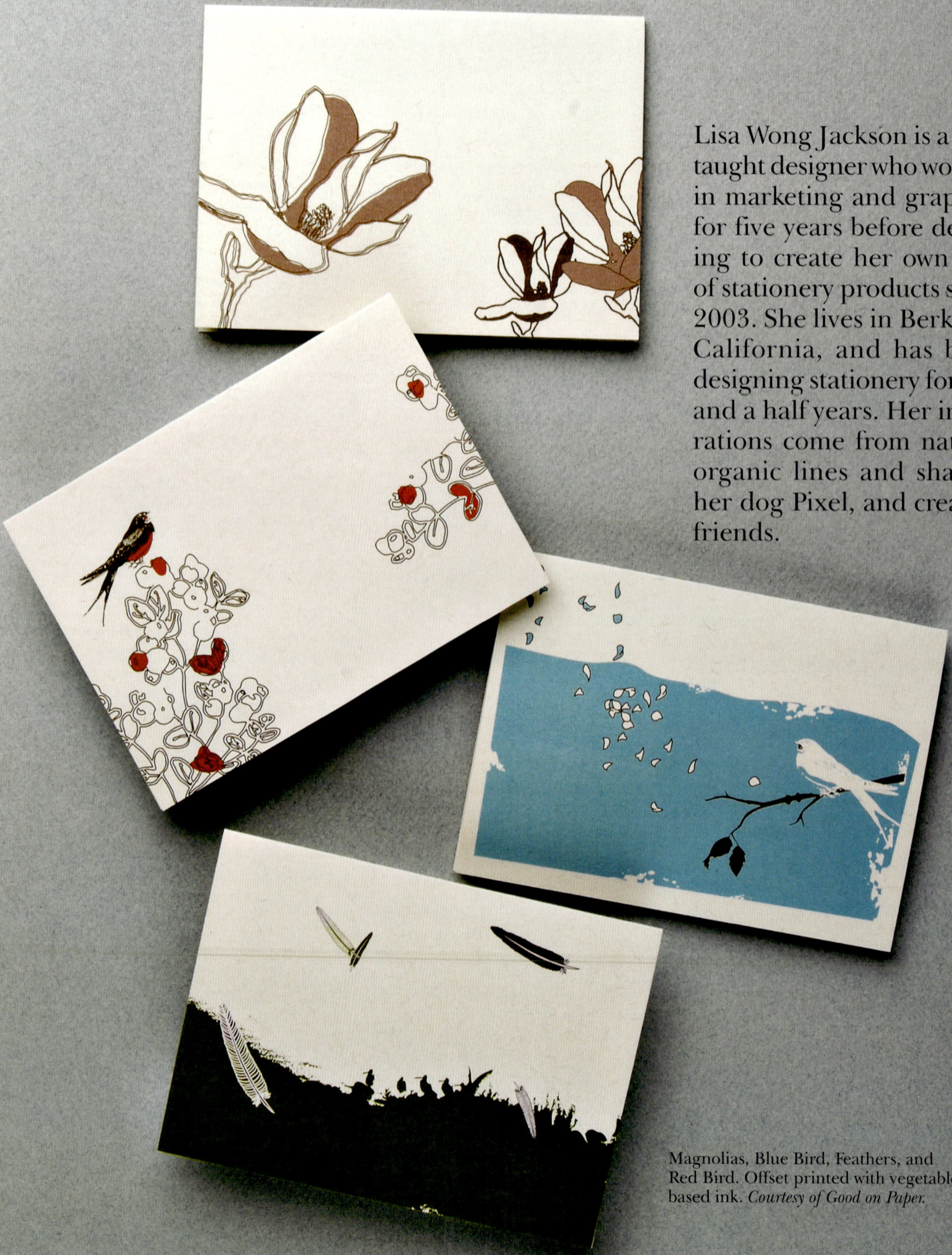

Lisa Wong Jackson is a self-taught designer who worked in marketing and graphics for five years before deciding to create her own line of stationery products since 2003. She lives in Berkeley, California, and has been designing stationery for two and a half years. Her inspirations come from nature, organic lines and shapes, her dog Pixel, and creative friends.

Magnolias, Blue Bird, Feathers, and Red Bird. Offset printed with vegetable based ink. *Courtesy of Good on Paper.*

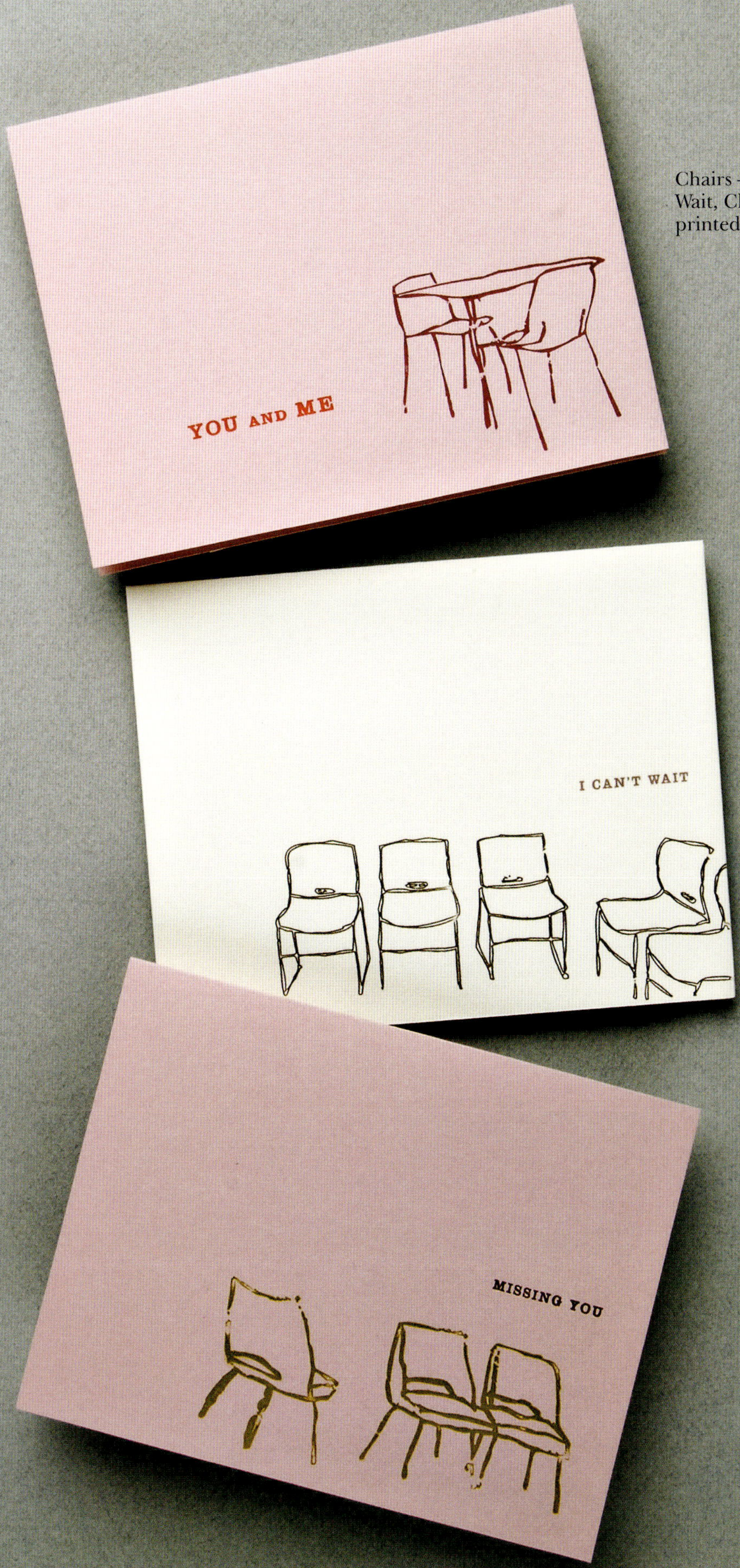

Chairs – You and Me, Chairs – I Can't Wait, Chairs – Missing You. Screen printed. *Courtesy of Good on Paper.*

Masha D'yans Design

www.masha.com

Masha D'yans has had her own company since 2002, but she has been making art and designing cards for her whole life. She even landed a freelance job for a card company while attending college. She draws inspiration for her artwork from fashion, animation, calligraphy, Japanese art, nature, and fairy tales. Her work was selected by the Museum of Modern Art for their Christmas card program and she won the International Louie Award in 2006.

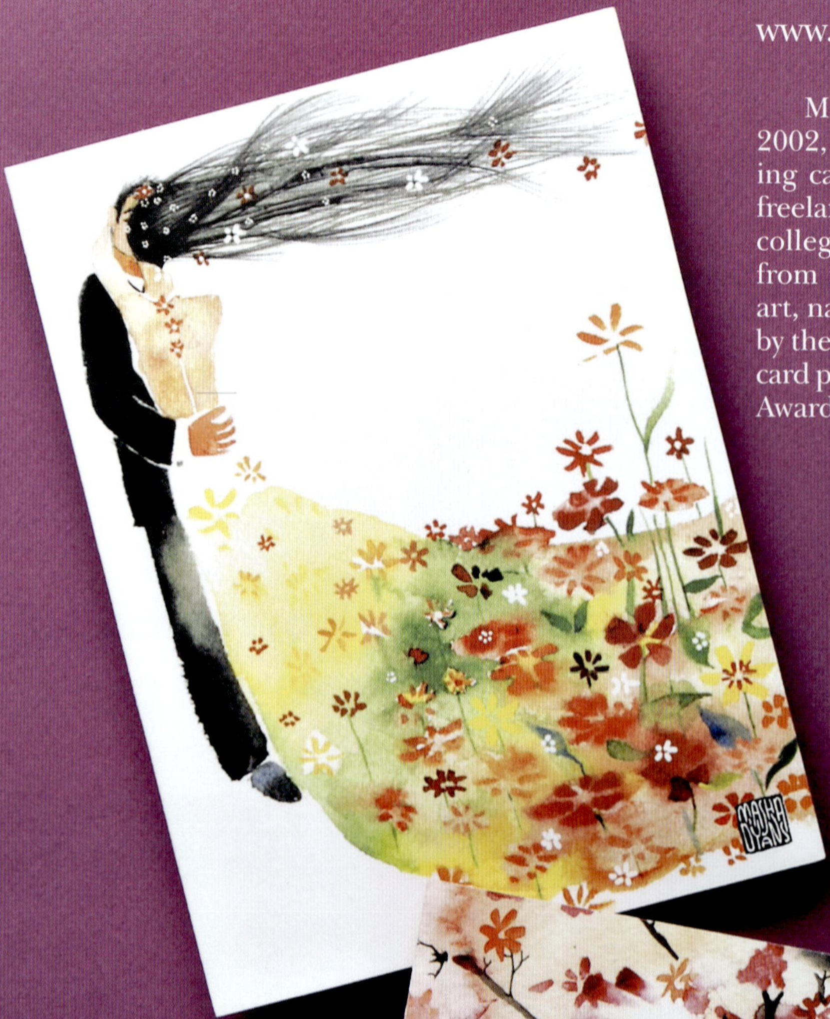

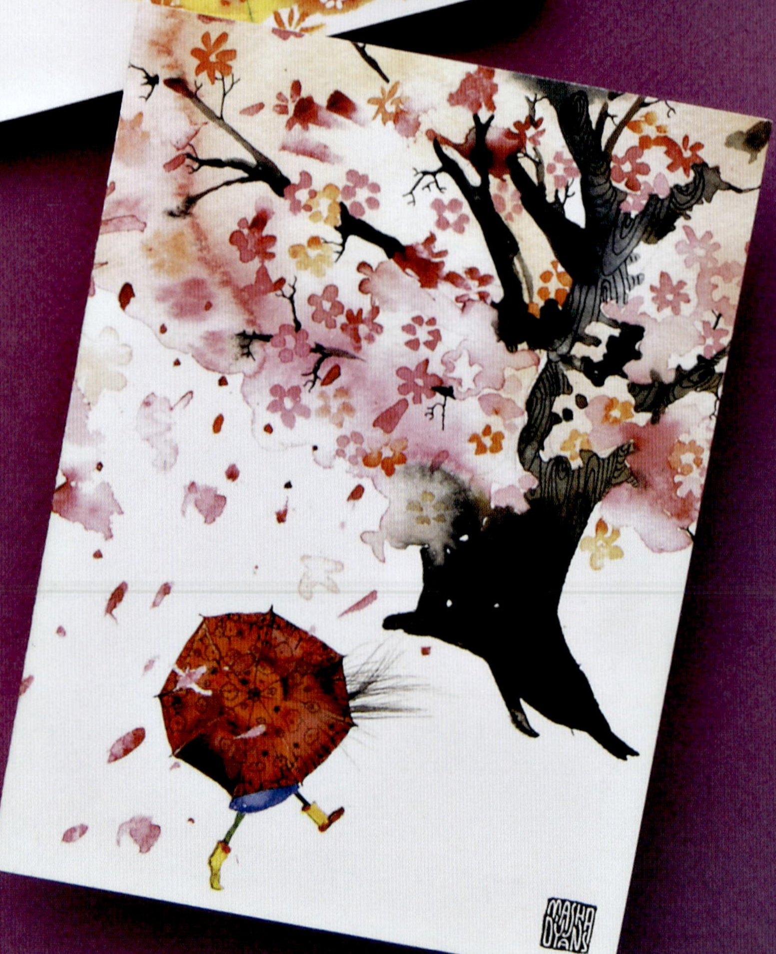

Bloom Kiss and Bloom Rain. Offset lithography with soy inks. *Courtesy of Masha D'yans.*

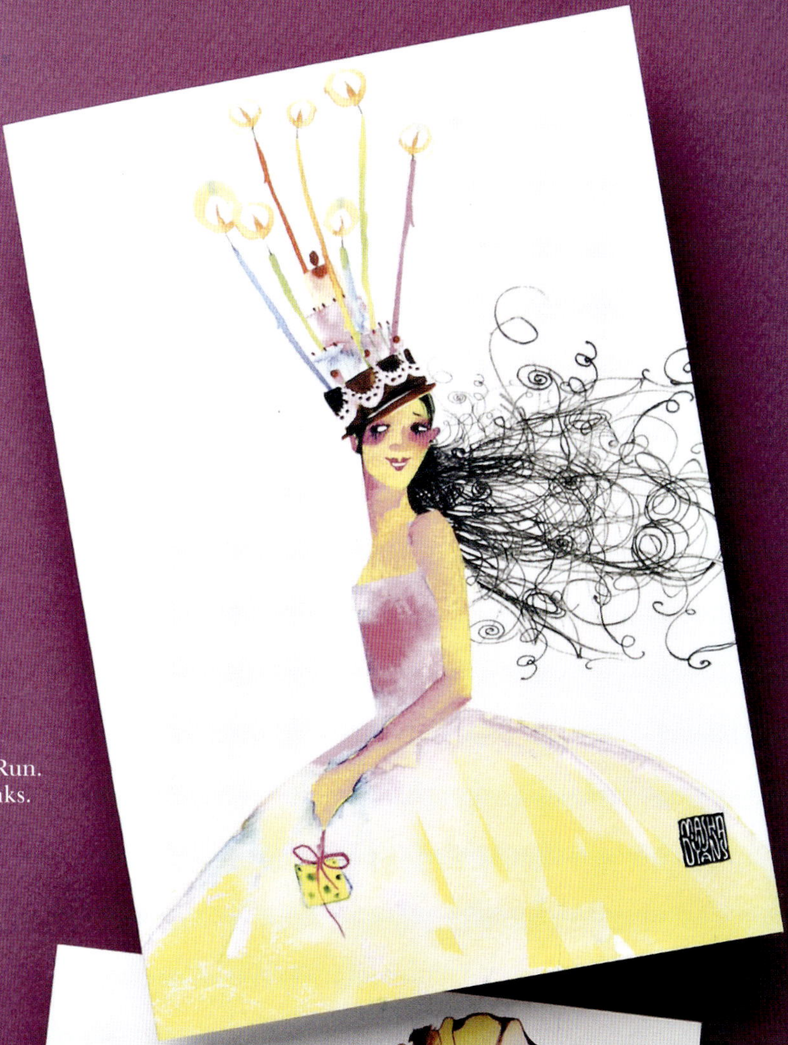

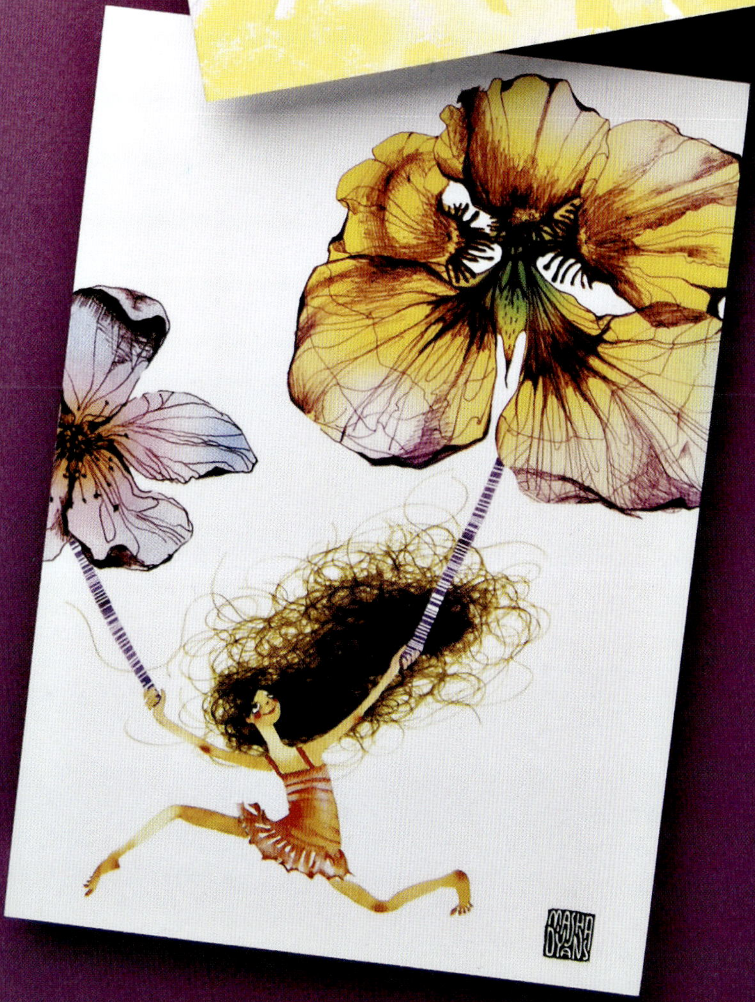

Birthday Queen and Flower Run.
Offset lithography with soy inks.
Courtesy of Masha D'yans.

Remanents

www.remanents.com

Monica Anderson launched her stationery line at the National Stationery Show in 2001. The wife of international shoe designer, Stuart Weitzman, placed one of her first orders. From that point on, her company has been growing and thriving. Monica loves fashion, movies, books, coffee, and running marathons. She is also a proud wife and mother of three. She currently resides in Haddonfield, New Jersey, with her family, who are very much involved and significant in her stationery business.

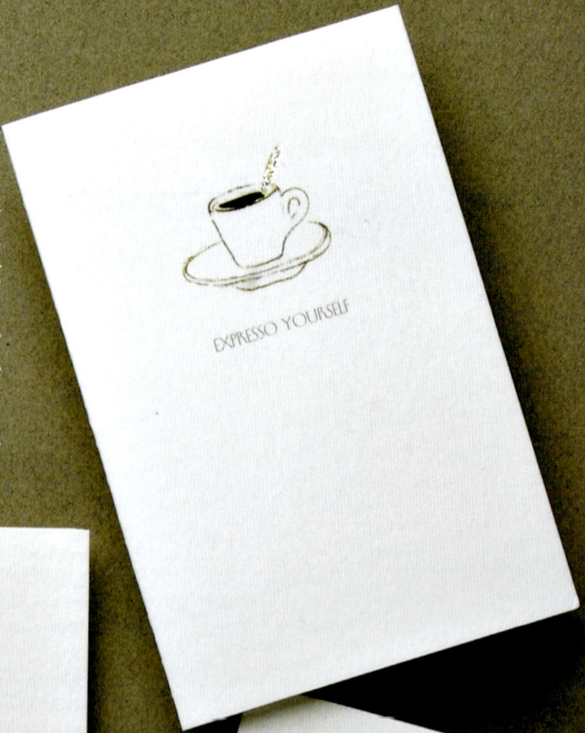

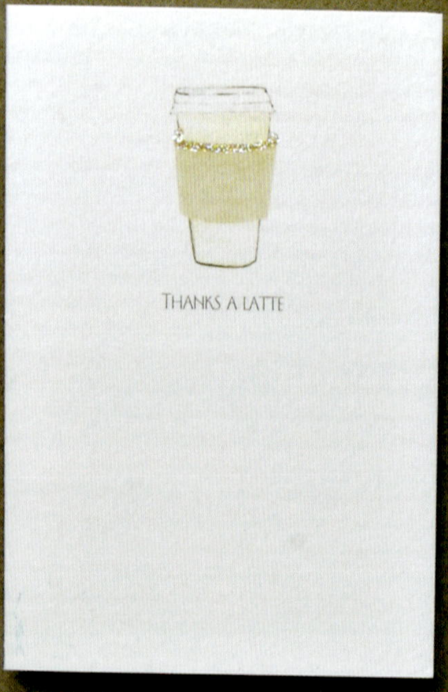

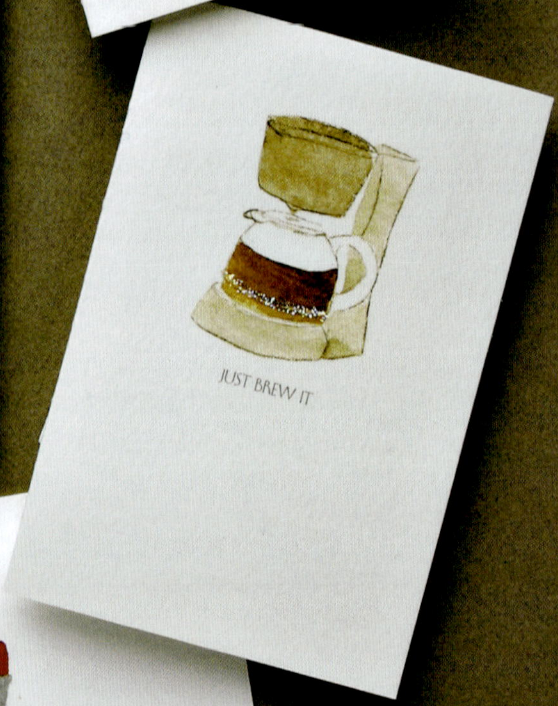

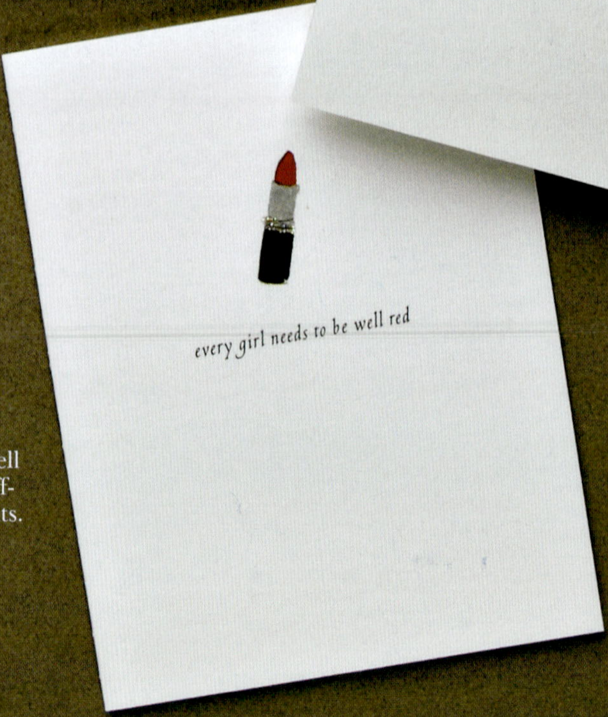

Expresso Yourself, Just Brew It, Every Girl Needs to be Well Red, and Thanks a Latte. Offset printed with glitter accents. *Courtesy of Remanents.*

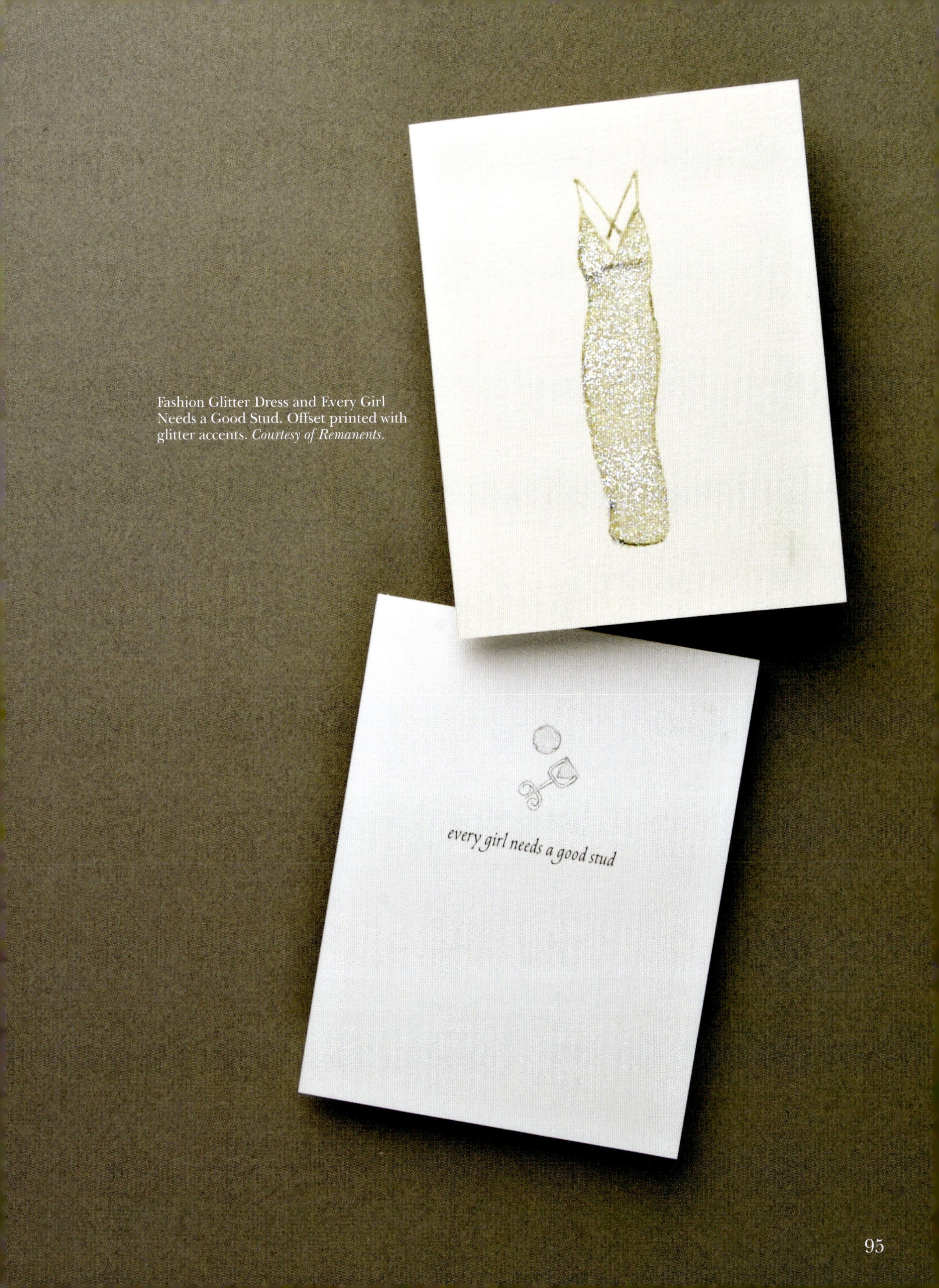

Fashion Glitter Dress and Every Girl Needs a Good Stud. Offset printed with glitter accents. *Courtesy of Remanents.*

Catseto

www.catseto.com

Catherine Seto holds a BFA in Painting and an MFA in Creative Writing. She began her stationery company in 2005 and can be found any given day in her design studio/ boutique in the "French Quarter" of San Francisco's Russian Hill neighborhood designing her collections and greeting customers. She is inspired by story, imagination, and the gift of giving.

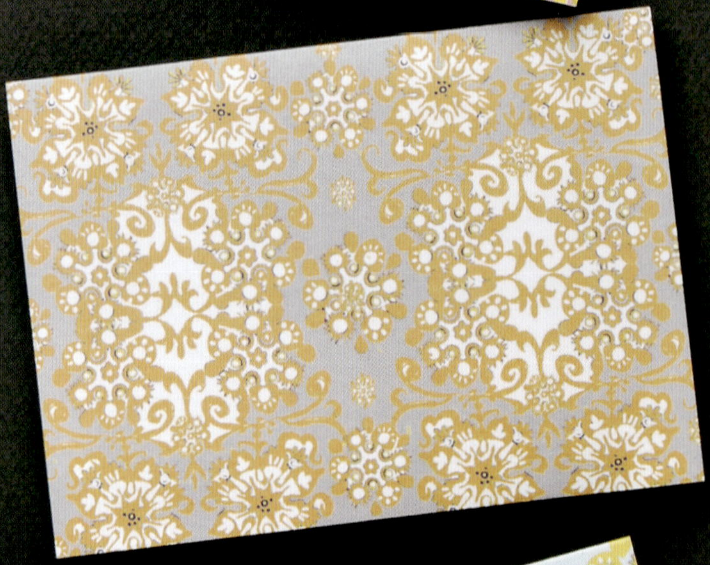

Pink Darjeeling Tea, Earl Grey Tea, and Tiffany Lace. Offset printed. *Courtesy of Catherine Seto.*

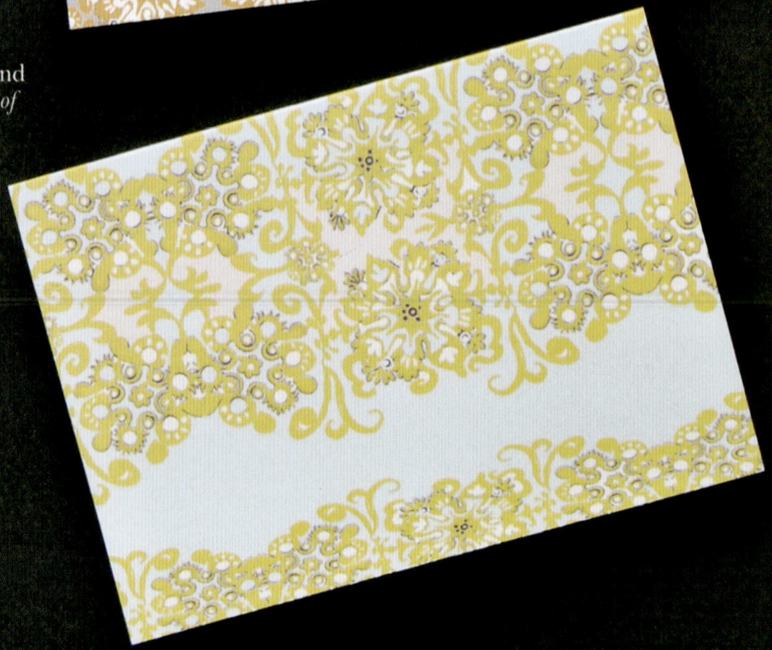

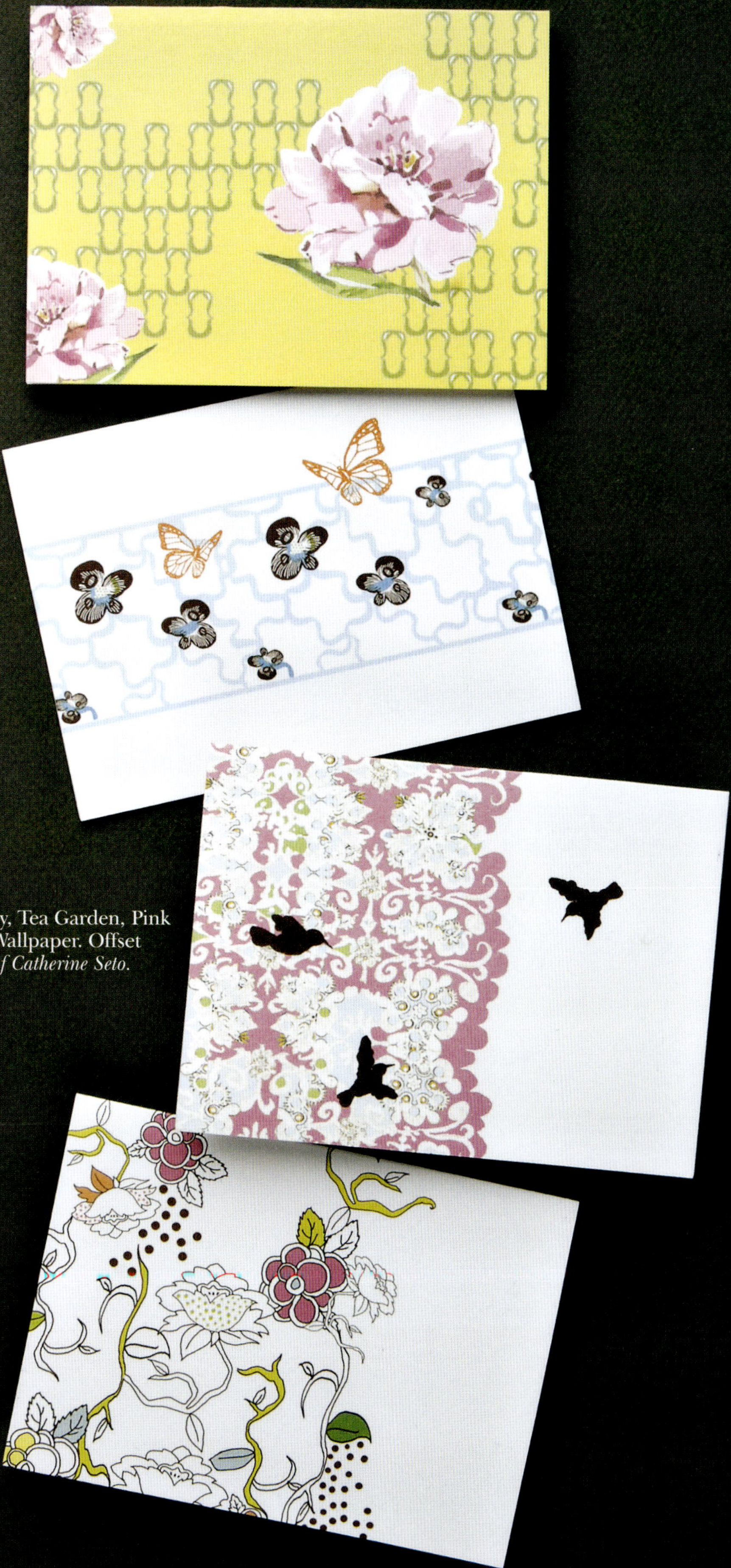

Yellow Glam Peony, Tea Garden, Pink Paris, and Louie Wallpaper. Offset printed. *Courtesy of Catherine Seto.*

Bonnie's Style Press

www.bonniesstylepress.com

With a background in fashion, wedding planning, and event coordination, Bonnie Marcus knew that she could find a niche in the stationery industry. She launched her company in her last trimester of pregnancy from her dining room table in Westport, Connecticut. A few years and two baby boys later, her designs can be found in hundreds of retail stores.

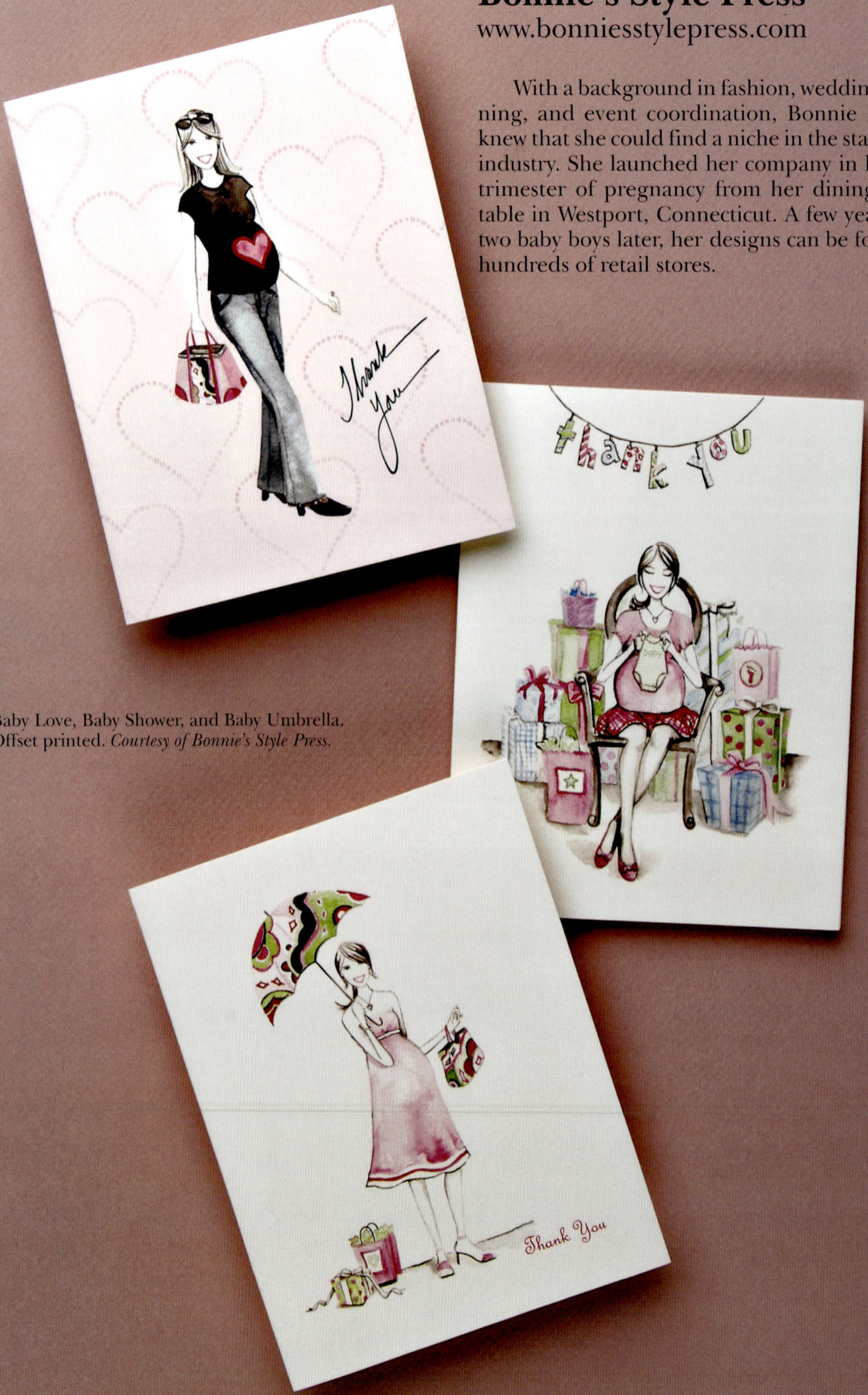

Baby Love, Baby Shower, and Baby Umbrella. Offset printed. *Courtesy of Bonnie's Style Press.*

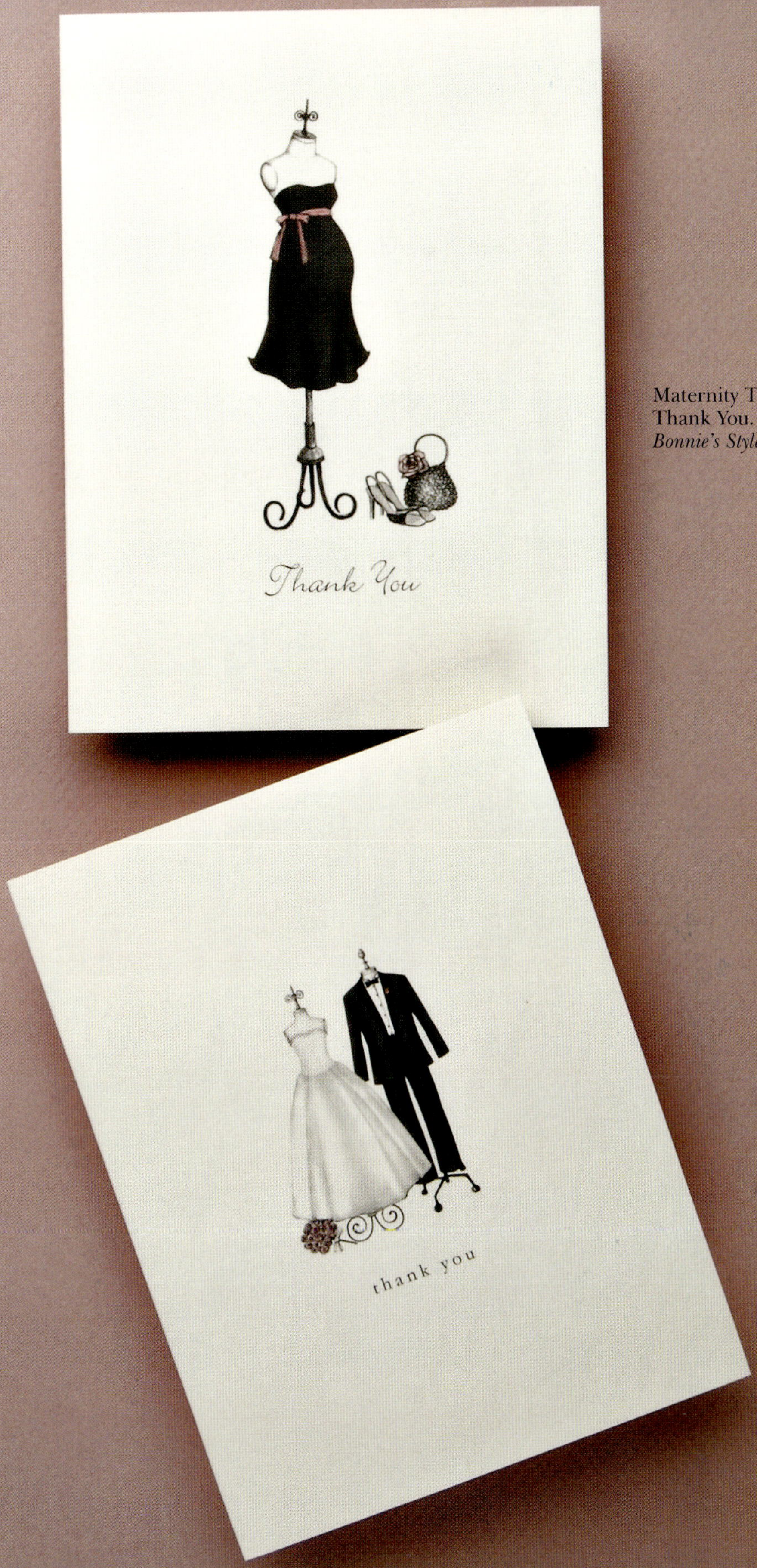

Maternity Thank You and Wedding Thank You. Offset printed. *Courtesy of Bonnie's Style Press.*

Waghappy

www.waghappy.com

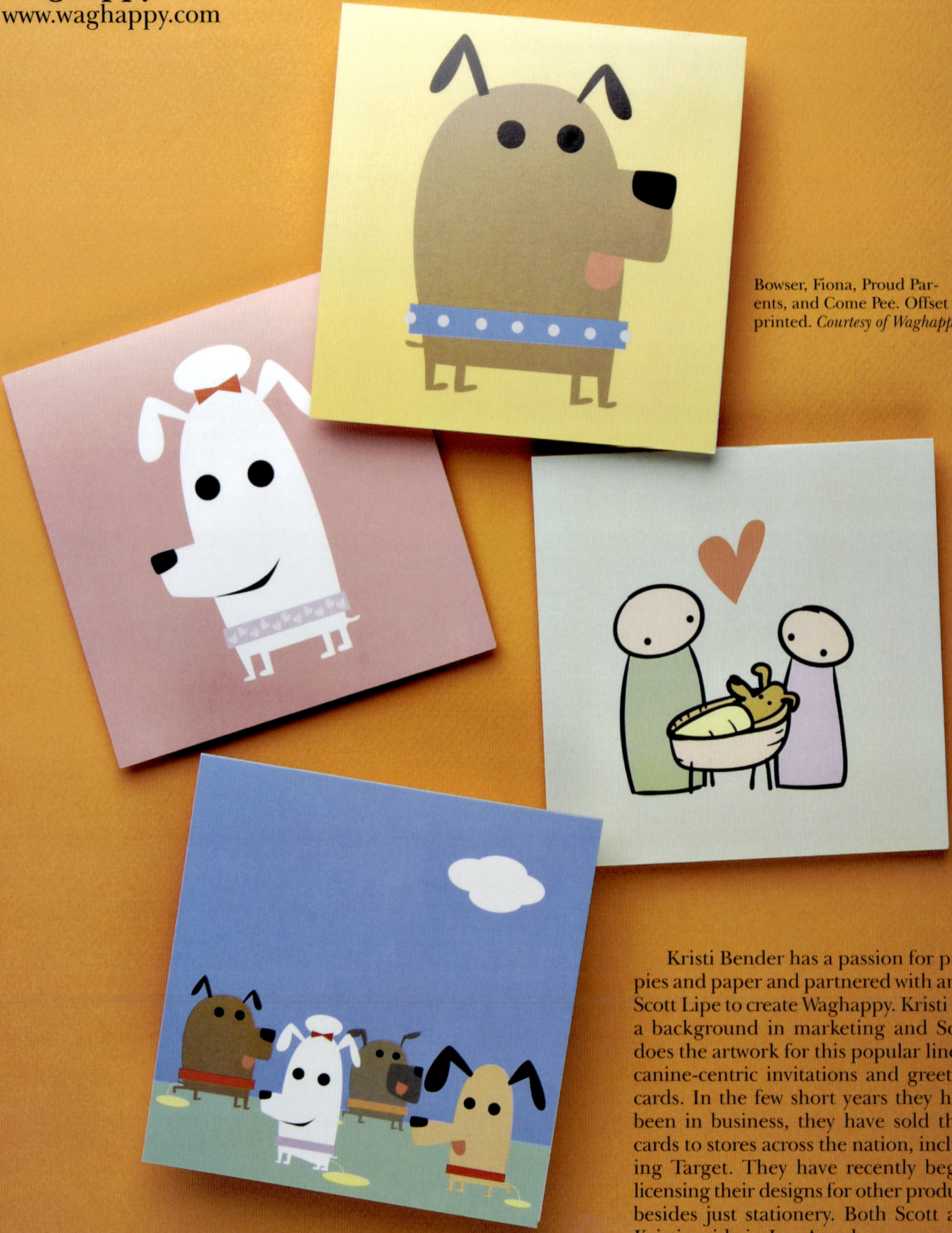

Bowser, Fiona, Proud Parents, and Come Pee. Offset printed. *Courtesy of Waghappy.*

Kristi Bender has a passion for puppies and paper and partnered with artist Scott Lipe to create Waghappy. Kristi has a background in marketing and Scott does the artwork for this popular line of canine-centric invitations and greeting cards. In the few short years they have been in business, they have sold their cards to stores across the nation, including Target. They have recently begun licensing their designs for other products besides just stationery. Both Scott and Kristi reside in Los Angeles.

Pupcake Time and Puppy Shower.
Offset printed. *Courtesy of Waghappy.*

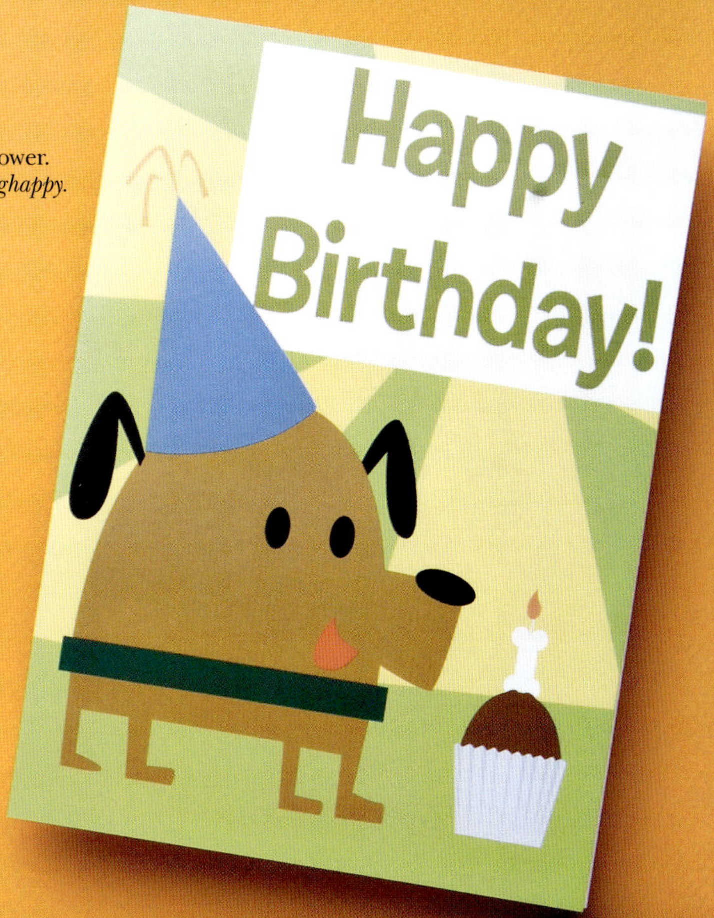

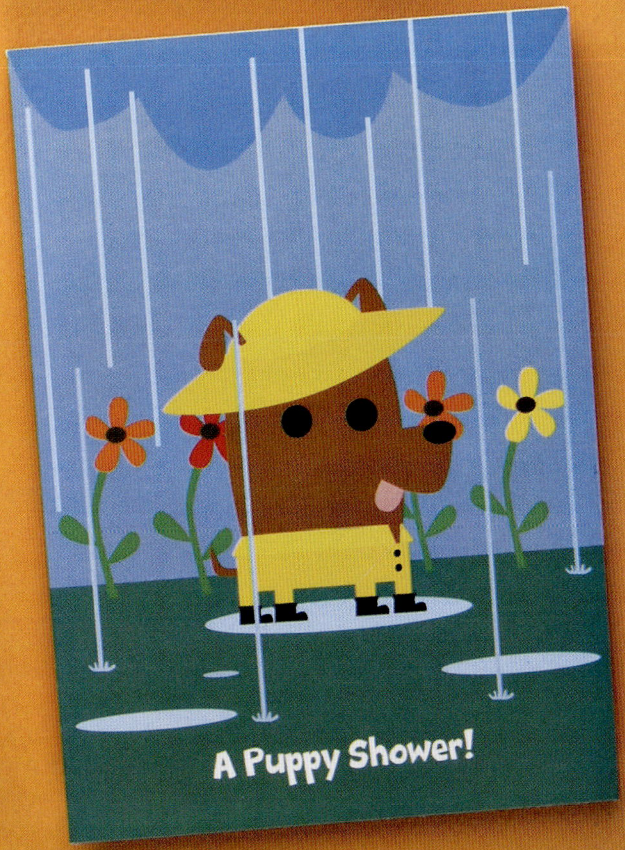

Fomato
www.fomato.com

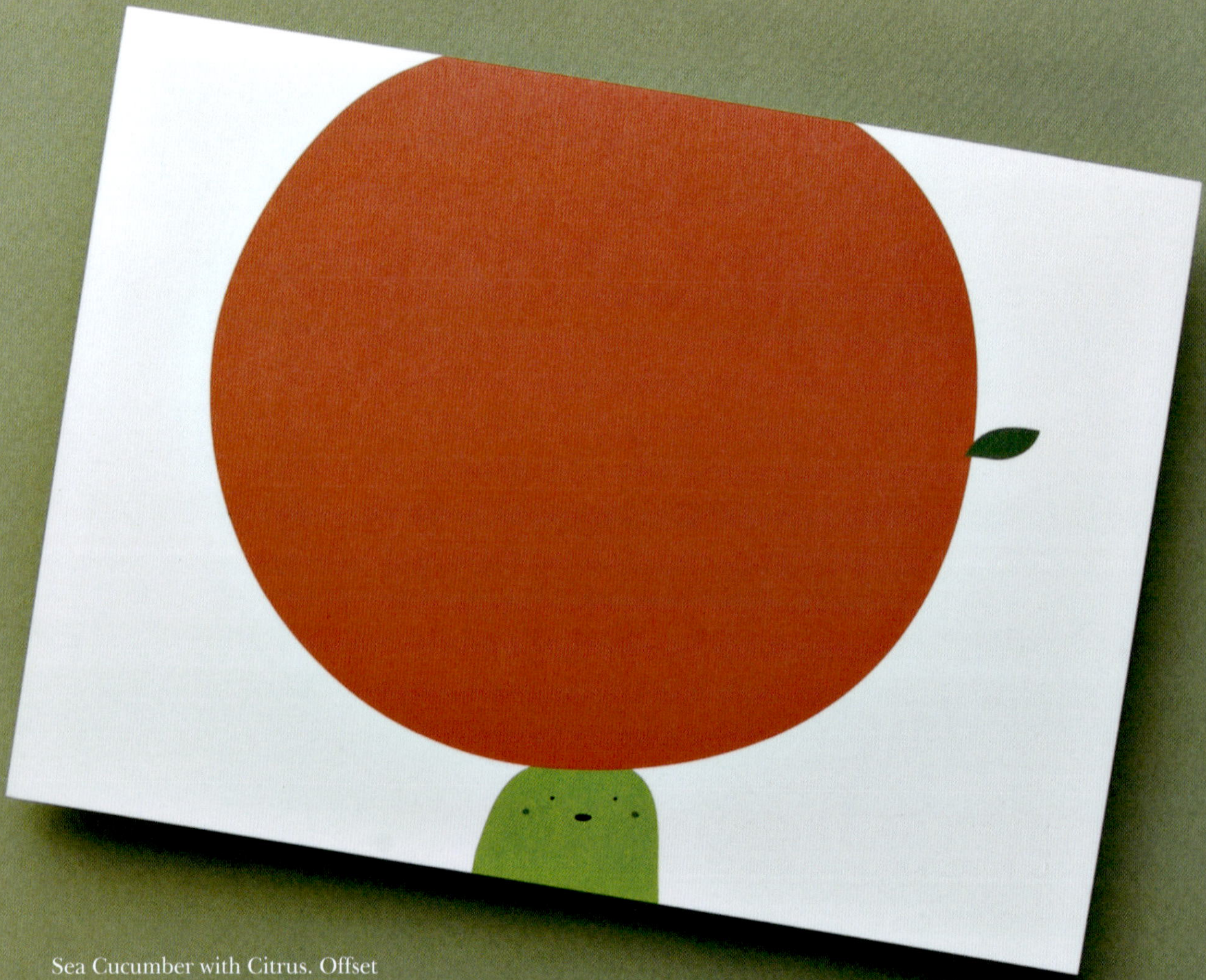

Sea Cucumber with Citrus. Offset lithography. *Courtesy of Fomato.*

Schmumu Tvörgenssen started her company in 2004 in Los Angeles, California. He doodled in primary and secondary school and didn't start drawing seriously until after college. After graduation, he decided that illustration was his profession (whether he was employed or not) and drew during most workdays. He finds inspiration in cities, human behavior, nature, and history.

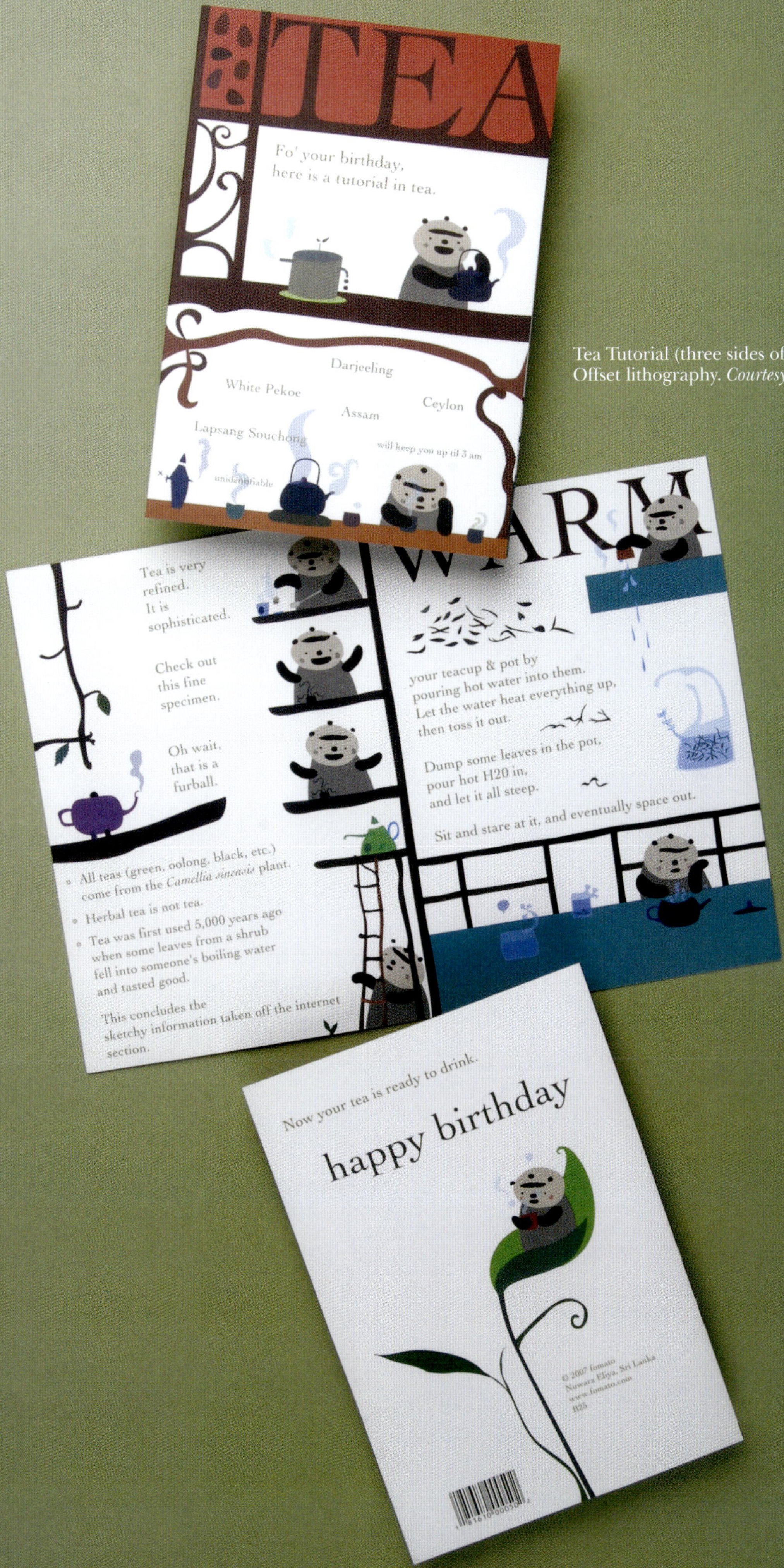

Tea Tutorial (three sides of one card). Offset lithography. *Courtesy of Fomato.*

Chapter Five
Hand Printed

Craftsmen have been using hand printing techniques for centuries. Methods like silkscreen and linoleum block printing require intimate knowledge of the craft and meticulous attention to detail. These traditional practices have become a new trend in contemporary stationery with each printing method resulting in a unique and beautiful piece of art ready to send…or suitable for framing.

The type of print quality and saturation that comes from hand printing is remarkable and truly sets it apart from other greeting cards. With companies like *Binth* and *Saturate* leading the way, these cards are closer to limited edition art prints than to typical greeting cards. The time and expertise it takes to individually handprint each card can be very demanding. The designers of *Spruce Avenue* say, "it's a lot of work but every bit worth the look and feel of the final product."

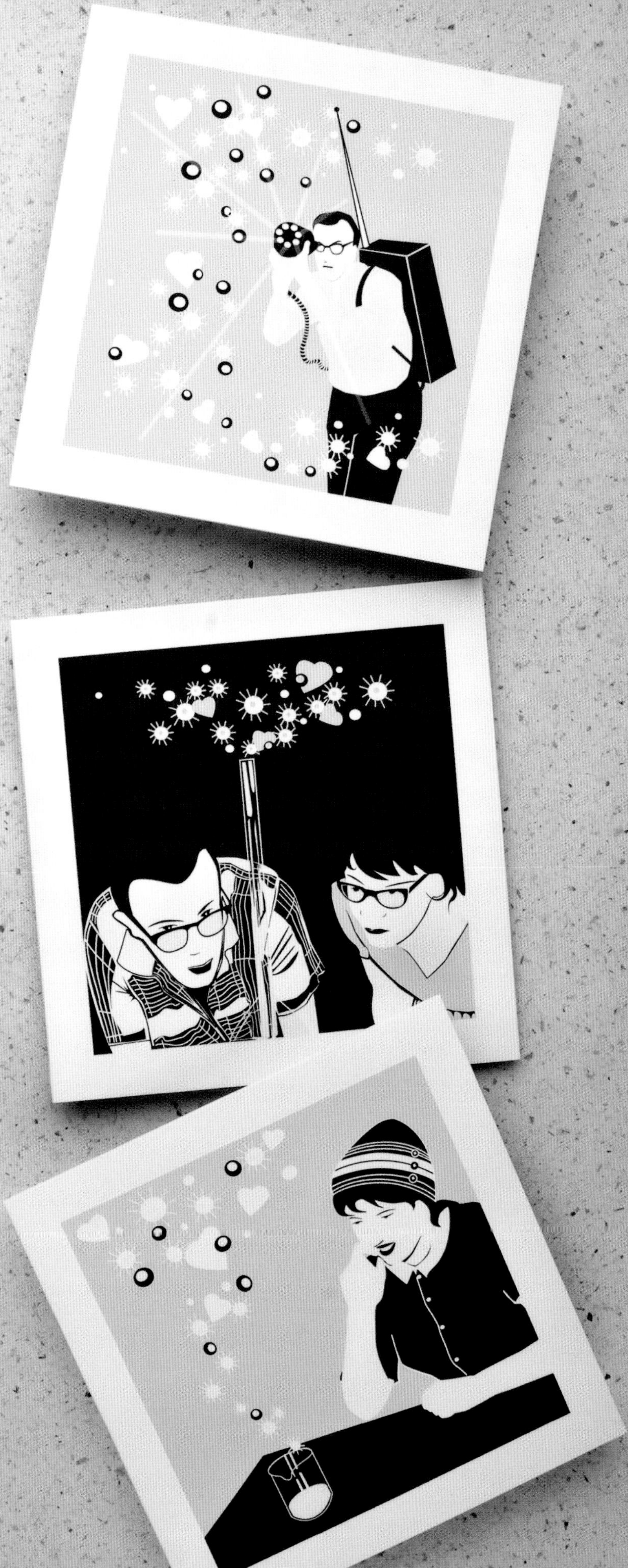

The Seeker, Chemistry, and Unexpected. Hand screen printed. *Courtesy of Linnea Gits of Binth.*

Binth

www.binth.com

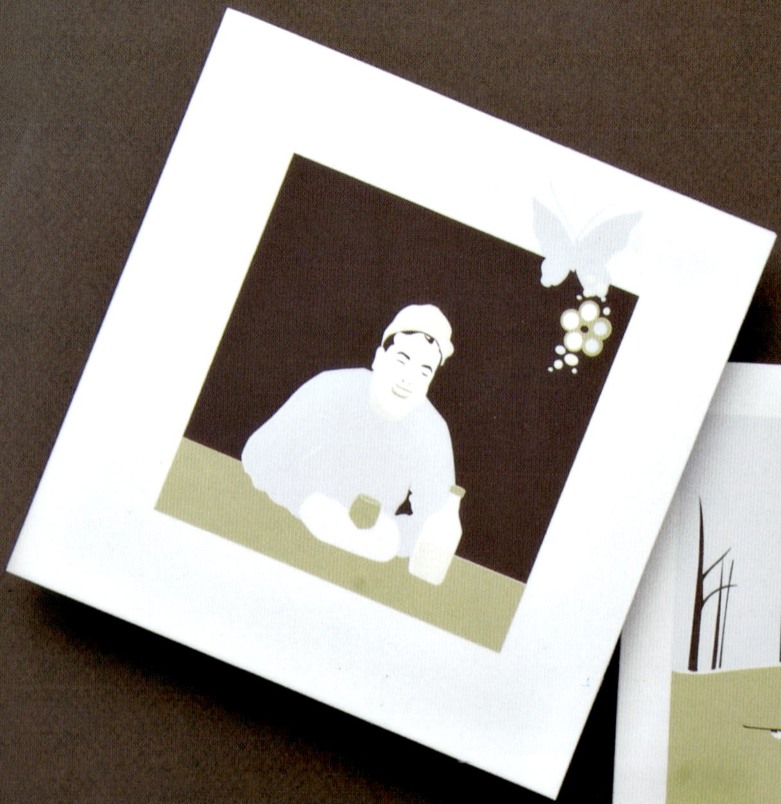

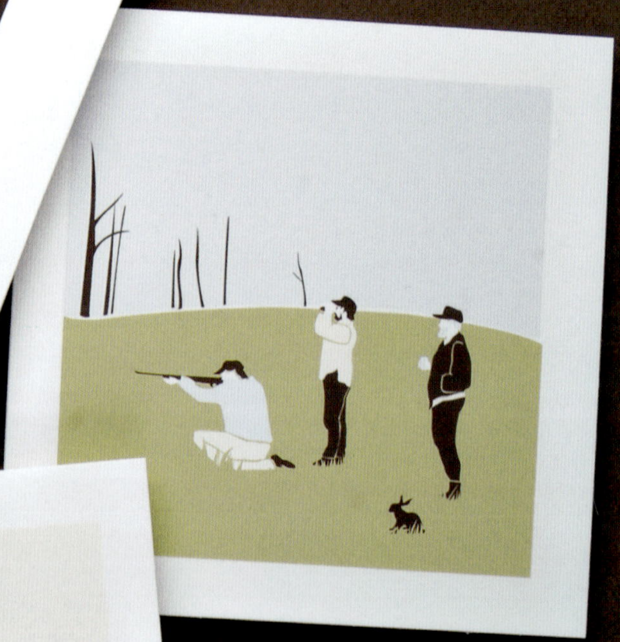

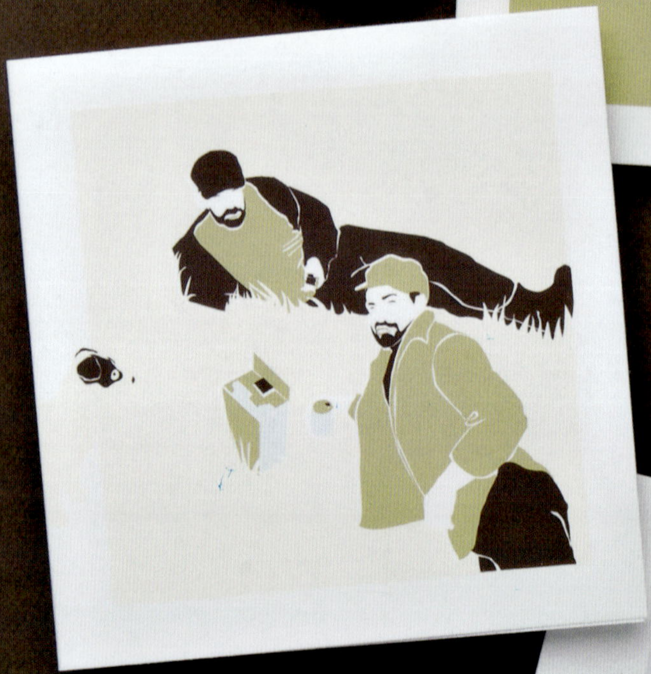

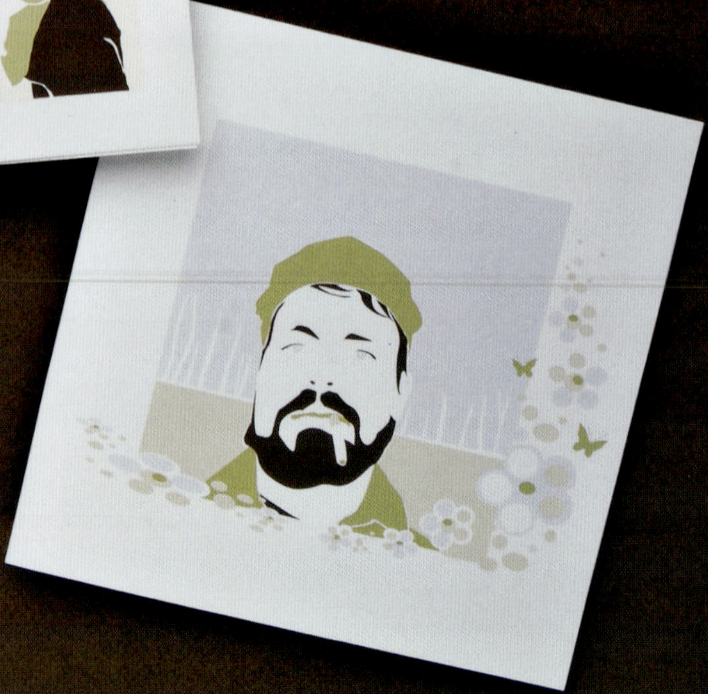

Bear Paw, Guy Squad, Grassy Beer, and Cam. Hand screen printed. *Courtesy of Linnea Gits of Binth.*

Suzanna Bierwirth, Peter Dunham, and Linnea Gits are the talented group of designers behind Binth. Suzanna has been a Creative Director for a global marketing company for the last ten years. Born and raised in Germany, she was originally trained as a photographer. Peter has a background in fine art and furniture design. Linnea is an artist who has shown her drawings and sculptures in galleries in New York, Chicago, and Los Angeles. Together, they each bring something unique to their Chicago based company.

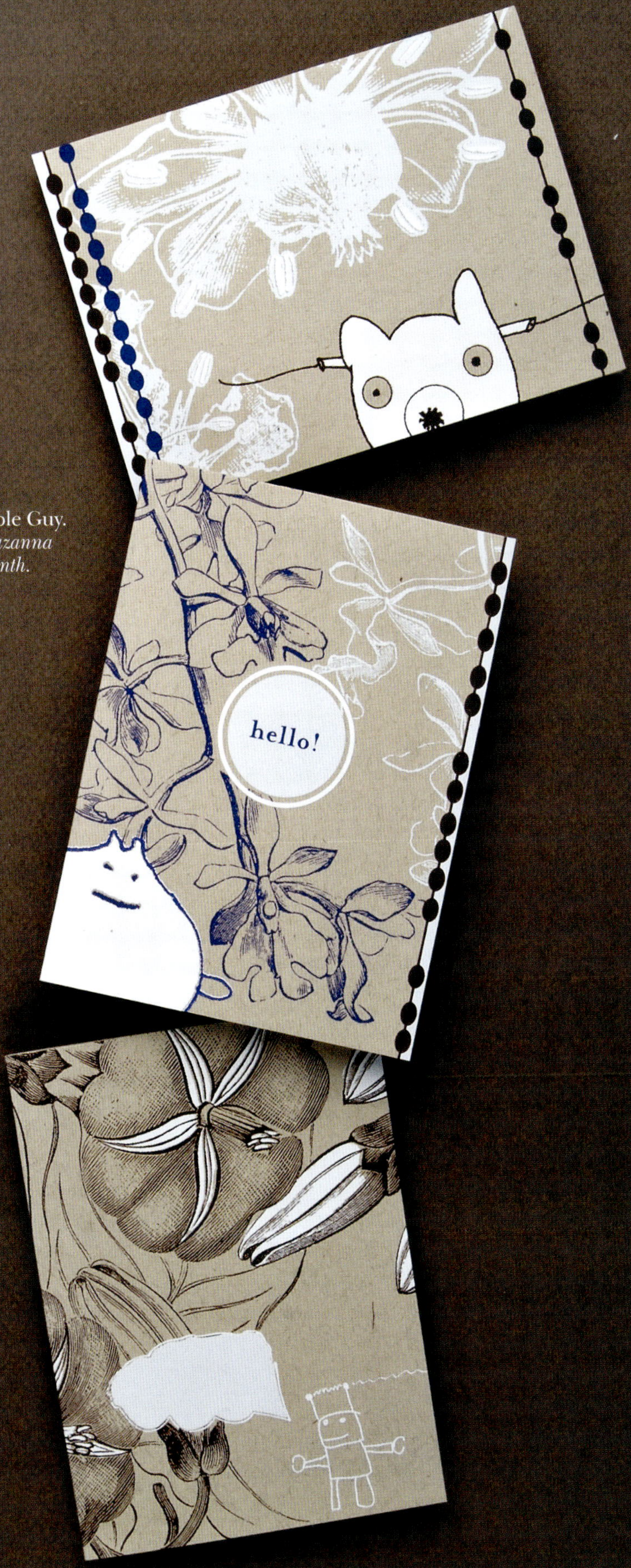

Smokey, Hello, and Speech Bubble Guy. Hand screen printed. *Courtesy Suzanna Bierwirth and Jarek Moorman of Binth.*

Perla Anne

www.perlaanne.com

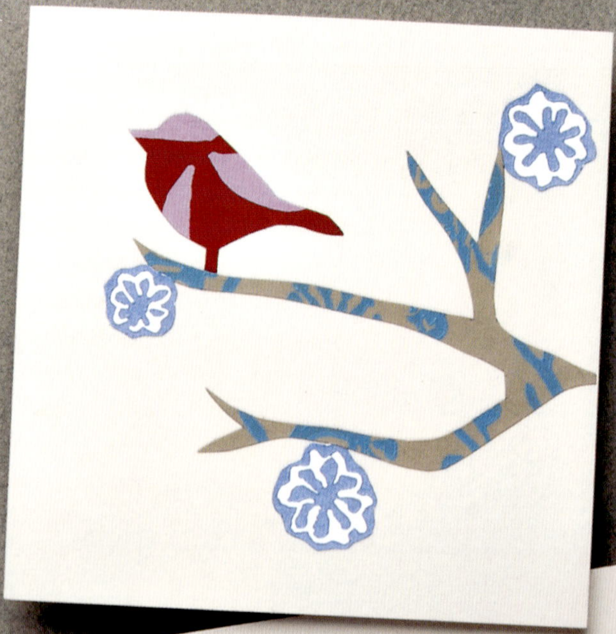

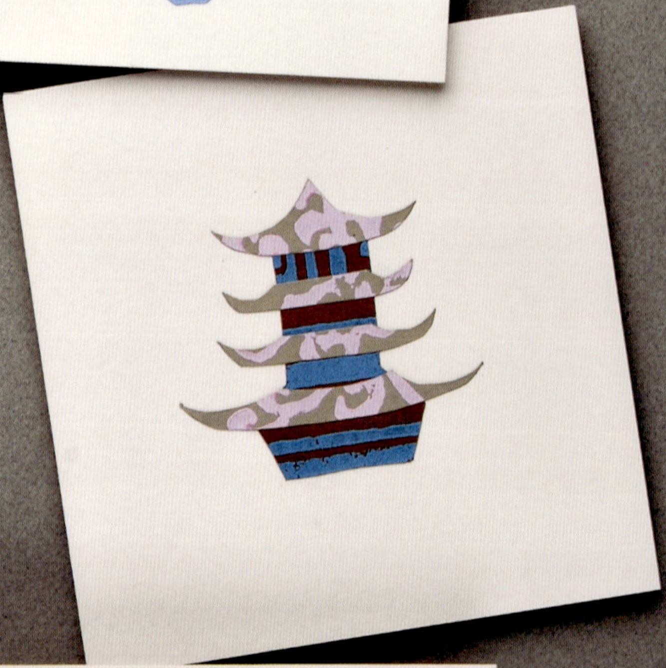

In 1997 Stacey Bradley began turning her six-year-old daughter's images into greeting cards. From there, her company was formed and has been growing and evolving ever since. She single-handedly runs her business from her Charleston, South Carolina, home selling to small boutiques and even designing a line for Target.

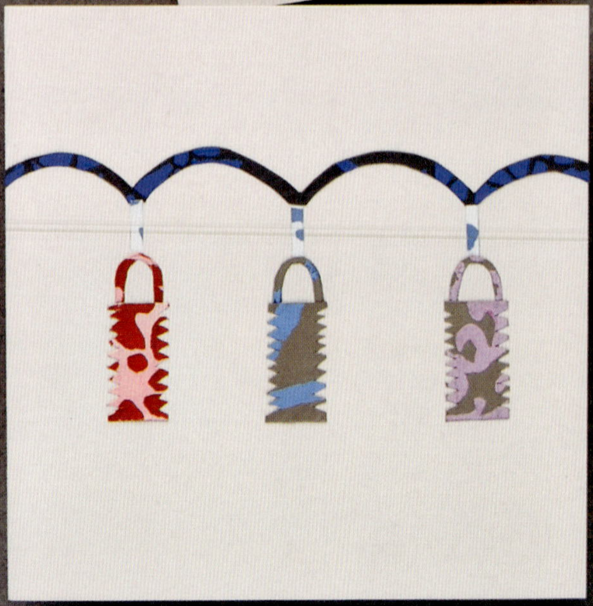

Bird on Branch, Pagoda, and Lanterns from Cut Paper Collection. Linoleum block printed and hand cut paper. *Courtesy of Perla Anne.*

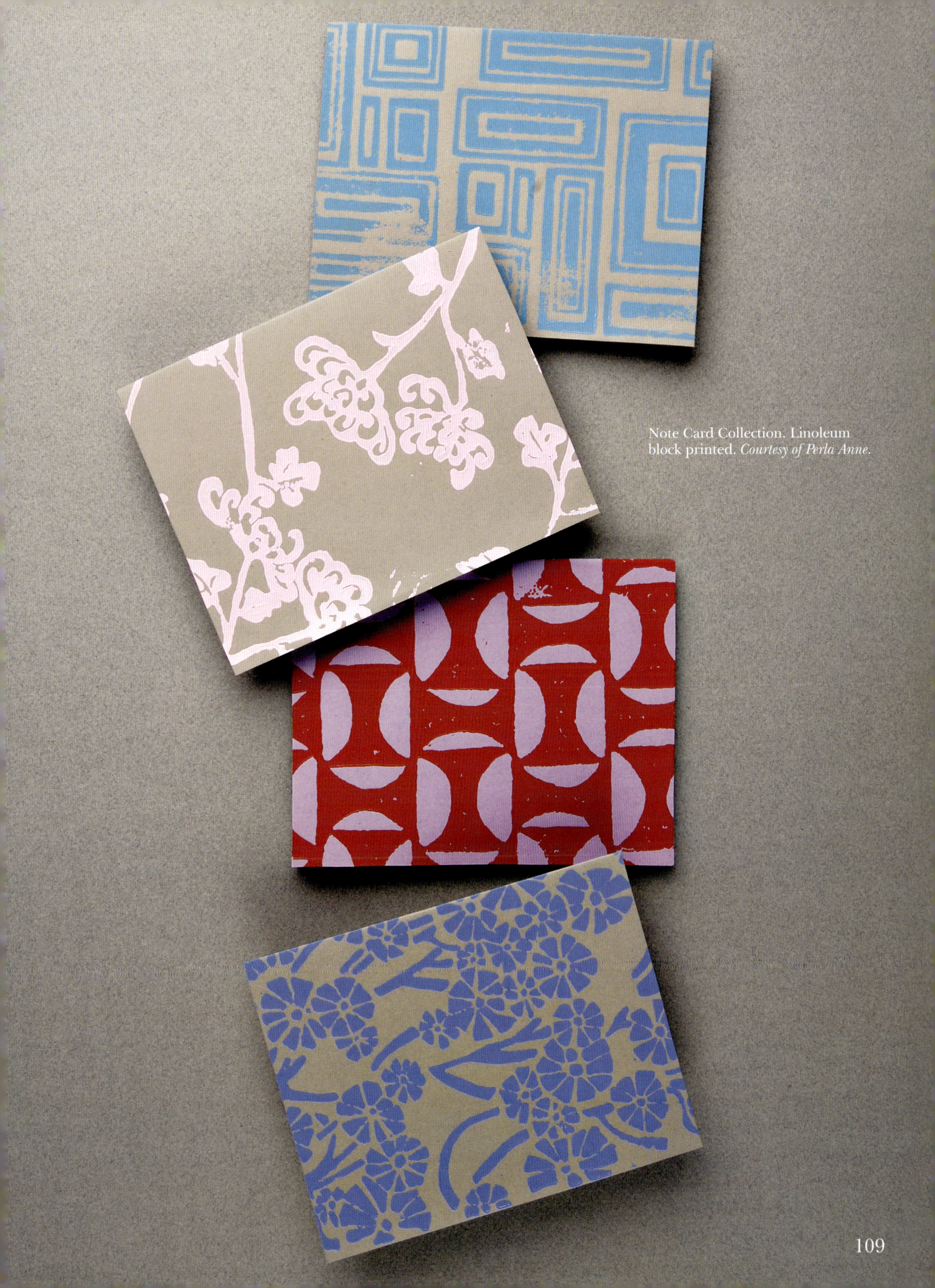

Note Card Collection. Linoleum block printed. *Courtesy of Perla Anne.*

Spruce Avenue

www.spruceavenue.com

Dana Wyatt and Melissa Bielecki have been designing stationery for their Westville, New Jersey, based company since the fall of 2004. Both artists have textile backgrounds, similar interests, and work experience in the wall covering/interior fabrics industry, which laid the groundwork for their partnership. Their decision to silkscreen over other mediums was influenced by their love of surface design and printmaking.

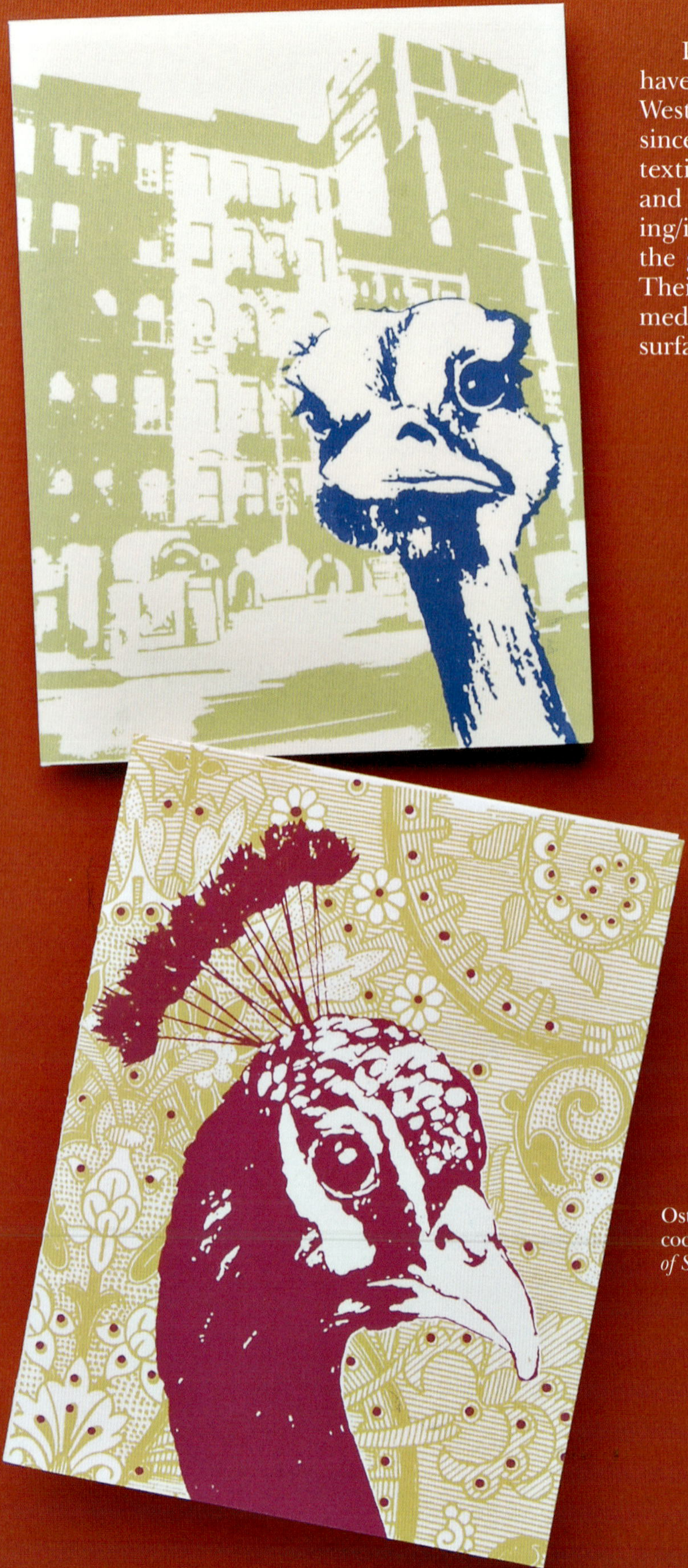

Ostrich in the City and Vintage Peacock. Hand silk-screened. *Courtesy of Spruce Avenue.*

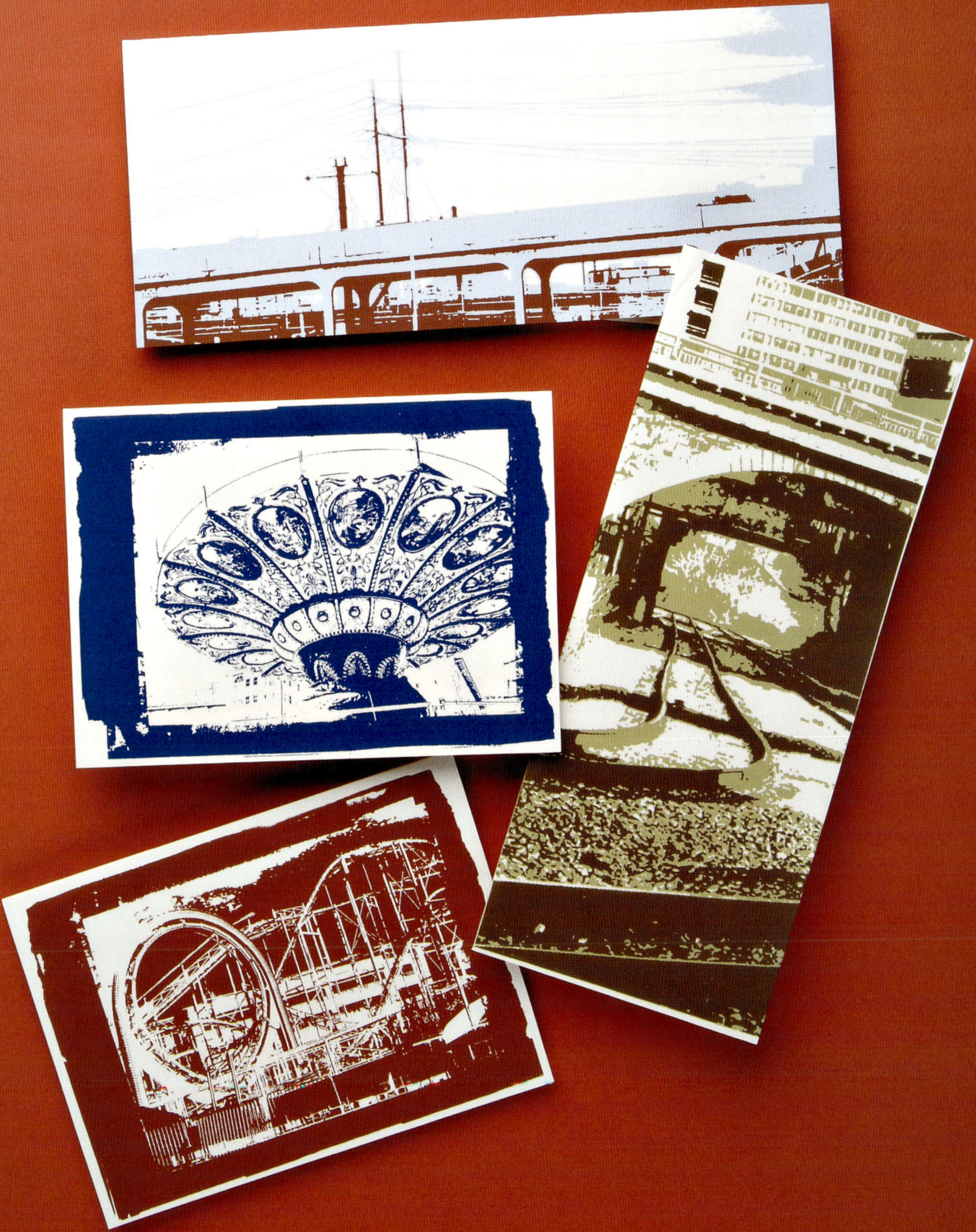

Bridge, Train Tunnel, Rollercoaster, and Swing.
Hand silk-screened. *Courtesy of Spruce Avenue.*

paper*ink studio

www.paperinkstudio.com

Le Vu is a multifaceted designer. With a BA in Urban Studies and City Planning from UC San Diego and a Masters in Architecture from the University of Pennsylvania, she has also studied photography, ceramics, oil painting, letterpress and silk screening. While she continues to practice architecture, paper*ink studio has become her immediate creative outlet for expressing her minimalist style and her love of color. She currently lives in San Francisco with her husband (and fellow architect) and their two young, energetic boys.

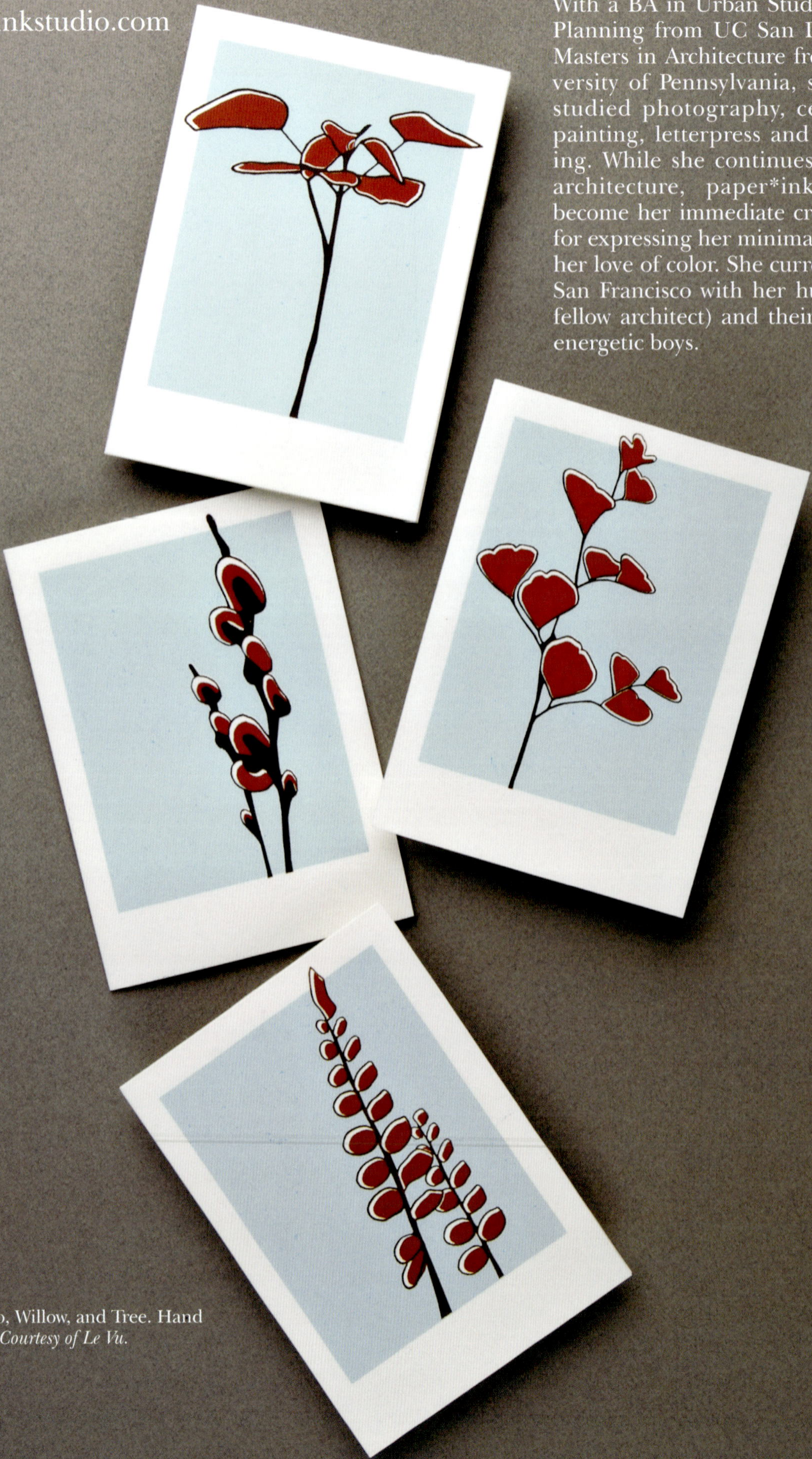

Canopy, Ginko, Willow, and Tree. Hand silk-screened. *Courtesy of Le Vu.*

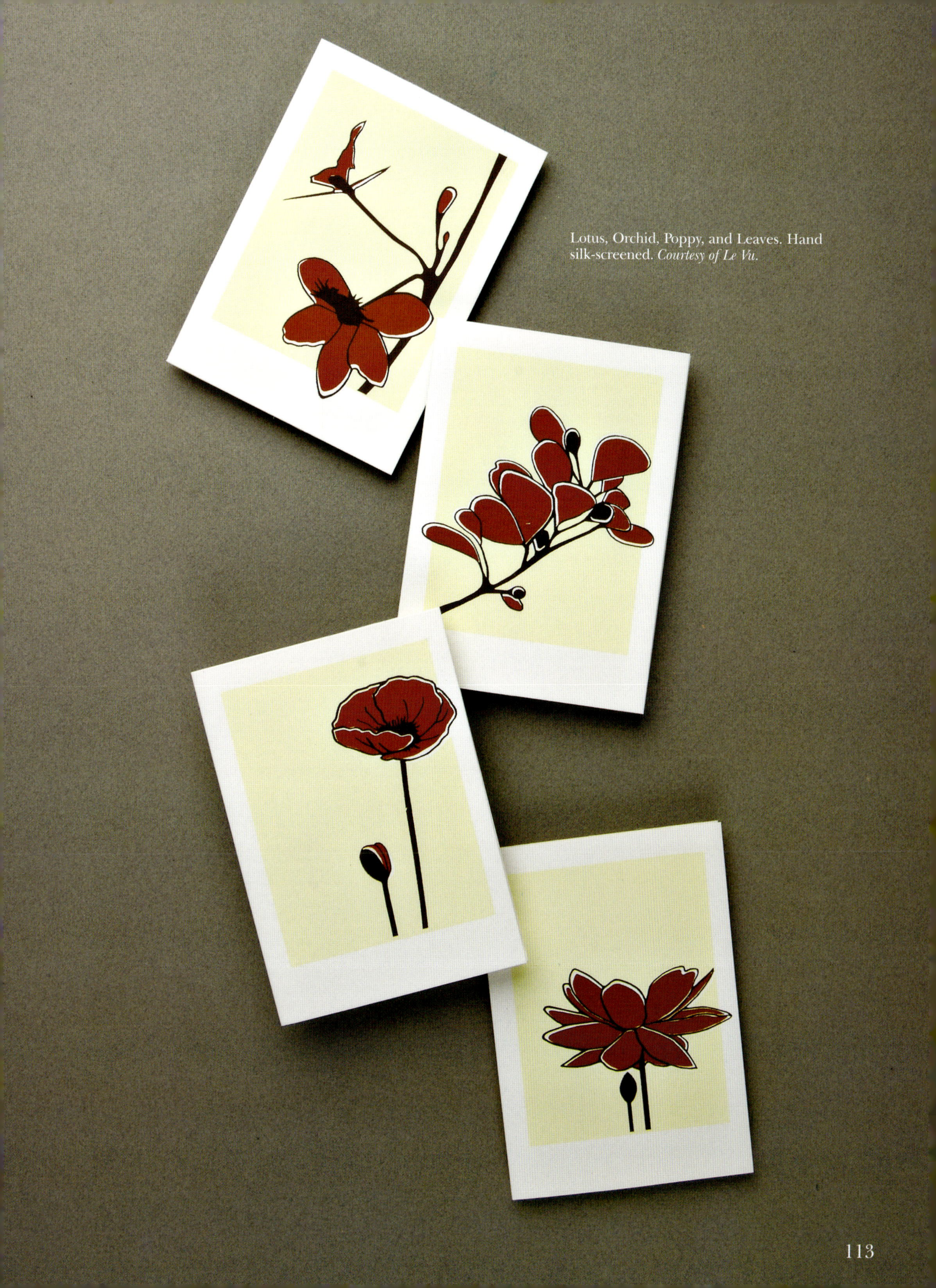

Lotus, Orchid, Poppy, and Leaves. Hand silk-screened. *Courtesy of Le Vu.*

Cielo Blu

www.cieloblustudios.com

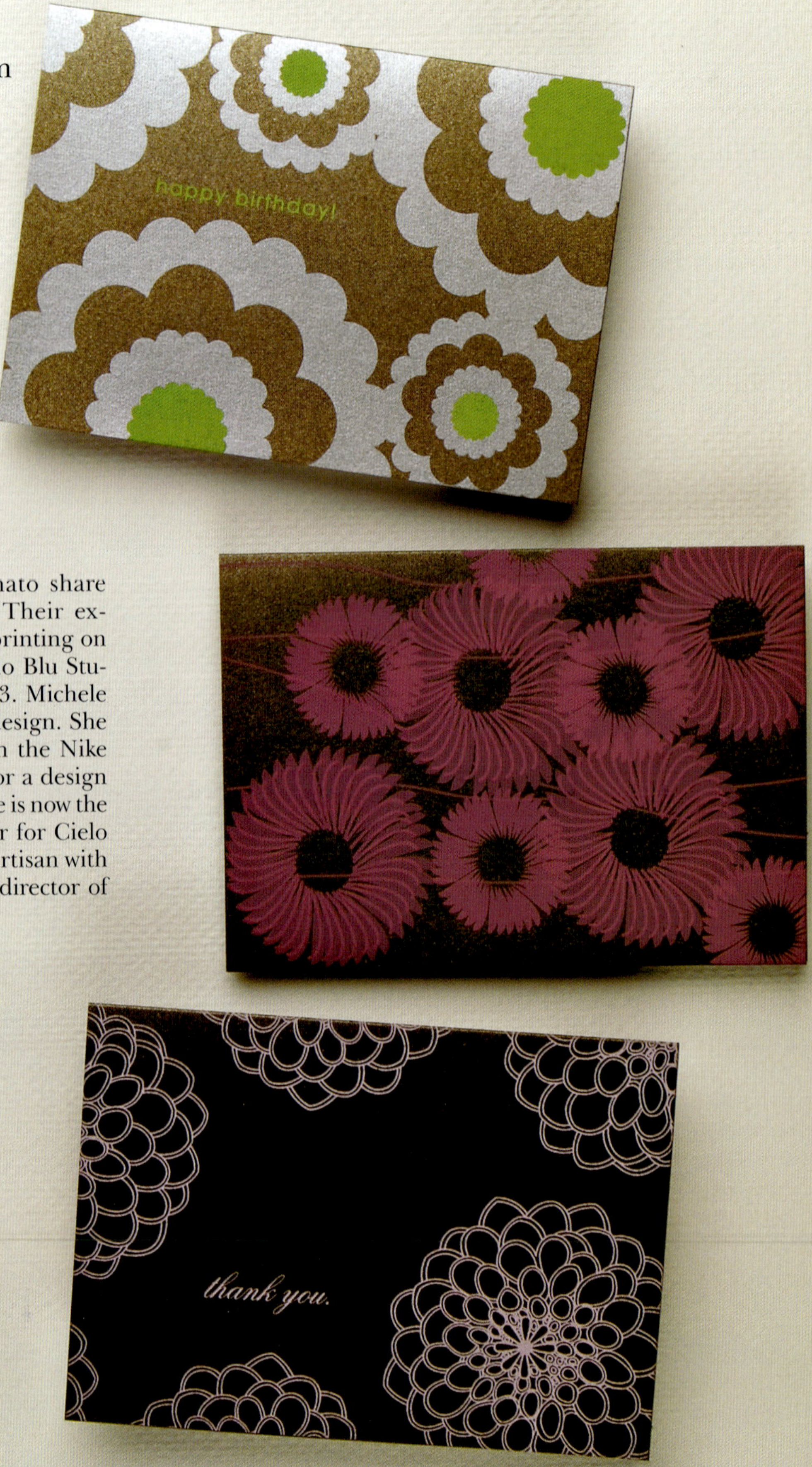

Michele and Guy Luminato share a passion for printmaking. Their experiments with hand screen-printing on paper led to the birth of Cielo Blu Studios in New York City in 2003. Michele has a strong background in design. She worked as a color designer in the Nike Footwear division as well as for a design agency called Imagination. She is now the creative director and designer for Cielo Blu Studios. Guy is a master artisan with the highest standards and is director of operations and printing.

Flowerpatch, Bloom, and Dahlia. Hand silk-screened. *Courtesy of Cielo Blu Studios.*

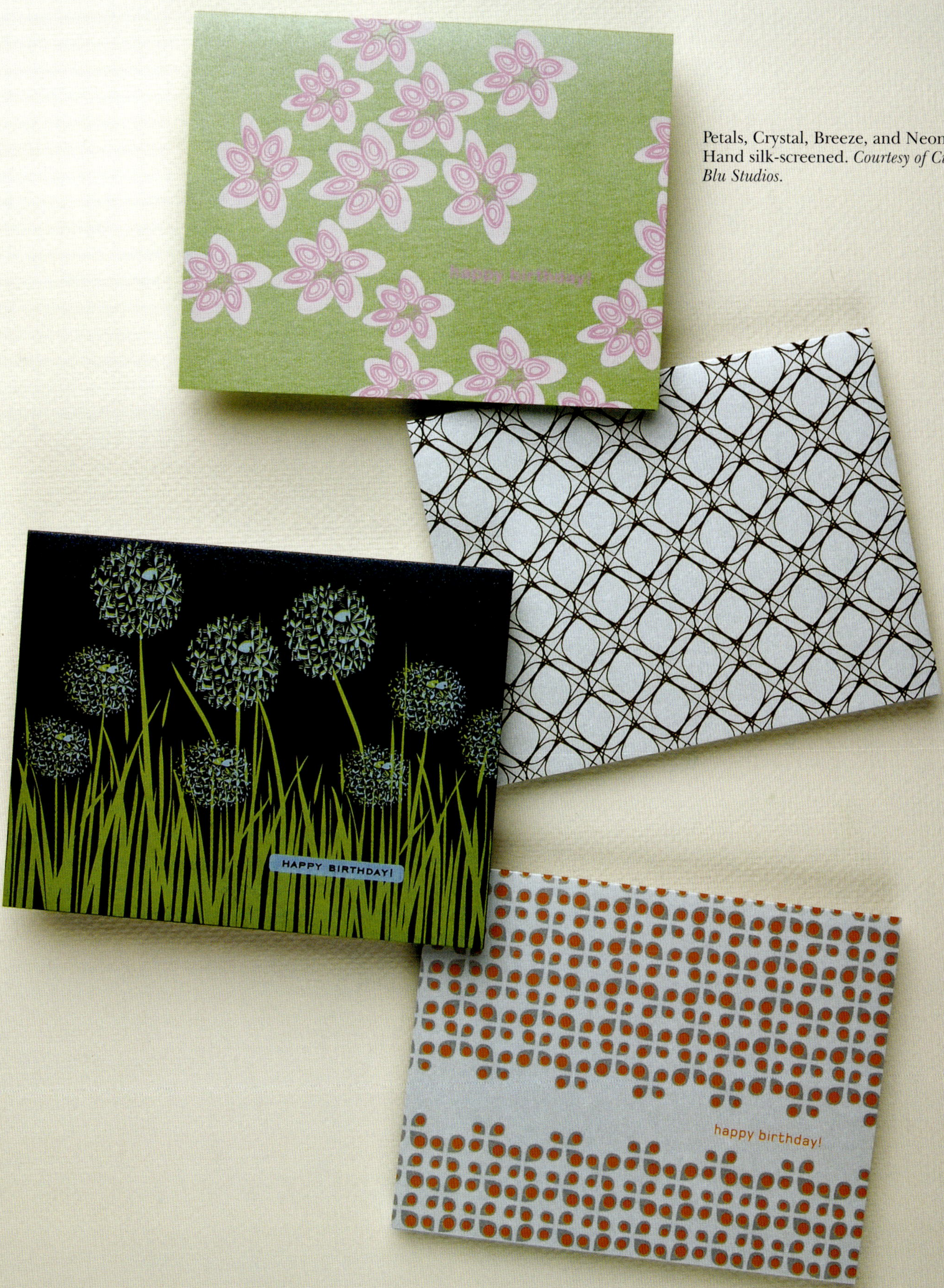

Petals, Crystal, Breeze, and Neon. Hand silk-screened. *Courtesy of Cielo Blu Studios.*

Saturate

www.saturatedesign.com

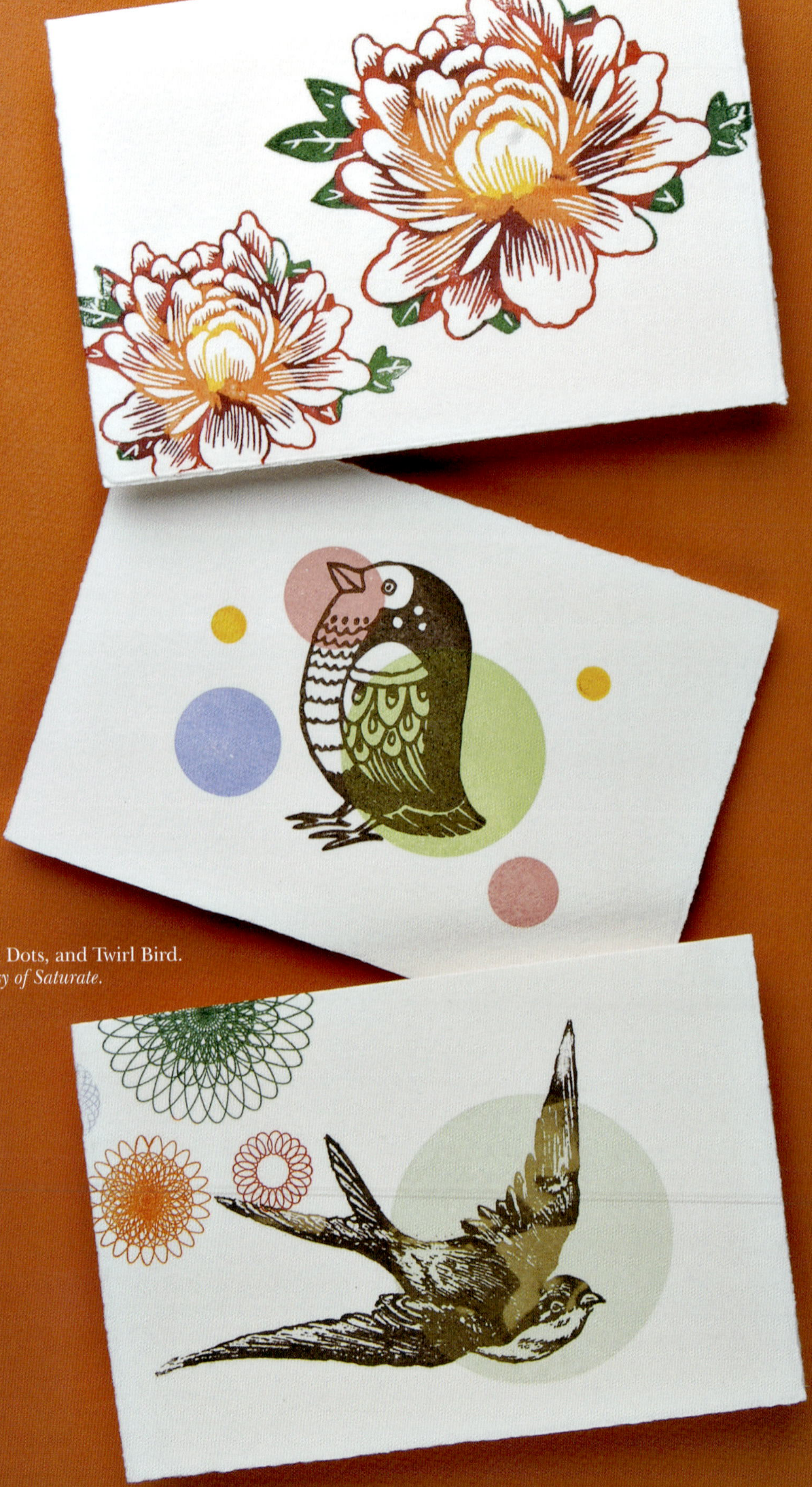

Bright Lotus, Baby Bird on Dots, and Twirl Bird. Hand silk-screened. *Courtesy of Saturate.*

Kate Lydon has been making cards since she was a child and has enjoyed a life of design ever since. She has worked as a graphic designer, art director, and even holds a degree in architecture. After designing party flyers, posters, and invitations, Kate founded Saturate in the spring of 2004 in Berkeley, California. She finds inspiration in candy wrappers, branch coral, full moon hikes, travel, and walking everywhere.

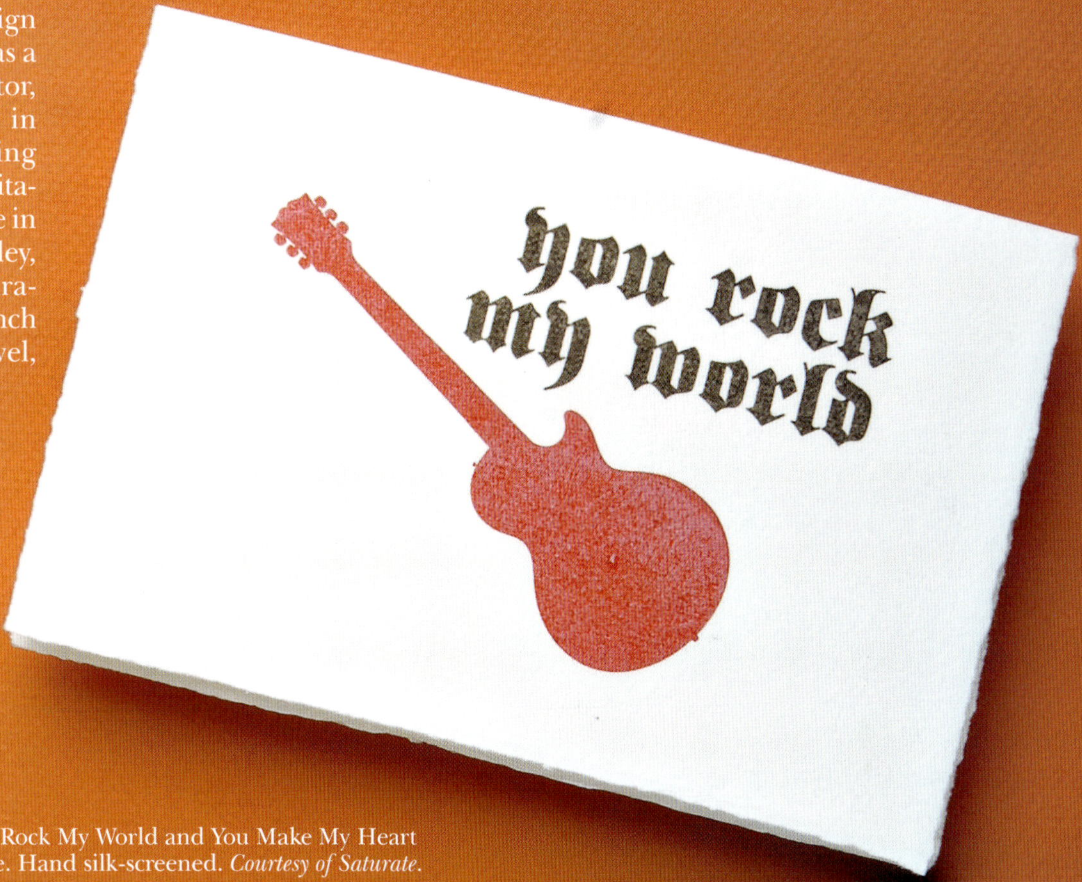

You Rock My World and You Make My Heart Race. Hand silk-screened. *Courtesy of Saturate.*

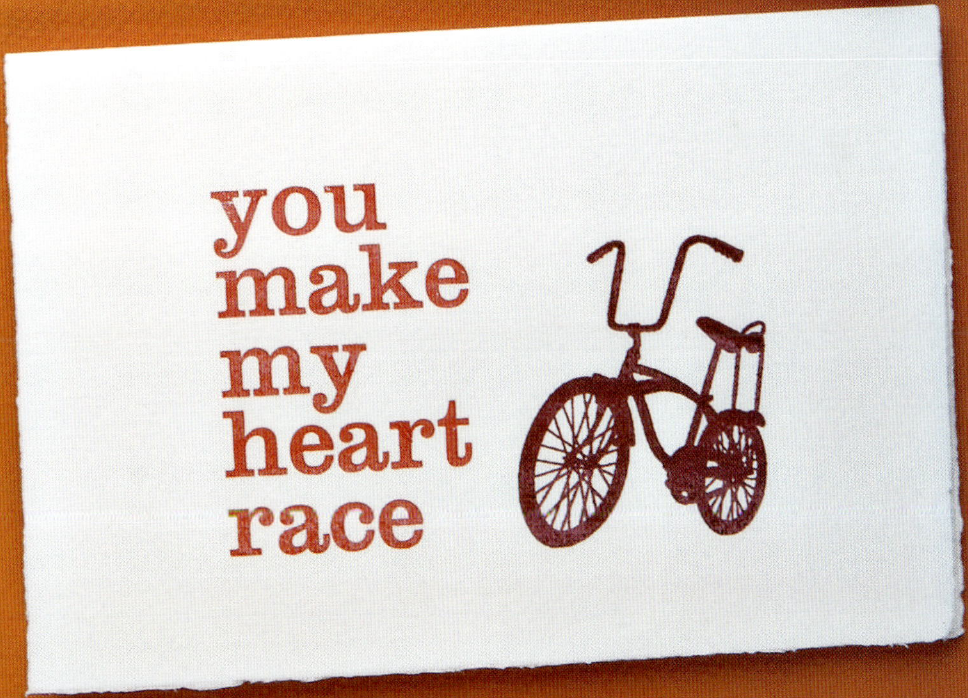

Pie Bird Press

www.wetfootpublications.com

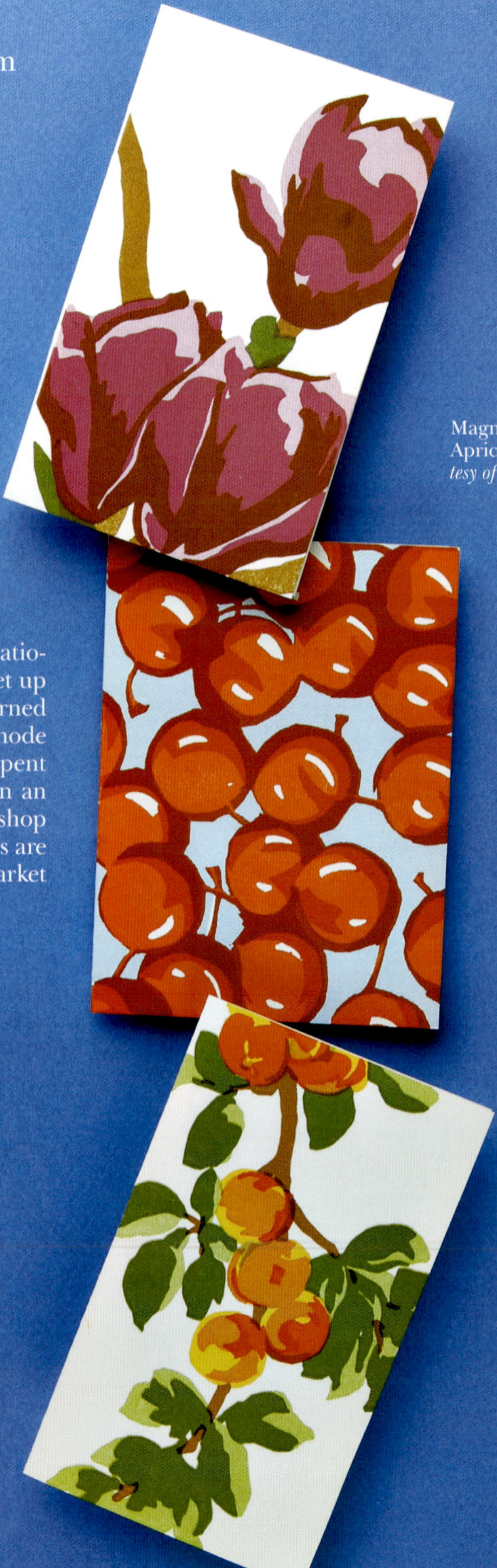

Magnolia, Blue Maraschino, and Apricots. Letterpress printed. *Courtesy of Pie Bird Press.*

Hannah Berman has been a stationery artist for five years and has set up shop in Berkeley, California. She earned a BFA in Printmaking from the Rhode Island School of Design and also spent three years perfecting her trade in an apprenticeship at the letterpress shop of Peter Koch Printers. Her designs are inspired by many years of flea market hunting and collecting.

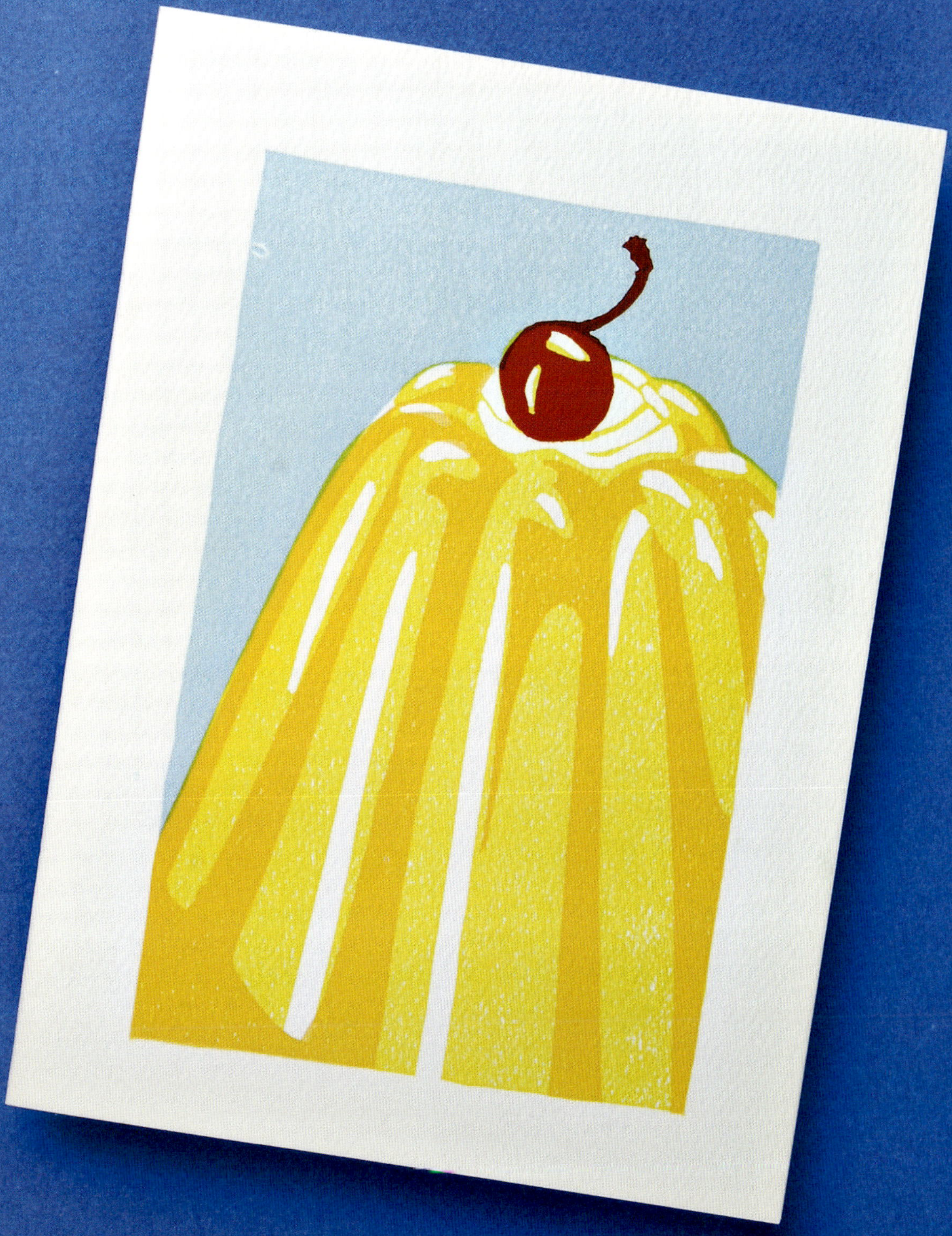

Jello. Letterpress printed. *Courtesy of Pie Bird Press.*

Foxy and Winston

www.foxyandwinston.com

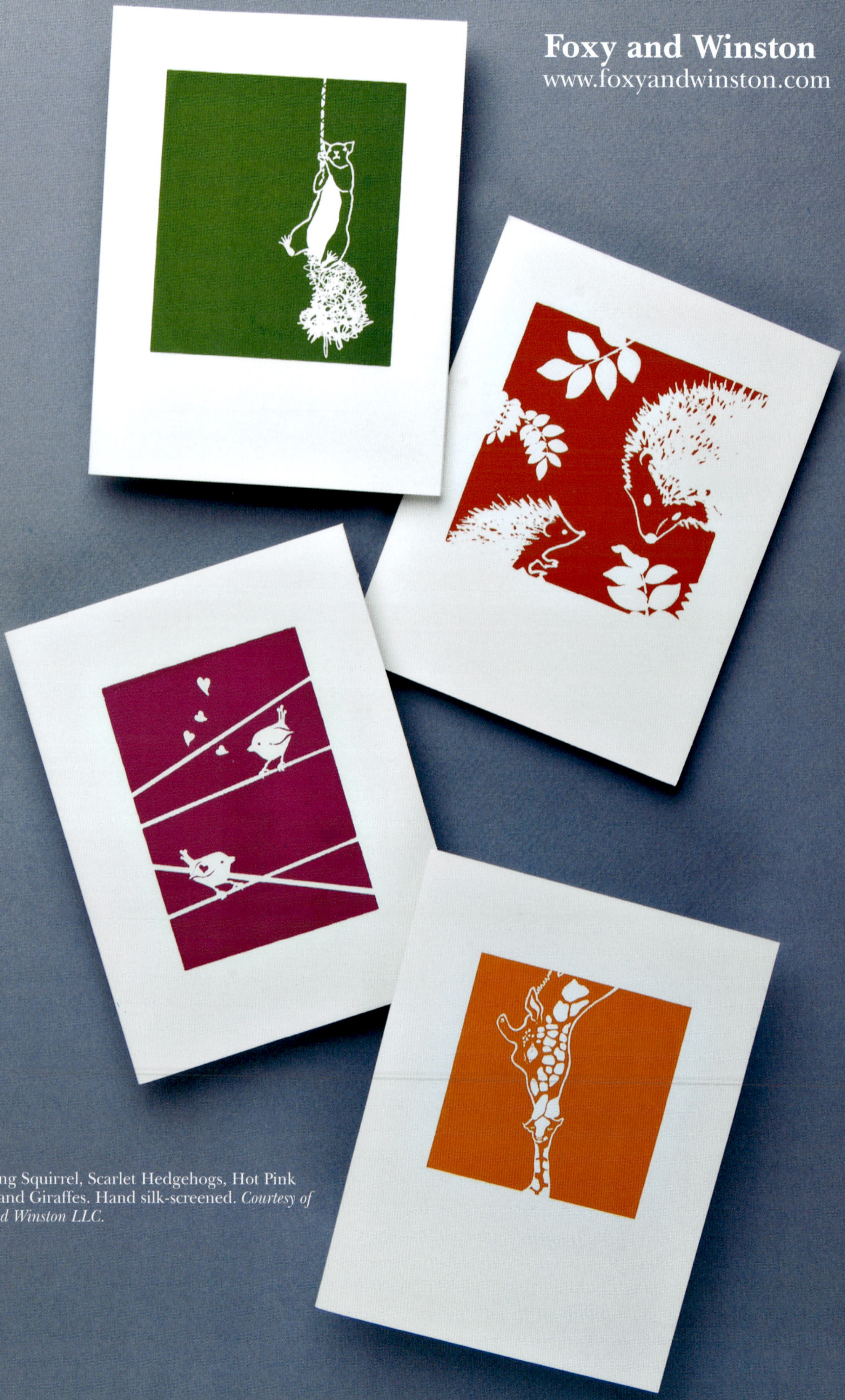

Swinging Squirrel, Scarlet Hedgehogs, Hot Pink Birds, and Giraffes. Hand silk-screened. *Courtesy of Foxy and Winston LLC.*

Jane Buck is originally from England and currently resides in Brooklyn, New York. Before she became a stationery artist in 2005, she worked at Paper Source and learned all sorts of crafty tricks. Her concepts are generally drawn from nature and the creatures that she meets on her visits to the botanical gardens. She continues to work on select freelance projects such as a new line of gift bags for the Gift Bag Factory. Her artwork can also be seen on children's clothing, as well as limited edition large wall prints.

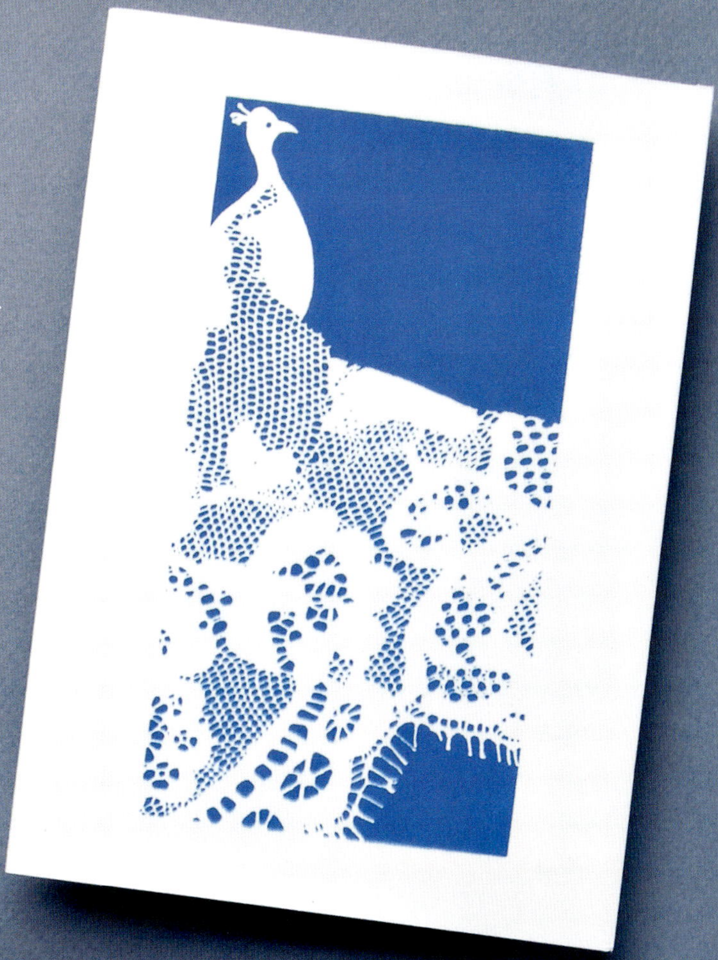

Blue Peacock and Deer & Toadstools. Hand silk-screened. *Courtesy of Foxy and Winston LLC.*

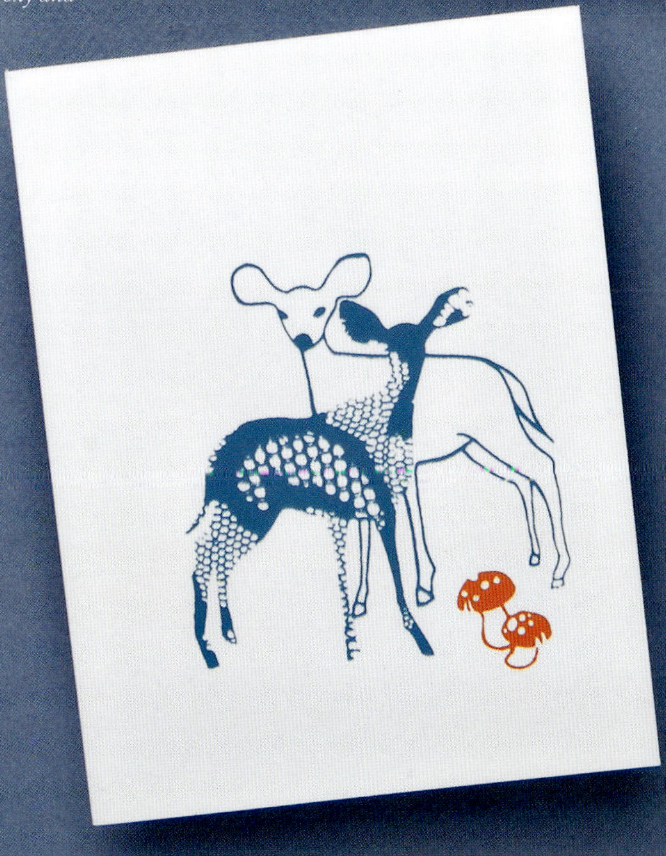

Katie Muth

www.katiemuth.com

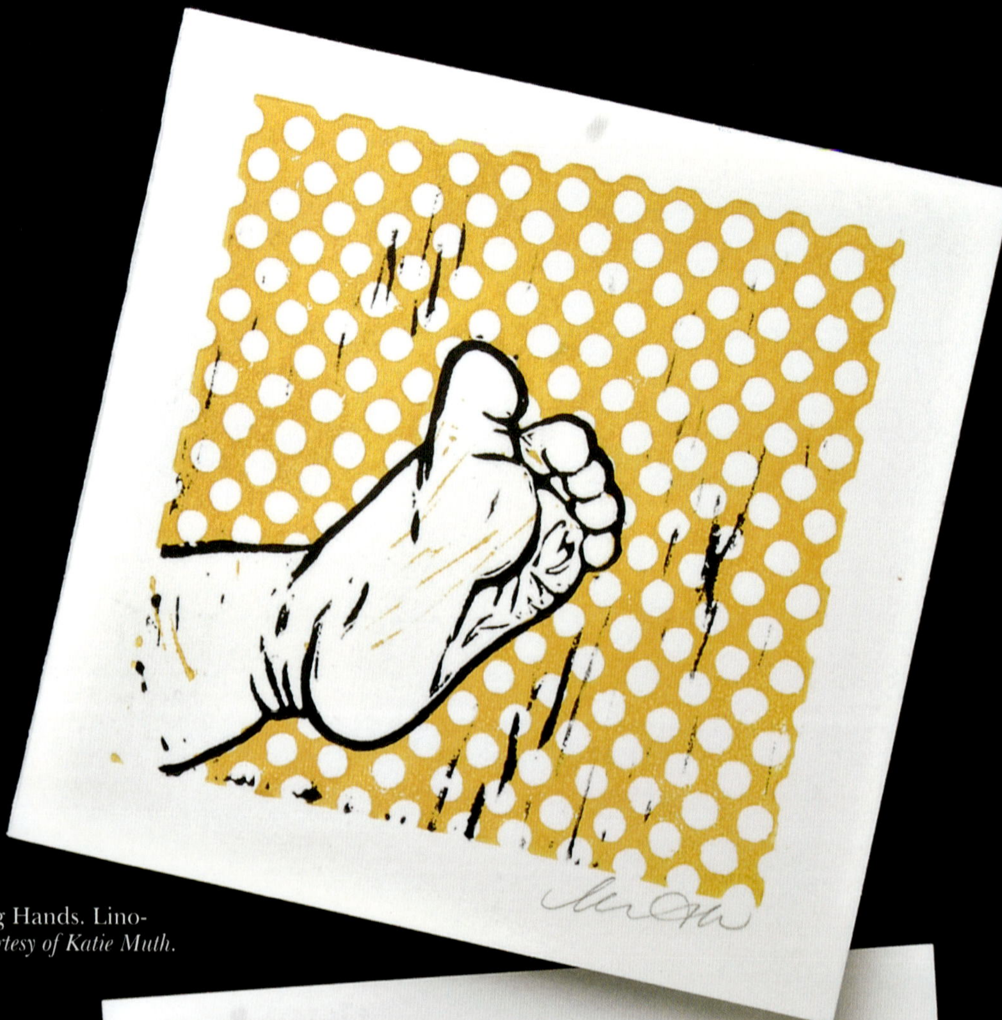

Baby Foot and Knitting Hands. Lino-cut/Relief Printed. *Courtesy of Katie Muth.*

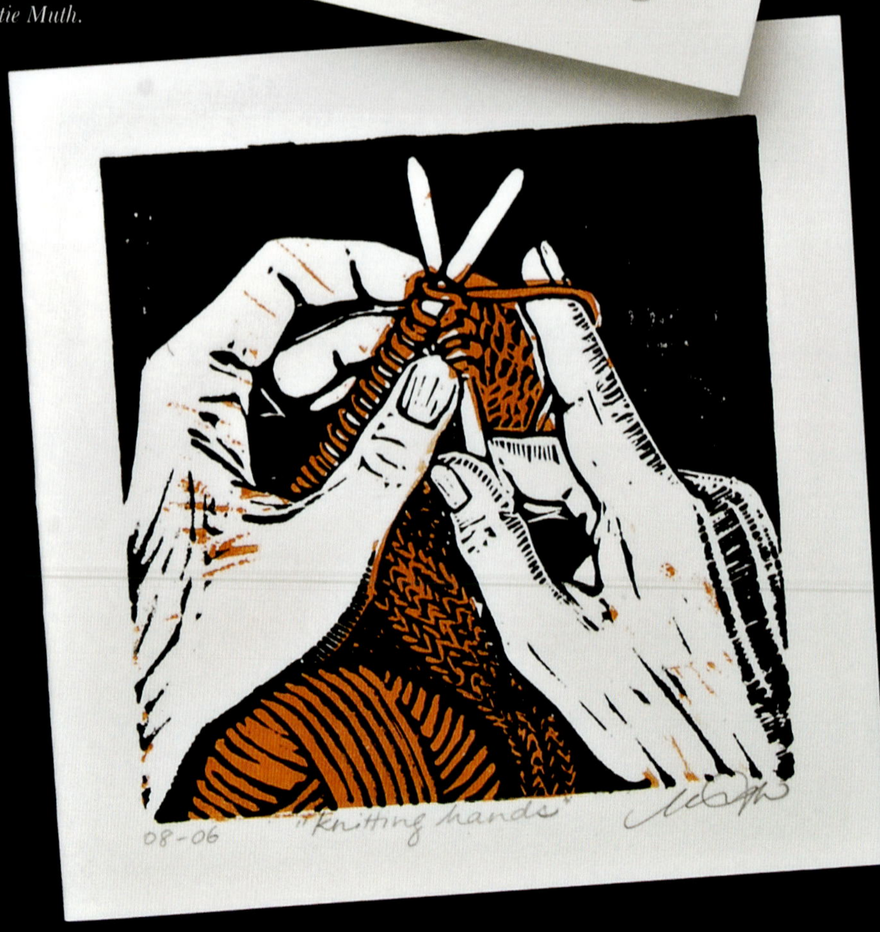

Katie Muth has handmade cards and decorated letters that she made for her grandparents going back to when she was five years old. After studying printmaking and graduating from the Ontario College of Art and Design in 2002, she launched her company a few short years later. Katie lives in Toronto, Canada, and enjoys knitting, sewing, bike riding, and camping – which are all common inspirations for her design work.

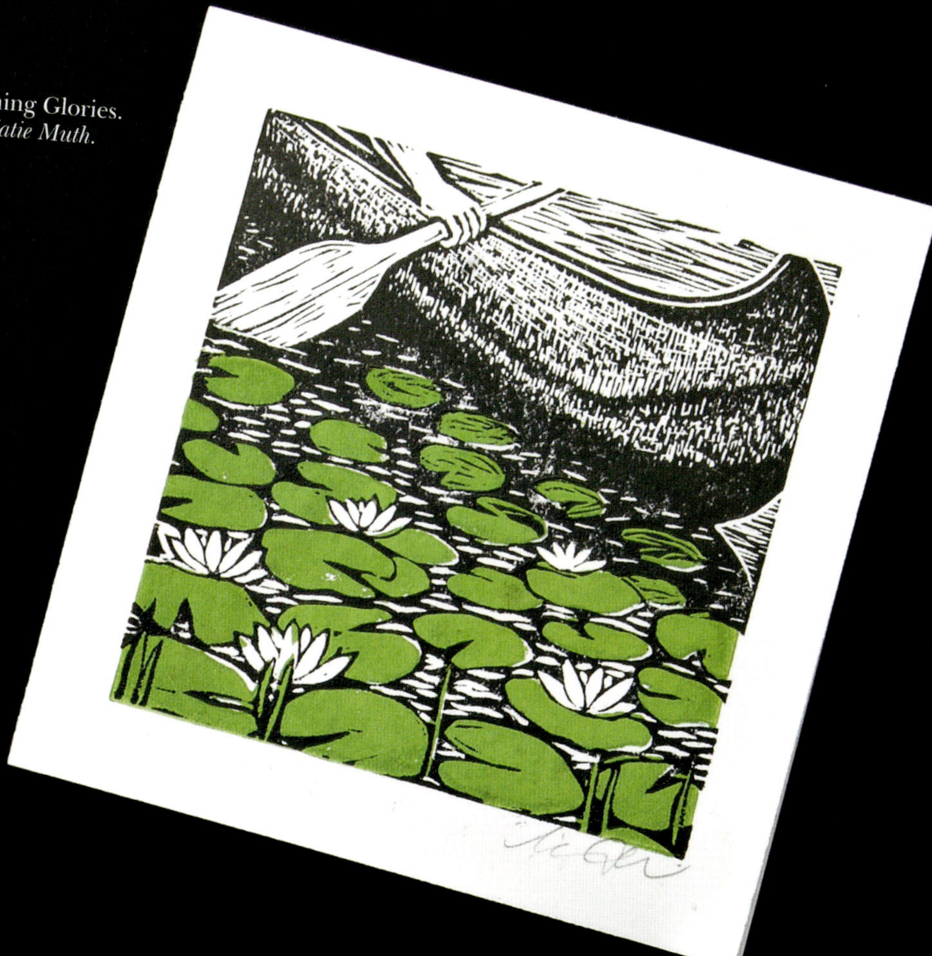

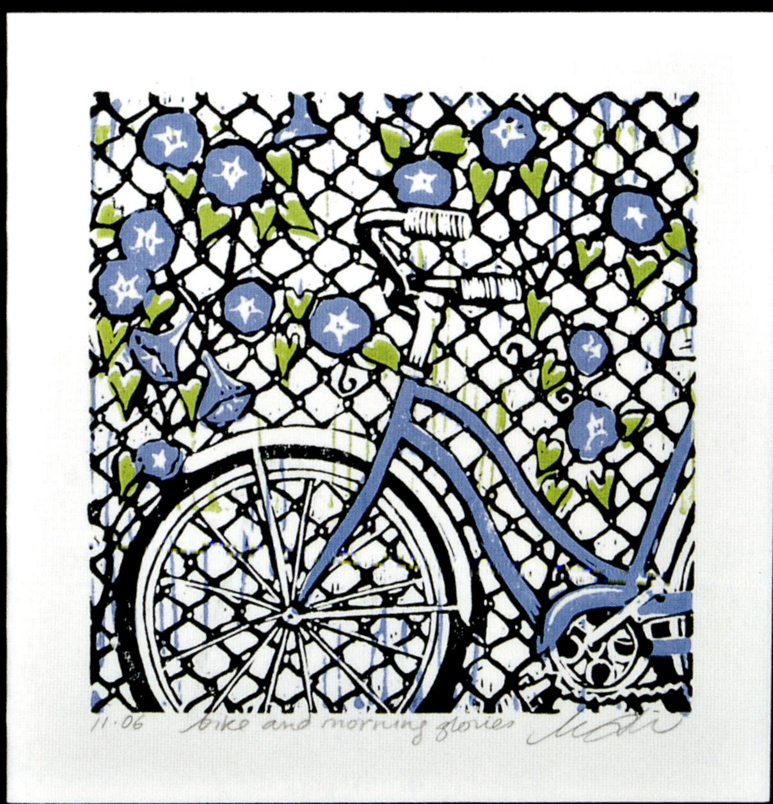

ily Pads & Canoe and Bike & Morning Glories. ino-cut/Relief Printed. *Courtesy of Katie Muth.*

Tall Cow
www.tallcow.com

Deanna Ebner started Tall Cow in 2004, but has been making her own cards all of her life. Art has always been a part of her life in one way or another. She is a self-taught artist with a jewelry design background. In addition to her stationery company, she and her husband, Lucas Manteca, own and operate a restaurant in Stone Harbor, New Jersey, called "Sea Salt."

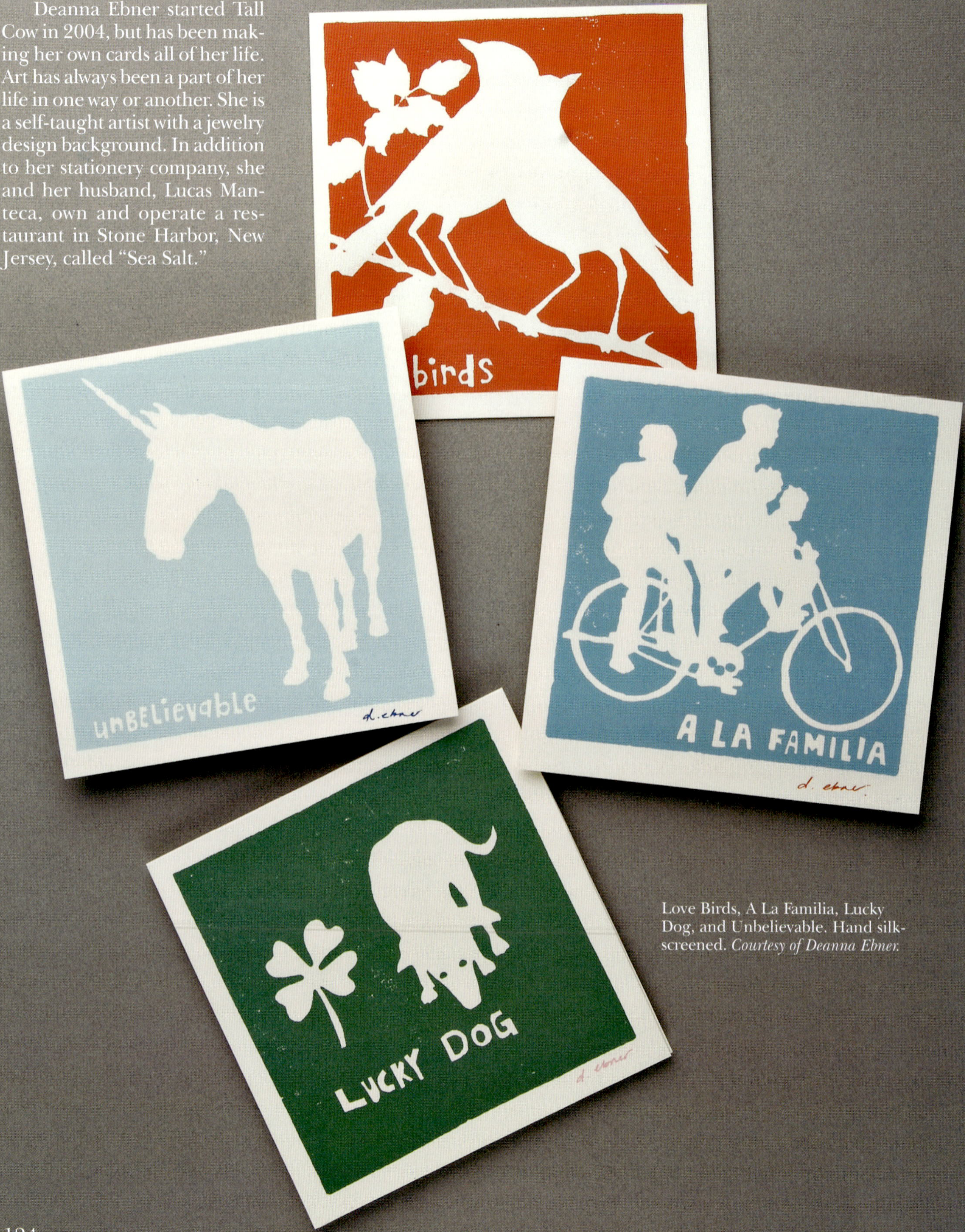

Love Birds, A La Familia, Lucky Dog, and Unbelievable. Hand silk-screened. *Courtesy of Deanna Ebner.*

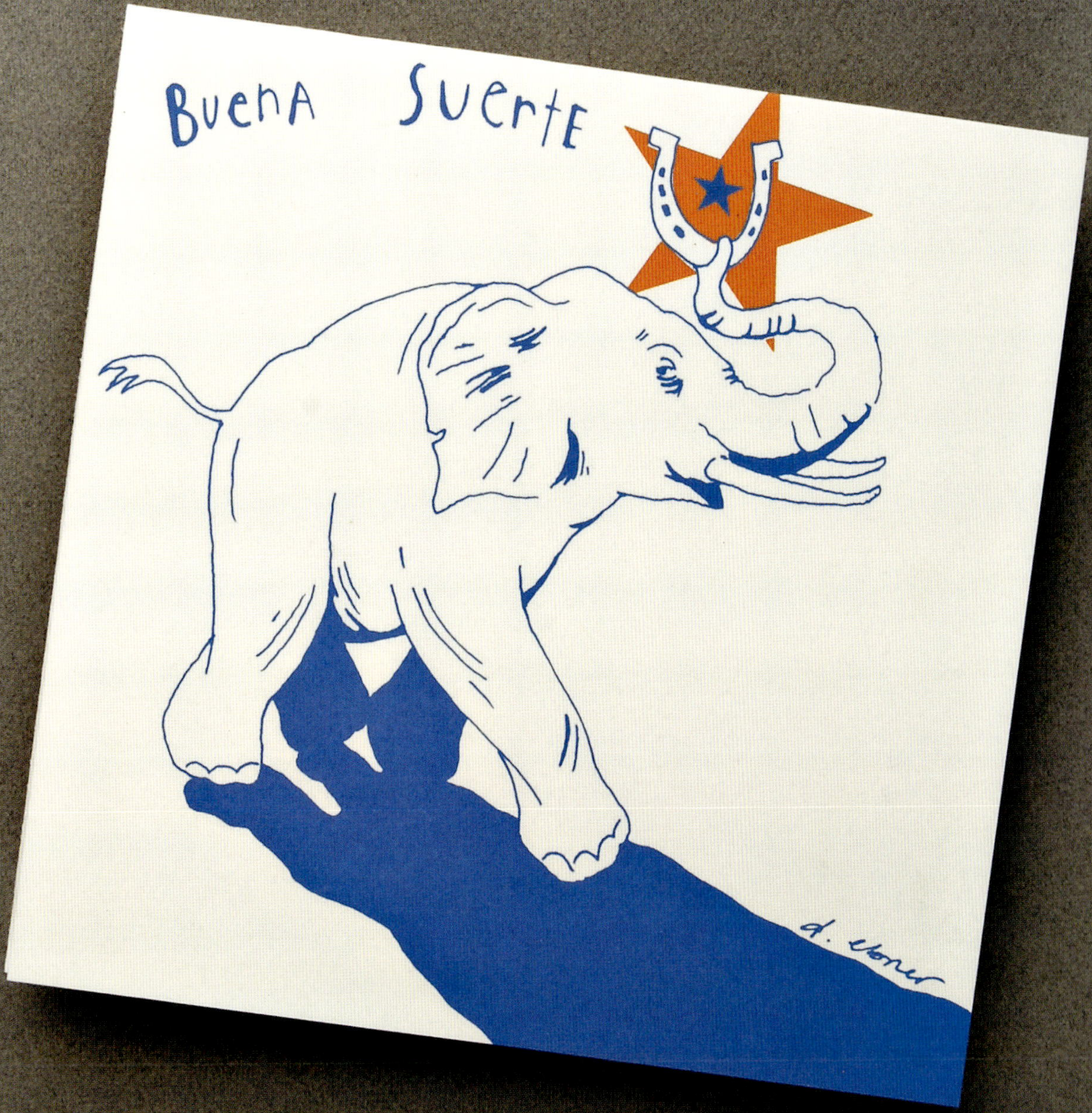

Buena Suerte. Hand silk-screened. *Courtesy of Deanna Ebner.*

Acknowledgments

I would like to extend a heartfelt thanks to all of the designers who are featured in this book. Their enthusiasm and excitement for this industry is apparent. I truly feel honored to have had the chance to work with each of them. I thank them for taking the time out of their busy schedules to work on this project and make this concept a reality. Their work has been an inspiration to me and I am thrilled to be able to share it with others in a compiled book.

A very special thank you to my editors, Tina Skinner and Jeff Snyder, whose knowledge, patience, and expertise made the entire process incredibly smooth for a first time author.

I express deep thanks to my husband, Branden, not only offering a great deal of moral support, but throughout the entire process he has been a sounding board, proofreader, ghostwriter, and overall greeting card specialist.

I am so grateful to have such supportive parents who have always encouraged me to follow my bliss. They never laughed at me when I told them I wanted to major in fine art in college and eventually become a designer. Because of them, I believe I have had the confidence to pursue my artistic goals and dreams.

Lastly, I would like to thank my close friends, who have heard me talk about this concept for quite some time. Their support and friendship mean so much.

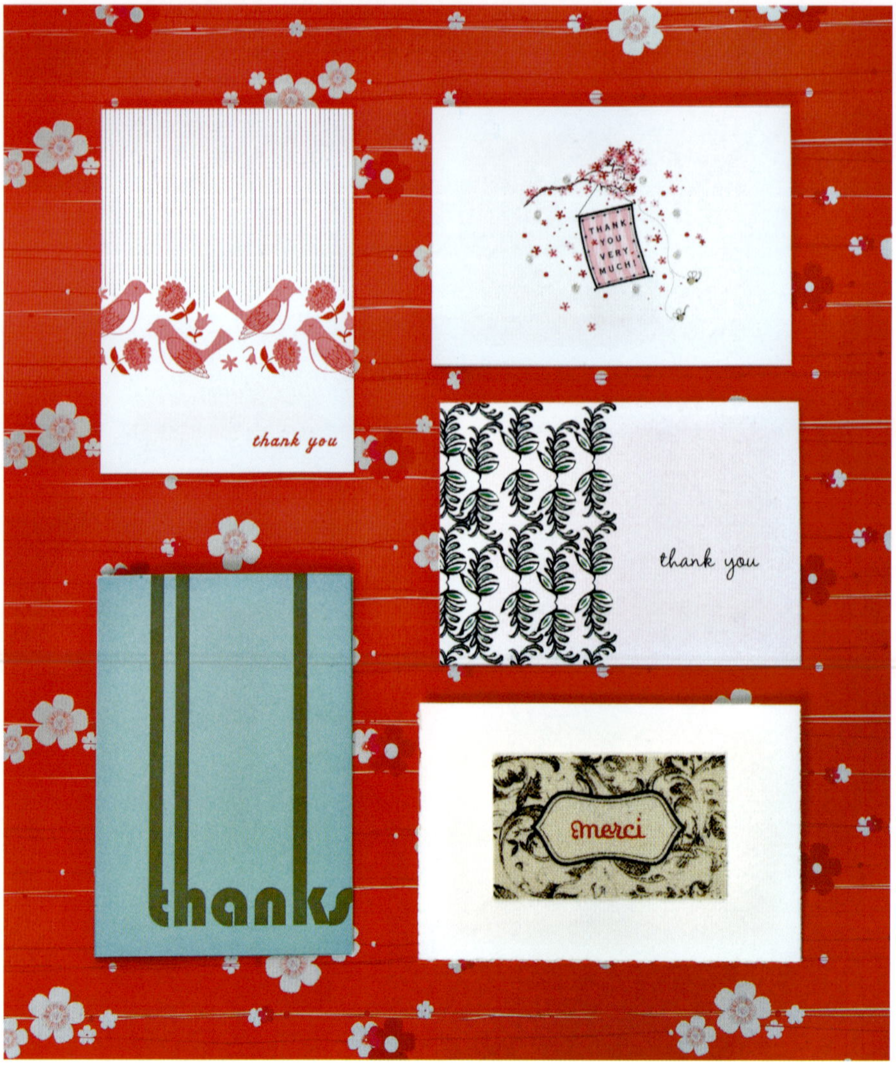

Note cards by (clockwise) Hello!Lucky, Driscoll Design, Cat Seto, Ess & Jae, and Paper + Cup. Wrapping Paper by Snow and Graham. Photograph by Casey Figlewicz.

Index